INTEGRAL PUBLISHING HOUSE

The Coming Waves

The Coming Waves

Evolution, Transformation, and Action in an Integral Age

Edited by
Dustin DiPerna and H.B. Augustine

The Coming Waves
Copyright © 2013 by Dustin DiPerna
All rights reserved.

Published by Integral Publishing House

First Edition

IntegralPublishingHouse.com

ISBN 978-0-9892289-0-9

Printed and Bound in the United States

Integral Publishing House

Table of Contents

Contributing Authors

Introduction
Dustin DiPerna and H.B. Augustine

EVOLUTION

Chapter 1. The Evolution of
Evolutionary Thinking
Michael Wombacher   3

Chapter 2. The American Roots
of Evolutionary Spirituality
Jeff Carreira   31

TRANSFORMATION

Chapter 3.
Wake Up, Grow Up, Clean Up, Show Up
Dustin DiPerna   55

Chapter 4. Waking Up: The Path
of Spiritual Awakening
John Churchill   61

Chapter 5. Growing Up: Your
Capacity for Developmental Growth
Clint Fuhs   75

Chapter 6. Cleaning Up: The Reciprocal
Dance of Psyche and Spirit
Michael Brabant 113

Chapter 7. Showing Up: The Power
and Potential of "We"
Andrew Venezia 137

Chapter 8. The Biggest Taboo
H.B. Augustine 157

Chapter 9. The Gateway into the Future:
Mysticism for Our Times
Thomas Hübl 185

ACTION

Chapter 10. Embodiment
Rob McNamara 203

Chapter 11. Activism
Jana Espiritu Santo and Eliot Bissey 215

Chapter 12. International Development
Gail Hochachka 235

Chapter 13. Leadership
Mikyö Clark 265

Chapter 14. Service
Mick Quinn and Debora Prieto 293

Concluding Remarks
Dustin DiPerna 313

Contributing Authors

H.B. Augustine has been extremely passionate about writing since age nine and with integral theory and practice since age 17. After writing a book titled "An Introduction to Integral Philosophy" (later published on Integral World), his work helping to publish *The Coming Waves* awakened him to the world of social entrepreneurship and integral business. He graduated from Denison University with degrees in Philosophy and Communication and is co-founder of Aupportunities and Taggle.

Michael Brabant is finishing his PhD at Saybrook University where he is co-designing, co-teaching, and studying an embodied and integrally informed leadership curriculum at an undergraduate university as part of a greater cultural evolution movement on campus. He is a teacher at the intersection of relational spiritual practice, collective intelligence, and embodiment of an integral approach to awakening. He is most interested in how we can synthesize the great wisdom traditions and other potent transformational technologies in order to provide the most benefit for the most amount of people on the individual, institutional, and cultural levels. www.integralawakening.com

Eliot Bissey has always been interested in philosophy, psychology, and spirituality; other interests have included guitar, tennis, and martial arts, where he trained under Cheung Hok Kin (Hawkins Cheung) in the Yip Man (Ip Man) lineage of Wing Chun Kung Fu. Eliot learned meditation and metaphysics from "sensitive" Lewis Emil Downs as a teenager, and recently completed Landmark Education's "Curriculum for Living". Eliot's working background includes engineering, sales management, and caregiving. His current areas of inquiry include integral meta-theory and context/content relationships, Neuroeconomics, NLP, hypnosis, Technical Analysis, Trading Psychology, emotional/heart integration and peak performance. Eliot is a living, loving, learning, doing, human, being.

Jeff Carreira is currently the co-leader of The Evolutionary Collective where he supports and facilitates the development of individuals through an intensive yearlong program of engagement. Previously he was the director of education for the educational nonprofit called EnlightenNext where he created and organized a global network of spiritual and philosophical education programs and trained over one hundred other individuals to teach worldwide. He is passionate about philosophy because he is passionate about the power that ideas have to shape the way we see ourselves and the way we live. He has been invited to speak to university students in the United States and Australia, has taught courses on American philosophy, spoken at conferences, and led seminars worldwide.

John Churchill is founder of Samadhi, an Integral Life Practice center in Newton Massachusetts. He holds an undergraduate degree from Naropa University as well as a Masters Degree in Acupuncture. John leads Body Based and Concentration Meditation programs. He also co-leads, Living Meditation classes and Mahamudra retreats alongside Dr. Daniel Brown, Ph.D, John is currently pursuing his Doctorate in Clinical Psychology at the Massachusetts School of Professional Psychology.

Mikyö Clark was born into the Dzogchen lineage of Tibetan Buddhism, where he has studied and practiced for the past five years. He is currently focused on developing leaders within the startup community, as well as helping companies harness the power of innovation to drive change. Check him out at www.mikyo.me

Dustin DiPerna was educated at Cornell University and Harvard University. He is founder of Integral Publishing House and co-founder of the Foundation for Integral Religion and Spirituality. For the past decade he has been a student of Integral Theory and currently studies under the mentorship of American philosopher Ken Wilber.

Clint Fuhs serves as the Executive Director of Integral Institute, Inc. and the co-founder of Core Integral, Inc., where he has worked as a senior student and advisor to Ken Wilber over the last 11 years. He is also a senior analyst at Lectica Inc., where he builds adult developmental assessments in conjunction with his doctoral research on the relationship between cognitive growth and perspective-taking growth in leaders.

Gail Hochachka has worked in international sustainable development for 18 years, unwaveringly seeking a more integral approach to the complex global issues of our time. In her work with the nonprofit organizations One Sky and Drishti, and as the Co-Director of the global network Integral Without Borders, and through mentorship with Ken Wilber, Gail pursues greater synthesis in approach, a truer sustainability of outcomes, and more coherence of vision with action for global wellbeing.

Thomas Hübl is a contemporary spiritual teacher, author, and founder of the Academy of Inner Science. He gives workshops, talks and individual guidance worldwide. His passion is a renaissance of spirit in the postmodern age. Through his work he explores how timeless mystical wisdom informs cultural and societal evolution and creates 'spiritual competency.'

Rob McNamara is author of *The Elegant Self* and *Strength to Awaken*. He specializes in helping people resolve their persistent painful limitations to become more powerful, proficient and aligned with what matters most in life. Rob is a skilled Psychotherapist, leading Performance Coach, Psychology Professor at Naropa University and an Integral Zen Practitioner. He runs his private practice in Boulder Colorado serving clients world wide. Rob works with a broad range of executives and professionals, undergraduate and graduate students and athletes ranging from high school to Olympic and professional world champions.

Debora Prieto graduated from the University of Madrid as an educator of mentally handicapped children. She spent the following 10 years working with her skills in the Spanish healthcare system. Debora is also a trained facilitator of the Big Mind Process, a counseling tool that combines Western psychology and Zen teachings, which she uses in this work.

Mick Quinn is as an Irish immigrant who fully embraced the American Dream, Mick's life path brought him from his native home in Athlone, Ireland, to New York City where he founded several successful businesses, to the publication of a book on the future of human potential - The Uncommon Path - to his current work in the slums surrounding the the Spanish Colonial city of Antigua Guatemala.

Jana Espiritu Santo is a multi-media artist, traveling the coast of California preforming face/body art and vending fine art creations as a "New Renaissance" merchant. She is constantly studying philosophy and the occult and occasionally puts it into writing when holistically inspired, as seeker of the Good, True, and Beautiful.

Andrew Venezia recently completed a Master's Degree in Integral Theory, conducting a research project on Intersubjective Awareness (We Space) Practices. At the time of publication he is enjoying cooking for his wife at their home in Ghent, Belgium, and his newborn daughter is training him in concentration under adverse states of bodily fatigue.

Mike Wombacher received his Master's Degree in International Relations from Florida State University in 1983. During his time at university he became compelled by the pursuit of Spiritual Enlightenment and its significance for the evolution of culture. In 1994 he met the American spiritual teacher Andrew Cohen who ignited in him a passion for awakening in an evolutionary context. Over the years he became one of his close students. In 2008 he published *11 Days at the Edge: One Man's Spiritual Journey into Evolutionary Enlightenment*, which was endorsed by two-time Nobel Peace Prize nominee Ervin Laszlo as well as by Barbara Marx Hubbard, who called it "epic in scope and purpose." He is currently working on a new book, a comprehensive exploration of evolution and the search for meaning.

Introduction

Dustin DiPerna and H.B. Augustine

It is an honor to present to you *The Coming Waves: Evolution, Transformation, and Action in an Integral Age.* We as editors have done our best to collect a handful of inspiring articles written by cutting edge authors around the globe. Each contributor was selected for the particular gift that he or she brings to the table. In our opinion, you hold in your hands the words and stories of several of today's brightest shining stars.

Our initial intention with this book was to provide a platform for the next wave of integral thinkers to share their thoughts and work in the world. In this light, we have tried to balance the offerings in this book across several generations. The majority of the contributors are young integral leaders in their twenties, thirties, and forties. Our hope is that the inclusion of younger writers provides a fair representation of the coming waves of integral thinking and action that are on the horizon. Our sense from putting this project together is that there is an immense amount of hope for our future.

The book is divided into three parts: In part 1, we begin with a general introduction to evolution and set the theoretical context for the book as a whole. In chapter 1, Michael Wombacher introduces a brief history of evolutionary philosophy. Contrary to conventional belief, Wombacher notes that evolutionary thinking and theories date as far back as ancient Greece. Wombacher offers a voice for the "nonmaterial evolutionary thinkers," who see that the force of evolution transcends the existence of matter. German idealism offered a counter to this materialist evolutionary account, but it was and is overruled by what began with Darwin and positivism in England during the late 19th century, ensuing the all-too-familiar disenchantment of modernity. Wombacher goes on to describe the role of American pragmatic philosophy in relation to the evolution of evolutionary thinking, arguing that it was this collective stream of consciousness, fused with Eastern wisdom traditions in the early 20th century, which gave rise to the most current forms of evolutionary thinking, these being Integral Theory/Integralism and Evolutionary Enlightenment.

In chapter 2, Jeff Carreira offers a more focused account of evolutionary philosophy and spirituality, emphasizing the roots of this tradition in American pragmatic philosophy. American scholars such as Wilber, Cohen, and Hubbard owe a decent portion of their findings to earlier thinkers such as Peirce, Dewey, and James. These late-19th-century American academics, members of Harvard's Metaphysical Club (along with individuals such as Emerson and Thoreau), shared a worldview of an infinite, continuous, interconnected universe, made up of pure creative potential, which perpetually grows and becomes increasingly more self-aware. The force of evolution itself is this pure creative potential, with the power to alter itself as any number of forms. Peirce, Dewey, and James saw the value in studying and pioneering an evolutionary ethics, in accordance with this worldview, which served as the foundation of their evolutionary metaphysics, epistemology, and logic. The American character, a utilitarianism-idealism hybrid, reflects such pragmatism—the will to believe that which results in the greatest possible good. After describing in detail the individual perspectives of key American evolutionary thinkers, Carreira connects this commentary with the current American evolutionary thinking community.

We then move onto part 2 to more deeply consider the role of transformation in the coming waves of reality set to hit the shore. We begin in chapter 3 with a piece from Dustin DiPerna where he introduces a simple frame he calls "Wake Up, Grow Up, Clean Up, Show Up." Here, DiPerna sets the stage for part 2 to show how this simple phrase holds the key to the emergence of a fully integrated, healthy, coming wave of integral practitioners on the planet. The four chapters that follow take each of the notions outlined by DiPerna and fills them in with broader detail.

In chapter 4, John Churchill shares an experiential expression of what it's like to "wake up." He begins his chapter with marking the difference between the process of awakening itself and levels of structural development capable of understanding it. Then, with direct instruction, Churchill leads the reader step by step through a guided experience of awakening using the body and its senses. Anyone curious about waking up will appreciate this gem. We highly recommend taking your time with this piece. (An audio version of the guided meditation is available on the book's website—www.IntegralPublishingHouse.com).

Next, in chapter 5, Clint Fuhs takes us through the process of "growing up." As the chapter unfolds, Fuhs offers a comprehensive and full articulation of development through structure-stages across multiple lines of intelligence. Fuhs's chapter takes the reader through a full rainbow spectrum of developmental altitude ranging from infrared and red at one end to violet, ultraviolet, and clear light at the other. When Fuhs's chapter is seen in conjunction with Churchill's preceding chapter on "waking up," the reader can begin to see a clear distinction between two fundamental types of growth: waking up through state-stages and growing up through structure-stages.

In chapter 6, Michael Brabant incorporates the role of "cleaning up" into the process of spiritual growth and development. He explores the reciprocity of psychological integration and spiritual awakening and how the two can dance together both skillfully and unskillfully. He makes the case that our spiritual growth is deeply hindered and tainted without psychological integration and healing. Conversely, he also asserts that psychological integration work cannot offer us a sense of freedom without the context of spiritual practice. By offering practical, intellectual, and experiential understandings, Brabant lays out a guide to support us in not getting stuck placing too much emphasis on either facet. This balancing effort, Brabant argues, is the key to embodying a deep, clean, and stabilized integral awakening.

Chapter 7 offers a newly emerging dimension of "showing up." Here Andrew Venezia provides an extraordinary account of the *power and potential* of We Space. We Space practices are an emergent phenomenon in integral circles (and beyond), and represent exciting potentials for opening up an integral cultural space and reworking our understandings of what it is to be human consciousness. Giving an introductory account of different ways of working with We Spaces, from practices which introduce individuals to a personal and empathic relationality all the way to radically experimental practices which are revealing an awake and self-reflexive intersubjective consciousness, Venezia highlights the implications of such practices for fostering psychological growth, healing, and development, on meditative and spiritual development, for community building and in the emergence of a global integral culture, for how practitioners show up in their daily lives in the world, and for Integral Theory and evolutionary philosophy in general.

In chapter 8, H.B. Augustine offers us a communication essay he wrote for a class titled "The Trouble with Normal." In his article, "The Biggest Taboo," he argues that "trans-mysticality" ("transpersonal" + "mystical" experiences/claims) is the biggest taboo we face on a cultural scale. He also claims that it shouldn't be this way because of the epistemic normativity, or truth, underlying trans-mystical phenomena. Augustine received the Orlando Taylor Top Student Paper Award for the Denison University Communication Department. The central thesis is that people who believe in or claim to experience "transpersonal," "mystical," and/or "paranormal" things aren't necessarily crazy or delusional. In many/most cases, they are quite the opposite: healthy, fully functioning human beings, contributing an extraordinary amount to society.

In chapter 9, Thomas Hübl rounds out part 2 with a visionary take on the role of mysticism in the third millennium. He shows how modern mysticism carries the timeless wisdom within it, while simultaneously acknowledging the need for our outer lives to develop in more depth. The future is accessible to us now, he tells us, although not as "tomorrow"—which would simply amount to a repetition of our today—but rather as the potential that we can become and embody. Hübl explains this as a radical path of awakening, placing our alignment to God, to the One, at the very center of our lives. Deeply connecting with the insights of the Absolute and then returning to the world of the Relative, anchoring life through our body-mind (our physical sensations, emotions, and thoughts), allows for total immersion in the life of this world, while knowing that we are not of it. In his chapter, Hübl also introduces a practice he calls Transparent Communication and suggests that it can serve as the foundation for a new culture of "We." His vision is one based on transparency between and within us as we attune with other people and situations. Hübl suggests that we can potentially perceive everything in everyone else, understand others in their depth, and allow the mystical aspects of life to reveal themselves in our everyday experience.

In part 3, we turn our attention to action and application. Rob McNamara begins in chapter 10 and invites the reader to practice integral embodiment. As McNamara explains, this entails the art of embracing and inhabiting one's (physical) body so as to optimize awareness, experience, and wellness. Integral embodiment is being inside the body that is your exterior expression. Depending on how effectively one is embodying, one can be a feeling anywhere on a "continuum of aliveness." On the back end of this continuum is disembodiment, or poverty of embodiment, which leads to wanting/craving more. On the front end of this continuum is the peak state that is optimal aliveness, an authentic, ecstatic feeling of electrical charge and vibrancy. McNamara goes on to instruct the reader on how to cultivate greater integral embodiment through various concepts, perceptions, intentions, and practices.

In chapter 11, Jana Espiritu Santo and Eliot Bissey give life to Wilber's Integral Theory by applying it to the culturally relevant topic of activism. Choosing to tackle a deeply complex subject matter, they elegantly deconstruct and integrate a spectrum of perspectives on activism appropriate for both those with no knowledge of Integral Theory and advanced students alike. Also drawing from Spiral Dynamics, Harvard psychologist Robert Kegan, and nondual sages, they hope to gently push the evolutionary edge on this topic with our transformative potential. Through the vehicle of coauthorship, they also give life to another form of the We Space, as a single voice in a shared perspective.

Chapter 12 turns the gaze on to international development work. Here, Gail Hochachka describes how an integral approach is being applied to alleviate poverty and enhance human wellbeing in remote corners of the planet. She explores the question, "what is integral?" in the context of current global statistics that report 1.75 billion people living in multidimensional poverty, with indicators reflecting acute deprivation in health, education, and standards of living, and another 1.24 billion living on less than $1.25/day. Hochachka shares some of the principles for integral action and provides examples from development projects in Peru, El Salvador, and Nigeria.

Next we turn to the all-important topic of leadership. In chapter 13, Mikyö Clark's article explores the future of leadership through a developmental framework. He focuses on the design and implementation of a specific networked-leadership platform intended to support the quickening of transformational processes, competency building, and the establishment of healthy mentor and mentee relationships. It outlines a social technology that aims to support rapid leader development, emphasizing the importance of this and similar tools for the cultivation of members of the millennial generation who are facing unprecedented global challenges. Through an examination of the relationship between artifacts and the intersubjective and techno-economic systems in which they arise, the article points to the role of artifacts as developmental pathways for the creation of new social systems. Finally, through an examination of the author's own developmental and typological orientation, the article further investigates the role of psychological and spiritual development in the cultivation of the highly complex forms leadership needs today.

We close the book with a fantastic chapter on a fuller look at the meaning of service when it is deeply informed by consciousness and spirit. In chapter 14, Mick Quinn and Debora Prieto inspire the reader to create Conscious Service, which, as they describe, is "karma yoga on steroids." Selfless action arises from the mind's ability to understand the concepts/realities of emptiness and interconnectedness, and from new maps of human potential (including Integral Theory, Evolutionary Enlightenment, Spiral Dynamics, and Big Mind). This wisdom is a powerful tool allowing luminaries to address and alleviate poverty issues such as 80 percent of humanity living on less than $10/day. Wisdom alone is insufficient, though, as the greatest leaders primarily value action rather than theory. Even traditional enlightenment is only the beginning of Conscious Service. Quinn and Prieto take the reader on an adventure through their world, their lives, in the slums of Guatemala, pioneering an educational/philanthropic model with the potential of eradicating poverty for good.

We are thrilled about each author's message in this book. Our hope is that each article positively influences the world. May the coming waves of integral wisdom prophesized in these pages come to full fruition here on Earth. May each of us stand more deeply with our feet in Eden as we set forth into infinite potential together.

Dustin DiPerna & H.B. Augustine

Part 1: Evolution

Chapter 1
The Evolution of Evolutionary Thinking

Michael Wombacher

I should preface this brief chapter by stating that what follows is extremely cursory and focuses in particular, though not exclusively, on a spiritualized understanding of the question of evolution. Strict materialists have been excluded from this discussion as their views are, to be frank, already the common currency of the culture. Instead we want to turn our attention to some of those individuals who, in their consideration of the course of both cosmic and human events, have detected patterns and purposes of a spiritual nature in their flow and given thought and voice to them.

The Greeks, anticipating so much of modernity, touched on the rudiments of evolutionary thinking—described most simply as change over time from the lesser to the greater—though in time these notions gave way to the predominant conception of a static cosmos, one that ruled the Western mind for several millennia. Some exceptions to this trend can be found in the thinking of Giordano Bruno (1548–1600), Gottfried Leibniz (1646–1716), Johann Gottfried von Herder (1744–1803), and Johann Wolfgang von Goethe (1749–1832).

However, while strands of evolutionary thinking were to be found throughout the history of Western thought, and with increasing frequency in the seventeenth and eighteenth centuries, none of them coalesced into a formal system until after the French Revolution in 1789 firmly established the rational values of the Western Enlightenment in Europe's collective consciousness. During this time of turmoil and the ascendancy of a new worldview, it was in Germany that a spiritualized evolutionary philosophy congealed into an increasingly coherent metaphysical system. There a constellation of powerful intellects—Kant, Fichte, Schelling, and Hegel—banded together and in turns, both through collaboration and conflict, gave birth to what has since been referred to simply as German idealism. This emerging philosophical perspective, itself embedded within the larger movement of Romanticism, was a reaction against the "rational mind's tendency to brusquely reduce the full grandeur and beauty of life to stale scientific abstractions,"[1] a view that was, with the growing success of the Scientific Revolution, increasingly casting its shadow over European intellectual life.

The first of these, Immanuel Kant, the father of German idealism, gave primacy to the subjective aspect of experience by pointing out that the world we see "out there" is structured in our perceptions by a priori categories in our minds. This identification of the laws of thought with the laws of reality itself would later give to Hegel much of the starting point for the further development of his own philosophy. With respect to biological evolution, Kant, throughout the course of his career, also gave intermittent attention to the question of the transition of forms over time and became an early evolutionary theorist of sorts. Nonetheless, Kant never articulated a robust theory of evolution on par with his seminal insights into the nature of subjectivity, and thus his contribution to philosophy would ultimately not include the notion of development in time. In other words, Kant thought he could give an adequate account of human nature purely in philosophical terms without taking into account that human nature itself could evolve as a function of the unfolding of history.

Upon his heels, and commonly considered a bridge between Kant and Hegel, came Fichte and Schelling. Johann Gottlieb Fichte (1762–1814), initially considered one of Kant's most talented followers and protégés, ultimately developed his own system of transcendental philosophy, which in part challenged some of Kant's conclusions and perceived oversights. Chief among them was Kant's failure to account for a source of subjectivity that transcended its status as a mere product of blind, determined nature, those noumenal "things in themselves" upon which so much of his thinking was based. Thus, a primary question with which Fichte wrestled was how an objective and entirely determined reality of "things in themselves" could give rise to a free and radically undetermined subjective experience or sense of "I." In attempting to approach this conundrum (which, incidentally, still plagues philosophers

Chapter 1 - The Evolution of Evolutionary Thinking

of mind and neuroscientists today) he argued that one can start either with "things in themselves," which exist outside our experience, or with the "I" or sense of subjectivity as the ground of all experience. Fichte believed that the two approaches are mutually exclusive and himself chose the latter, arguing that consciousness does not have a grounding in the so-called real or objective world but rather that consciousness is not grounded in anything other than itself. It is, he believed, self-originating and inherently and utterly free. Moreover, he argued, that consciousness contains an infinite striving to know itself yet in so doing runs up against the limits of nature, which constrain the potentials of that infinite striving.

In response to this, Friedrich Wilhelm Joseph Schelling (1775–1854) took the conversation one step further, arguing that while nature may on the one hand present a limit to the infinite striving of spirit, it is also more than that. That is, it cannot stand in conflict with spirit, rather nature and spirit form a complementary whole, each relatively complete but ultimately correlative with the other. In Schelling's words, "Nature is visible Spirit; Spirit is invisible Nature."[2] That being the case, he concerned himself with the essence of the interaction between these two aspects of a seeming duality, how that interaction expresses itself in the world, and to what ends. That expression, he argued, occurs through a dynamic series of evolutionary processes in which spirit struggles toward an ever-increasing consciousness of itself in nature. In the course of that struggle, he went on, when the freedom of unlimited spirit runs up against the concrete pushback from the objective world, the final point of reconciliation is to be found in works of art and genius. Moreover, through this encounter between the infinite and the finite self-consciousness continues to develop toward an ideal form, seeking ever-higher expressions of subjectivity in spirit's encounter with the material world. In the end, Schelling was a mystic, arguing not only that the Absolute or "Godhead" is the ultimate ground of reality but that its true character can only be known through transcendent insight. Expanding these notions out to the human condition writ large Schelling, in his *System of Transcendental Idealism* (1800), writes that "History as a whole is a progressive, gradually self-disclosing revelation of the Absolute."

Which brings us to Georg Friedrich Wilhelm Hegel (1770–1831) who, more than all the others, applied these intuitions and arguments to the development of world history. "History," Hegel powerfully argued, "is none other than the progress of the consciousness of freedom."[3] Despite the chaos and bloody turmoil that has defined so much of the historical record, Hegel argued, an increase in reason and order as well as an ultimate purpose can be detected in its forward march. Specifically, he posited that history progresses through the famed dialectic of "thesis-antithesis-synthesis" and through that process Spirit, or the Absolute, comes to know itself increasingly more fully in nature and through mankind. More specifically, each historical stage of human development, Hegel believed, contains within itself a contradiction, an "antithesis," that needs to be resolved by a higher synthesis or more comprehensive way of grasping the world. Once resolved, the higher synthesis itself becomes the new thesis, once again containing within itself the seeds of contradictions, spurring the process onward to repeat the cycle, albeit at a higher level. In this way Hegel understood the Divine, which on the one hand was always the ground of everything that exists, to exist most fully in the collective future of humanity, to be revealed with increasing depth and clarity as consciousness evolved. In adopting this dialectical and historically dynamic perspective, Hegel rejected Kant's static notions of timeless categories of knowledge and acknowledged the powerful interplay between consciousness and culture in the evolution of humanity.

In his own time Hegel's influence was enormous, overshadowing those upon whose work his own ideas were founded, particularly Fichte and Schelling. From Germany his influence spread across the continent and as far as England, where it provided the spiritually and intellectually inclined a powerful system of defense against the growing tide of secularism and materialism sweeping Western Europe. However, he was not without critics and ultimately, largely due to the rise of naturalistic philosophies and the secular philosophical juggernaut set in motion by the Scientific Revolution, idealism in any form could not hold. This was particularly true after the publication of Darwin's *Origin of Species* in 1859. With its publication the secular tide overwhelmed idealism with positivism (the notion that the only valid truth is based on sense experience and positive verification), which was rapidly drawing in both the European and American intellectual life. As Will Durant put it, "After a generation of Absolute intoxication, the mind of Europe reacted by taking a pledge against metaphysics of any kind."[4] And it seems to have been a final pledge, as "With Hegel's decline there passed from the modern intellectual arena the last culturally powerful metaphysical system claiming the existence of a universal order accessible to human awareness."[5] The last

Chapter 1 - The Evolution of Evolutionary Thinking

great system builder of the European intellectual tradition had ironically gone down in the very cycle of thesis/antithesis predicted by his own system. And to date, no further grand systems of historical unfolding have gained traction in the Western psyche.

With the reaction against high-minded metaphysics, contemplation regarding the nature of life, the nature of knowledge, and the role of human beings now moved boldly and rapidly in the naturalistic direction. One of the key figures of positivism and exemplars of the new thinking was the Frenchman Auguste Comte (1798-1857) who argued powerfully that science functioned in concentric circles of complexity, with mathematics being the simplest and most general, moving up to astronomy, physics, chemistry, biology, and ultimately sociology. Each science, he noted, was built on the foundations of the broader and more general science that preceded it and therefore it made sense that the social life of human beings should be the last to yield it secrets to the increasingly powerful light of scientific method. He viewed that life as having moved through three historical stages: the theological stage of mythical conceptions, the metaphysical stage of obscure forces, and finally the positivist stage in which everything is explained naturalistically and in which the preceding stages are gratefully discarded. He viewed metaphysics of any sort as a stage of arrested development and in his old age went so far as to set forth, in symbolic opposition to it, a "religion of humanity" within which humankind itself would become the object of worship, with the heroes of human progress herein taking on the role of saints.

Ultimately positivism, though French in its roots, found its greatest philosophical resonance with the English worldview. There utility trumped metaphysics owing to the fact that England was a country busy with trade, industry, and a worldwide empire, which "looked up to matters of fact with a certain reverence."[6] And it was here that one of the greatest intellects and synthesizers of the day, Herbert Spencer, took evolutionary thinking, stripped of metaphysics, to new heights. Like Comte, Spencer advocated the idea that the discovered laws of nature could be directly applied to understanding the complexities of human culture and the nature of the mind. He also held that the result of evolution was progress, but not in the teleological sense embedded in the above mentioned metaphysical systems. Rather, he coined the phrase "survival of the fittest" and argued that rational self-interest drove human culture forward toward increasing levels of complexity. With respect to the nature of mind, while allowing that it evolved in tandem with the brain, he refused to endorse the dualism of the mind and brain being separate and ultimately viewed the entire process in strictly mechanistic terms.

Spencer's ideas were widely influential during his own time and his renown in intellectual circles was on par with Darwin himself. Among those he influenced were William James (1842–1910), Charles Sanders Peirce (1839–1914), and John Dewey (1859–1952), the founders of a uniquely American philosophical movement referred to simply as pragmatism (or radical empiricism), which essentially held that the truth of a philosophical statement can only be evaluated by its pragmatic results in the lives of individuals. In a subsequent chapter Jeff Carreira will explore the contributions of these three thinkers to the current development of evolutionary spirituality in a good deal more detail than I will do here, where I will offer only the briefest summary of some of their contributions. There are three that are most significant. First, their thinking itself was powerfully informed by an evolutionary perspective; second, their philosophical insights bring together both logical realism and metaphysical idealism; and third, they contributed to the foundations of process philosophy which is becoming increasingly influential in helping to interpret the significance of human emergence in an evolving universe.

All three start from an essentially positivist standpoint, that our knowledge of life comes first from positive, verifiable experience. But their universe is not the strictly determined one of scientific materialism. Rather, as you will see in Carreira's essay, it is a teeming process that is unstable, dynamic, geared toward development, and laden with teleology. For Peirce the universe is an ever-expanding continuum in which thought, feeling, and matter are increasingly fused together into greater degrees of harmony.[7] For James the universe is not one of objects but of a "blooming, buzzing confusion" of processes that one organizes through experience and that is continuously evolving. James, like Peirce, viewed nature as a constant striving to bring order and intelligibility into chaos and he emphasized the human freedom of choice as central to this process. Thus, the appearance of novelty in the evolutionary process was, to James as to Peirce, more than the mere random chance so commonly cited by scientific materialists. That is, James argued that to "an observer standing outside of its generating causes, novelty can appear only as so much 'chance,' while to one who stands inside it is the expression of 'free

Chapter 1 - The Evolution of Evolutionary Thinking

creative activity.'"[8] Thus, in James's conception teleology enters the process of evolution through the free action of intelligent individuals. John Dewey, whose central influence was in the field of education, concurs, arguing in his *Evolution and Ethics* (1893), that "the forces bound up with the cosmic have come to consciousness in man. That which was instinct in the animal is conscious impulse in man. That which was 'tendency to vary' in the animal is conscious foresight in man. That which was unconscious adaptation and survival in the animal . . . is with man conscious deliberation and experimentation."[9] And Dewey, no doubt, speaks for all three when he questions "whether the spiritual life does not get its surest and most ample guarantees when it is learned that the laws and conditions of righteousness are implicated in the working processes of the universe; when it is found that man in his conscious struggles . . . is . . . buoyed up by the forces which have developed nature; and that in this moral struggle he acts not as a mere individual but as an organ . . . carrying forward the universal process."[10]

These three thinkers, and in particular William James, had considerable influence on two very significant figures in the furtherance of evolutionary thinking: Henri Bergson (1859–1941) and Alfred North Whitehead (1861–1947). Let us turn our attention first to Bergson whose writings were wildly popular between the world wars and for which he was awarded the Nobel Prize in Literature. Bergson's fundamental reaction to the philosophical trends of his own times was profoundly anti-materialistic and anti-mechanistic. He rejected the notion that space, quantity, and mathematics alone can offer a sufficient account of reality as a whole. Such stable concepts, he argued, can never capture the fluidities of a reality ever in flux. Nor, he added, is the intellect, which tends to divide and categorize, the primary means by which to apprehend the deeper movements and structures of that reality. In fact, the intellect, he argued, shaped by evolution to deal with life's pragmatic problems, is precisely what causes us to erroneously interpret reality as a collection of fixed objects and consequently cut us off from life's deeper flow. On the contrary, it is intuition by which life's totality—a stream of fluid and interconnected processes, not things—is most adequately apprehended. And that totality is best understood not as a collection of objects related to each other through mechanistic laws but as an unbroken stream of events occurring in *duration*. Duration for Bergson was distinct from clock time, which he viewed as a mathematically fixed abstraction. In actual experience there is no place where one moment ends and another begins. There is one stream of experience, a "succession without distinction . . . an interconnection and organization of elements, each one of which represents the whole, and cannot be distinguished or isolated from it except by [the distorting transformation of] abstract thought."[11] "Duration," Bergson tells us, "is the continuous progress of the past which gnaws into the future and which swells as it advances." By extension, then, "the past in its entirety is prolonged into the present and abides there actual and acting." To put it differently, he points out that ". . . we think with only a small part of our past; but it is with our entire past . . . that we desire, will, and act."[12] Bergson also argued that the evolution of consciousness, having awakened in man the intuitive dimension, now afforded him direct apprehension of the creative force, the *élan vital*, underlying all of life. And that all-pervasive force, the engine of evolution itself, he saw as a raw spiritual impulse emanating from the source of life itself to bring into being in the natural world higher and deeper expressions of creativity.[13] Moreover, the *élan vital* acts neither in accordance with mechanistic determinism nor notions of final causation (a drive toward a preplanned goal)—both ultimately static notions—but is rather an expression of pure creative freedom and the true source of unforeseeable novelty. And it is in man, through his highly evolved freedom of choice (which coevolves with consciousness), that the pure creative freedom of the *élan vital* has come upon the greatest opportunity to express itself in the theater of life. Thus, he argued, "man is no passively adaptive machine; he is a focus of redirected force, a center of creative evolution."[14] Extending this dynamic conception out to cosmic dimensions, he added that the universe itself is no blind, purposeless machine but a creative, open-ended process by which the human and divine wills are unified and that man is ultimately destined to become a living expression of the mystery of God in time.

Alfred North Whitehead's philosophy was powerfully influenced by the process-oriented thinking of Henri Bergson and the pragmatism of William James (which acknowledges the validity of nonsensory experience in philosophical speculation) as well as by Leibniz's notion of "appetition" by which all things strive to bring novelty and greater perfection into being.[15] However, the unexpected and dramatic collapse of Newtonian physics as the bedrock of reality under the weight of both Einstein's relativity theory and the birth of quantum mechanics gave a fundamental

Chapter 1 - The Evolution of Evolutionary Thinking

impetus to the development of a series of powerful ideas and insights whose significance—overlooked by mainstream philosophy for the better part of the twentieth century—is only today becoming increasingly appreciated. Whitehead's masterwork, *Process and Reality*, published in 1929, describes the universe as an unbroken stream of interrelated events within which "objects" are, as they were for Bergson, mere mental abstractions, pulled by the intellect from the unceasing flux of existence for practical purposes but not ultimately real in any sense. He contrasted his "metaphysics of flux" with the existing "metaphysics of substance" (which views life as a collection of objects or substances and their interrelations) but viewed them not as competitive but rather as complementary or correlative ways of approaching reality.

In this complementarity, however, Whitehead clearly considered time, change, and creativity as foundational philosophical concepts and viewed "process" as central to a full understanding of life. In such an understanding the basic building blocks of reality are not solid objects of any sort but rather moments of experience he termed alternately as "actual occasions" or "actual entities." Each such event or entity, conscious or not, contains within it all the influences from the past (which are "prehended" in the present moment and referred to as its "internal relations") as well as all the immediate objective influences from the environment (its "external relations") at that very moment and thus represents a kind of organic totality that, as Bergson said, swells forward into time, adding the totality of this moment to all future moments as the process surges ahead.

An "actual event or occasion," it must be understood, need not be a moment of human experience, but rather any event whatsoever. According to Whitehead's thinking, every actual occasion or actual entity —from electrons to human beings—both experience the world around them and have *some* essential degree of self-determination or freedom of choice in relationship to it. To be clear, experience here does not necessarily mean conscious experience. It can also be unconscious. To help understand this, consider the twentieth century's insights from depth psychology, which have revealed the influence of the dark and teeming world of the "unconscious" whose contents exist in inky depths and rise to the surface light of consciousness only in small and digestible portions. Nonetheless, its powerful influences affect our behavior in significant ways, all the while remaining utterly unknown to our conscious minds. In a very similar way, Whitehead argues, an experience need not be conscious and thus experience can be said to exist even at the most fundamental levels of reality. To put it differently, subjectivity, broadly defined, can exist without conscious awareness of it and through this understanding we can appreciate that some form of "interiority" runs straight down to the foundations of reality though conscious awareness clearly does not. This understanding, referred to as "pan-experientialism" is a rather dramatic departure from the conventions of Western philosophy, which has tended toward either idealism (subjectivity or mind is the foundation of reality), dualism (subjectivity and objectivity, mind and matter, are equally fundamental though separate), and materialism (only matter is real).

The question of freedom of choice deserves some extra attention here. According to Whitehead, all actual occasions—again, from electrons to humans—are influenced by the past in countless ways and carry that past forward in their responses. Yet while much of this is deterministic in the Newtonian sense, there exists at every level the possibility for some freedom of choice or novelty of response. Hence Whitehead's notion that the past *influences* the present rather than strictly determining it purely in accordance with Newtonian mechanism. Now clearly that influence can be very, very strong and additionally the degrees of freedom available for differing entities in responding to such influences will vary enormously and in accordance with their structural complexity. The range of options for a dog will always be greater than for an ant and for an ant it will always be greater than for an amoeba. Nonetheless, at every level of reality the potential for novelty exists by virtue of this fact, a fact which is therefore always pregnant with the promise of a continuously open-ended future.[16] New choices are possible. And it is by recognizing this freedom of choice or self-determination that Whitehead, and process philosophers in general, begin to address the notion of divine influence in the world. Before considering the nature of divine influence, however, we must first turn our attention to Whitehead's conception of God.

That conception reflected both Whitehead's commitment to naturalism as well as to theism, a tension he resolved by conceiving of God as having two "poles," one primordial and transcendent as well as one bound into space and time. To put it more simply, the two poles of God can be said to consist of pure being on the one hand and pure becoming on the other. And God's relation to the world can be summarized as "mutual transcendence, mutual immanence, and mutual

Chapter 1 - The Evolution of Evolutionary Thinking

creation."[17] In other words, God transcends the world in that whatever that mystery meant by the word "God" is always utterly free from the world and utterly one in its own imperishable perfection. On the other hand, the world transcends God "insofar as it is not subject to divine fiat and can disregard God's lures or presentation of novel possibilities."[18] As we all well know, it is one thing to be inspired by the new, the novel, and even the sacred, but another altogether to respond to that inspiration with the fullness of our humanity. In other words, in the process conception God is not all powerful and interventionist in the sense of directly interfering in human history through the performance of miracles. Rather, God is persuasive and lures all of existence towards truth, goodness, and beauty at the same time that freedom of choice always allows for the possibility of that lure being disregarded.

Additionally, God can be said to be the creator of the world in the sense of having set all the elements in motion at the beginning of time. However, the process itself, being a maelstrom of creativity, defies strict predictability in its outcome and thus God himself may be as surprised by the universe's emergent novelty as any onlooker might. Moreover, as much as God is the creator of the world, the world can conversely be said to be —and this is a tricky notion for traditionalists—creating God as well. That is, the "becoming" pole of God, in Whitehead's conception, actually evolves as the world evolves and becomes richer in experience, more complex in its inner and outer interconnectedness, as well as deeper in its conscious subjectivity. In addition to being both the creator of and created by the world, the God of process philosophy is a participatory God, being the ultimate subject of everything, and thus he deeply feels every experience of the world with subjective immediacy.

It should be fairly clear from this that the God of process philosophy is a significant departure from the traditional theistic God who is completely transcendent, supernatural, unchanging, omnipotent, and beyond time and space. On the other hand, Whitehead's conception of God is not one in which God is purely immanent or merely the sum of all the entities in the world, a position referred to as pantheism. Rather, Whitehead's conception may be referred to as "panentheism" (or to be very specific though inordinately confusing, "dipolar panentheism"), the notion that everything exists within God and that God is immanent everywhere in the universe while simultaneously being transcendent, more than and always free from the entire creative process of becoming.

An additional aspect of God is that in and through his creation He is ever striving for the realization of higher value, and that striving is directly reflected in all of His creatures and their striving.[19] In fact, one of the key characteristics of life that distinguishes it from nonlife is that it acts purposefully and strives first and foremost to survive and secondly to flourish or live as best as possible. This fundamental drive underlies all of creation and in humans, of course, such striving reaches to ever-higher levels. It is what the Greeks referred to as eros—the creative or evolutionary impulse underlying all of existence. Therefore God, though perfect in himself in the dimension of pure being, is striving for the realization of higher truth, goodness, and beauty, as well as deeper and more intense modes of being or subjectivity in the dimension of becoming. And the two, of course, are directly correlative to one another. The truth, goodness, and beauty at the source of things is directly correlative to the human utopian impulse or striving for truth, goodness, and beauty in the manifest world of imperfection where its nature is often not so evident.

Lastly, because Whitehead understands every actual entity to be an instance of creativity, experience, and self-determination, God is not capable of forcing them into compliance with some overall grand design. As we have already seen, in process philosophy God is viewed as persuasive rather than coercive, ever luring his creation forward with the promise of novelty and the realization of higher value rather than enforcing compliance through direct intervention in natural processes. This conception puts process philosophy in a position to address the problem of human evil by highlighting the human responsibility for their own freedom choice. To put it differently, God is powerless to act in the world except through the willing responsiveness of his most highly evolved creatures to his lures towards the greater realization of truth, beauty, and goodness. In other words, in a profound sense God is as dependent upon us to assure the furtherance of the realization of truth, goodness, and beauty as we are on him as the source of these transcendent values. Clearly there are enormous moral implications in that.

Let us sum up with a quote from a highly respected contemporary advocate of process philosophy, Nicholas Rescher, who tells us that Whitehead:

Chapter 1 - The Evolution of Evolutionary Thinking

> ... saw the evolution of living organisms on Earth as a particular manifestation of the most fundamental creative process of the universe in general. It is not directed by laws beyond itself but generated from large populations of entities all at once seeking their own fulfillment and contributing, over countless generations, to the great cycle of generational succession that makes for the advance of the whole. Evolution is of course not a thing of some kind but the name we give a process consisting in the ongoing succession of dynamic elements, each maturing its transitory contribution to the unfolding of existence. And time, like evolution, is also not a thing but the name we give to overall series of risings and perishings of concrete moments of satisfaction and sacrifice.[20]

It is because Whitehead's conception of God and evolution is so broad and deeply nuanced that I have given it as much space in the current discussion as I have. The subtlety and multidimensionality of its philosophical framework puts it in a position to embrace and seamlessly harmonize science, religion, and philosophy in a way that no prior system has. And while for the better part of the twentieth century process philosophy was by and large ignored in all three realms, as we enter into the twenty-first century limitations in the conventional thinking of these fields are becoming increasingly evident and problematic. Thus, a growing number of thoughtful individuals are turning their attention to process philosophy. Additionally, process thought has helped lay a major foundation for the even more comprehensive and increasingly influential field of integral philosophy, to which we shall turn our attention shortly.

However, before so doing there are at least two other individuals who deserve our attention in this discussion of the evolution of evolutionary thinking. The first is the French Jesuit paleontologist Pierre Teilhard de Chardin (1881–1955) and the second is the Indian revolutionary and spiritual visionary Sri Aurobindo (1872–1950). What sets both of these individuals apart from those already mentioned is that their first and most profound commitment was to the deeply lived spiritual life. Their scholarly pursuits and philosophical daring were a direct outgrowth of this primary passion. And in both cases their exposure to and understanding of evolution profoundly altered their understanding of the significance of the spiritual life and the purpose of human existence.

The Coming Waves

Pierre Teilhard de Chardin was naturally curious and spiritually sensitive from an early age, the pursuit of the spiritual life and the life of a naturalist growing in him side by side. At the age of twelve he attended a Jesuit boarding school and ultimately took up training as a Jesuit missionary. It was his reading of Henri Bergson's *Creative Evolution* that awoke him to the spiritual significance of evolution and catalyzed a fire that, by his own accounts, devoured his heart and spirit. After his highly decorated service as a stretcher bearer during the most brutal battles of the First World War he began writing and publishing some of his evolutionary reflections. Yet for all the bloody pain and death that surrounded him, his passionate conclusion was not nihilistic in the least. Rather, it was the life-affirming conclusion that existence was shot through with a hidden, mysterious, glorious direction and purpose and that evolution was the vehicle by which that divine trajectory was being worked out. It was during the war years that his thinking both on evolution and the nature of Christianity began to develop—and disturb his superiors. In 1925, the same year that saw the Scopes Monkey Trial unfold in Tennessee, he was firmly rebuked by his superiors and ordered to sign a statement repudiating his ideas. In a show of submission to his superiors he signed the document and returned to the Far East. Teilhard, now essentially exiled, spent the next eleven years in China where he became a renowned paleontologist and played a major role in the discovery and interpretation of Peking Man in 1929 and 1930.

As the years wore on he participated in numerous geological expeditions and his reputation in scientific circles steadily grew. His final period of exile in China spanned the years of the Second World War and saw the publication of one of his most significant and enduring works, *The Phenomenon of Man*, in 1940. In this work, many of his ideas concerning evolution that he had nurtured over the years found their full flowering. Teilhard here expressed evolution as a process that leads to ever-increasing levels of complexity, each level allowing for a greater concentration and articulation of consciousness. With Homo sapiens, that increased complexity allows for the emergence of a radical new phenomenon—the capacity for consciousness to turn upon itself, become aware of its own existence, and reflect on its own nature. This emergent capacity, according to Teilhard, raises the human species out of and above the animal world by leaps and bounds. With the birth of self-reflective awareness the evolution of the human species accelerates, leading ultimately to the

Chapter 1 - The Evolution of Evolutionary Thinking

forming of a collective identity that becomes increasingly nuanced and sophisticated as the network of trade and communication and the ever-growing transmission of ideas continues to grow around the globe. This deepening and increasing complexification of consciousness continues apace until it leads to a further leap in its own evolution, which Teilhard referred to as the emergence of the "noosphere." This noosphere he described as a thinking membrane encasing the Earth which, as such, represents the collective consciousness of the entire human species—a complex network of thoughts and emotions in which everyone is immersed and to which everyone both contributes and is subject. Eventually, according to Teilhard, this increasing convergence and complexification of consciousness will, ultimately and in cosmic time, culminate in a final convergence upon an "Omega Point." There has been much discussion about precisely what Teilhard meant by an Omega Point; many of the vagaries surrounding this notion no doubt stem from its deeply spiritual, profoundly utopian, and "very distant to even the most inspired imagination" nature.

What can be said is that the Omega Point represents some form of ultimate or supreme consciousness toward which the entire universe is driving. In addition to being the convergent goal of evolution, the Omega Point also, in some sense, already and simultaneously exists as the ultimate transcendent attractor for further evolution. Additionally, it can be thought of as a kind of intense super-personalization of the entire cosmos rather than a mere aggregation or collectivity of separate parts. Yet in that, individuals themselves are not suppressed but rather become super-personalized, autonomous centers of agency, constrained neither by space nor time, who exist in a fully awake universe. They are manifest reflections of the image of God who, when taken together literally, form a collective cosmic Christ. And for Teilhard this highly utopian and difficult to conceive outcome was the evolutionary goal of all existence. This powerful sentiment of purpose and direction as driving the entire evolutionary enterprise is beautifully expressed in the opening lines of his book *The Future of Man:*

> The conflict dates from the day when one man, flying in the face of appearance, perceived that the forces of nature are no more unalterably fixed in their orbits than the stars themselves, but that their serene arrangement around us depicts the flow of a

tremendous tide—the day on which a first voice rang out, crying to Mankind peacefully slumbering on the raft of Earth, "We are moving! We are going forward!"[21]

Unfortunately Teilhard was unable to share his evolutionary passion with a wider public for, ever-remaining respectful to his ecclesiastical superiors, he refrained from publishing his works during his lifetime. Only upon his death did his friends publish the considerable body of work Teilhard had accumulated during his extraordinary and adventurous life.

Interestingly, while Teilhard de Chardin was diving deeply into his evolutionary speculations both in Europe and in China, similarly inspired evolutionary contemplations were consuming the mind of an Indian man of whose presence Teilhard was entirely unaware: Aurobindo Ghose, later to become known as Sri Aurobindo.

Like Teilhard, Aurobindo led a life that spanned many diverse and extreme dimensions of the human experience. He was highly educated, exposed to many cultures, swept up in the conflict and political turmoil of his time, and deeply fueled by spiritual inspiration. Born in Calcutta in 1872 to Westernized Indian parents, he was sent to England at the age of seven to receive a British education and soon proved to be a brilliant student. Some years later, while pursuing his education at Cambridge as a young man, he not only immersed himself in the study of the German idealists mentioned above, but also became painfully aware of India's plight under the brutal heel of British rule. Thus, upon graduation, rather than pursuing a promising career as an English civil servant he returned to India intensely committed to freeing his motherland from the colonial yoke. It was during this time that he also began to commit himself seriously to the practice of yoga and meditation. Being driven, gifted, and passionate he excelled astonishingly in both areas. With respect to his revolutionary inclinations, he soon got the attention of the British authorities, who eventually came to refer to him as the most dangerous man in India. And with respect to his spiritual inclinations, it took him a mere three days after meeting a meditation master to be able to fully stop the activity of his mind and enter into a state of samadhi (a state of intense meditative absorption, often referred to as cosmic consciousness, in which the individual merges into the Divine and realizes his or her deepest and truest nature)—something that took his master years to attain.

Chapter 1 - *The Evolution of Evolutionary Thinking*

Both attainments had consequences. In 1908 he was arrested by British authorities and spent a year in jail. Yet there, rather than moldering away, he gave himself fully to spiritual practices—with dramatic consequences. Again and again he entered into the deepest states of consciousness and spiritual revelation; a year later and upon his acquittal he emerged a deeply enlightened soul. After his release he retreated to the French province of Pondicherry where he was able to commit himself fully to the pursuit of his spiritual practices. It was there that he was able to compose the many books, articles, and poems in which he articulated a dramatic new spiritual vision, wherein the traditional revelation of spiritual enlightenment was interpreted in the context of the newly emerging understanding of evolution. In what he would come to call "integral yoga," Aurobindo suggested that the purpose of spiritual enlightenment was not to free the soul from endless Earthly incarnation, as nearly all of Indian mysticism teaches, but to free the soul from its egoic constraints so that the spiritual power discovered at the source of reality could surge into life and help humanity evolve to as yet undreamed of spiritual potentials. From this basic insight Aurobindo formulated a profoundly sophisticated and deeply nuanced understanding of the future potential of the evolution of human consciousness.

Aurobindo was a prolific and gifted writer and any attempt to summarize his teaching here would be unacceptably inadequate.[22] That said, he committed himself to the articulation of the deepest human aspiration: "The divination of the Godhead, the impulse towards perfection, the search after pure Truth and unmixed Bliss, the sense of a secret immortality,"[23] in the context of an evolving universe. Understood in that context, he saw man as being pushed from "below" by the physical forces of material evolution and pulled from "above" by the Godhead and the spiritual aspiration its transcendent presence sparked in the human soul. Man in his current state represented for Aurobindo a transitional being between these two poles of reality through which the Godhead could ultimately come to full expression in the world of manifestation. Over thousands of pages of the most elevated prose and poetry Aurobindo laid out not only what he understood to be the relations between nature, man, and spirit, but also the many gradations and layers of spiritual progress that lie ahead in the unfolding evolution of the species.

At any rate, these last two figures in our brief overview of the history of evolutionary spirituality both passed on in the mid-1950s. And in truth, in their own time both remained virtually unknown as the great mass of their contemporaries had adopted either scientific materialism or religious fundamentalism as their creed for living—a cultural rift that has been bequeathed generation by generation to our own.

However, as the twentieth century drew to a close the conversation concerning evolution began to diversify both on the theistic and materialistic fronts, though in both cases still well beneath the notice of the culture at large. This diversification had to do, on the one hand, with the fact that an increasing number of scientists (though still a minority by far) began to challenge the neo-Darwinian framework (genetic determinism and natural selection are the *only* drivers of evolution) by suggesting that other factors such as symbiosis, epi-genetics,[24] and even the conscious choice of organisms[25] might have a role to play in evolutionary outcomes. On the other hand, a growing number of spiritually interested yet scientifically literate individuals began to suspect that perhaps there was a way of understanding evolution that was both scientifically rigorous and spiritually significant. The upshot has been a small but significant explosion of interest in evolution across its many dimensions.

As a consequence, there are now so many lines of evolutionary thinking that Carter Phipps, author of *Evolutionaries*, has identified as many as twelve distinct positions[26] which run the gamut from hardcore atheists to unapologetic theists; they include the neo-Darwinists, intelligent designers, process philosophers, progressive Darwinists, collectivists, complexity theorists, directionalists, transhumanists, theistic evolutionists, esoteric evolutionists, conscious evolutionists, and, last but not least, the integralists.[27] Now that is a full docket of ideas and debates indeed. And the debates between them, as often contentious as collaborative yet always spirited and lively, are without a doubt infinitely more nuanced, interesting and, most importantly, more relevant to the current cultural predicament than the one-dimensional and fundamentalist positions which we are usually fed both by hardcore neo-Darwinists and narrow-minded intelligent designers. That being the case, these are voices that need to be heard, and thankfully increasing numbers of people are clamoring to hear them. That is particularly evident with respect to what Phipps has called the integralists, a diverse group of people from all walks of life and a multitude of professions interested in Integral Theory.

Chapter 1 - The Evolution of Evolutionary Thinking

Integral Theory is largely associated with the work of the contemporary American philosopher Ken Wilber. Wilber launched his career in 1973 with the publication of his first book entitled *Spectrum of Consciousness* in which he attempted to categorize and organize along a developmental spectrum different levels and experiences of consciousness as described both in Eastern mystical literature and Western psychological traditions. Over two decades and a great deal of rumination later he published *Sex, Ecology, Spirituality* (1995), a monumental work of extraordinary breadth and depth whose publication is generally thought to mark the official birth of what has since come to be called Integral Theory. Integral Theory as conceived of and developed by Wilber is a response to the one dimensionality of scientific materialism (only matter is real) and is built around a number of key insights. First among them is an insight culled from process philosophy, namely that every exterior has an interior. Second is the understanding that each of those has an individual and a collective dimension. Bringing those two together gives us what has become the famous four-quadrant model of integral philosophy which, as Jeff Carreira will argue in the following chapter, was deeply influenced by his study of the work of Charles Sanders Peirce. These quadrants are: the individual interior (mind, soul, spirit, psyche, etc.), the individual exterior (one's physicality in all its aspects), the collective interior (culture), and the collective exterior (social institutions). Moreover, within each of these quadrants there are lines of development about which much has been learned from fields as diverse as developmental psychology, evolutionary psychology, cultural anthropology, systems theory, and a great deal more. Additionally, all of this is understood to take place in the context of evolution, about which integral philosophy has at least two further insights to offer. First is the understanding that evolution as a whole features certain characteristics that apply equally across all of its domains from the lowest levels of biological evolution to the highest levels of cultural evolution. And second is that evolution itself is a cosmic process progressing along an undivided, multidimensional trajectory in which spirit and matter form two sides of one unbroken, dynamic process moving forward in time to increasing levels of complexity, integration, and creative expression.

Taken together these insights have come to form the foundation of an extraordinarily flexible and increasingly sophisticated lens to view the human experience. One of the many things that comes into sharp relief when viewing the current human predicament through this lens is that our world is comprised of differing levels of cultural development or worldviews which, though often standing sharply against one another, form part of a predictable flow of development, a "spiral of development" to use integral language, that has a direction. Development, in this case, is defined primarily, though not solely, by increasing circles of moral inclusion. That is, a "higher" level is considered higher by virtue of the fact that its worldview extends moral consideration to a larger segment of the human race and life as a whole than the level below it. And again, Integral Theory holds that this developmental process is going somewhere, that greater and greater levels of moral inclusion lie ahead in the future evolution of human culture, as do increasingly nuanced and multidimensional perspectives on the entirety of the human experience and of the human understanding of its place in a living "Kosmos."[28] In short, the integral lens has much to offer not only to the understanding of human evolution but to the effort to construct a comprehensive and meaningful new worldview that can begin to sort through, organize, and harmonize many of the contentious issues currently dividing the culture at large.

One final newly emerging school of thought should be mentioned here: Evolutionary Enlightenment. Evolutionary Enlightenment is the product of the awakening, spiritual experimentation, and philosophical reflections of American spiritual teacher Andrew Cohen. Before embarking on a brief overview of Cohen's work and conclusions I should acknowledge up front that Cohen is a very controversial figure and that good reasons exist for that controversy. The bulk of these issues revolve around the fact that due to the power and nature of Cohen's spiritual awakening at the age of 30, and the impact he was having on those who came to him, he took up the traditional role of guru, as understood in the Eastern sense of the term. That meant that within the context of his own community he held absolute authority over every aspect of the students' lives—a risky undertaking at any point in history but particularly so in the modern and postmodern context that forms our world. The reasons for Cohen's assumption of this role are complex, but two are worth mentioning.

First, it was in the context of a traditional guru/disciple role that Cohen's own awakening occurred, and this relationship anchored itself as his reference point for the awakening of others. Second, due to his own

Chapter 1 - The Evolution of Evolutionary Thinking

relatively young age when he was unexpectedly thrust into the role of spiritual teacher he, in his own words, "had to assume total authority or my students would not have taken me seriously." There are additional very complex reasons for all this, which are far beyond the scope of this short chapter.[29] Suffice it to say that in his role as enlightened teacher and absolute authority figure, Cohen put enormous spiritual and psychological pressure on his students, and this has resulted in extremely negative fallout for both many of the students involved and Cohen himself. He now must deal with the harsh consequences of severely overstepping the bounds of legitimate authority.

And the current controversy around Cohen raises many important questions regarding the significance of spiritual enlightenment, its relationship to the development of the individual, its relationship to the development of culture, and a great deal more.

That said, negative fallout is not the only thing Cohen's work has produced over the years. In fact, Cohen's teaching of Evolutionary Enlightenment has contributed enormously over the last two decades to the emerging cultural conversation around Integral Theory in a multiplicity of dimensions. A great deal of this contribution came through *EnlightenNext Magazine*, the flagship cultural expression of his teaching, as well as through a spiritual practice developed by Cohen and his closest students that may most simply be referred to as "intersubjective enlightenment." Let us delve into the emergence of the latter because in it are found clues both to Cohen's significant contributions to questions of ultimacy in an evolving universe as well as to his controversial reputation as a spiritual authority figure.

At the age of twenty two, haunted by a spiritual awakening he underwent when he was only sixteen, Cohen began the pursuit of spiritual enlightenment. At the age of thirty he met H.W.L. Poonja, the last living disciple of the famed Indian Advaita master Ramana Maharshi. In Poonja's company Cohen underwent an enormous transformation. "I felt like I was being eaten alive by a conscious energy," he has said in various accounts of his transformation, which became complete with Cohen's conclusion that "Andrew is dead." After that, both by his own accounts and those of others who witnessed the transformation, Cohen became a living furnace for the transmission of enlightenment. Driven to set the world aflame with the fire of his own awakening Cohen began to teach relentlessly. However, after several years he began to question the sufficiency of the Advaita tradition as passed along to him by Poonja. The reasons are multifold.

First, it became apparent to Cohen that the interior revelation of enlightenment had to exert noticeable and significantly positive effects on the exterior expression of the personality and its moral stand in the world. To insist that inner awakening had little or nothing to do with outer behavior (as much of the Advaita tradition, including Poonja, insists) seemed not only not non-dual or unified, it also threw into question the ultimate relevance of spiritual enlightenment with respect to the issue of human relationship. And it was with the nature of human relationship that Cohen was concerned from early on. How, he wanted to know, are the unity and perfection revealed in the timeless source of one's being expressed in the world of becoming and imperfection? If there is only one Self, how can its undivided nature express itself in the world of division? These questions burned in Cohen and spawned further reflections.

Of those, one would become key for the future development of this thinking. To awaken to enlightenment, he realized, was one thing—a profound inner revelation of inherent freedom, immortality, and perfection—but how that revelation would be lived was determined by how it was interpreted by the individual. And that interpretation would clearly be influenced by any number of cultural factors. Moreover, since culture had so dramatically moved forward since the birth of the ancient enlightenment traditions, Cohen felt compelled to question traditional conclusions about enlightenment and explore potential new ones. In this, two factors profoundly influenced his contemplations. The first was the reality of cosmic, biological, and cultural evolution—an understanding of the greater context of human emergence that the great spiritual realizers of the past simply did not have access to. Their cosmologies, in one way or another, were all cosmologies of stasis and for them the goal of spiritual liberation was to be free from this world of illusion forever. For Cohen, however, the understanding of evolution—the fact that the universe exploded from nothing and seemed to have an enormous forward momentum—changed the picture considerably. And these considerations brought him into line with much of the evolutionary thinking already outlined above, though he had never heard of the German idealists, Teilhard de Chardin, Sri Aurobindo, and the others. In other words, it became clear to him that while Spirit as the interior revelation of the timeless and immortal Ground of all Being was ever unchanging, radically

Chapter 1 - The Evolution of Evolutionary Thinking

transcendent and always prior to anything that ever happened in time, in the external world of evolutionary becoming Spirit was striving for ever greater expressions of harmony and integration. It was this latter dimension that became key for Cohen and upon which he would focus most of his teaching and philosophical exploration.

Second, from very early on in his teaching career Cohen intuited the potential for the emergence of a new kind of enlightenment —"intersubjective" (between subjects) enlightenment—which could only emerge through the interactions between individuals who had transcended their egos to a significant degree. Following this intuition and working with a very committed group of students led to a series of significant breakthroughs in which a new potential in human consciousness began to emerge. That is, Cohen and his students found that through a committed, ego-free engagement with one another a new form of consciousness was able to emerge between the individuals that radically transcended the significance of any particular individual. And yet it simultaneously and utterly depended upon their committed engagement. That new consciousness, or what Cohen came to refer to as the "New Being," was characterized by two unique and seemingly contradictory qualities. On the one hand, in such a gathering it was impossible for the individual to tell where "they" ended and "the other" began as the living experience of One Self overwhelmed everyone in the room. And on the other, each individual, now radically free from fear and self-concern, felt more authentically themselves than they ever had. In this paradoxical fusion of autonomy and communion what became apparent to all was that a newly emergent and miraculous human potential was beginning to express itself in the world through them. "It was as if a portal to another dimension was opened and God was becoming aware of Him, Her, Itself in the world of time through the collective," many who participated in such emergences would say. And through that collective new and astonishing human potentials—new expressions of Spirit in time—began to reveal themselves, potentials that stand poised to redefine the nature of human relationship and point the way forward in the further evolution of consciousness, culture, and our species as a whole.[30]

These initial eruptions of what Cohen came to call the Authentic Self were and are for Cohen only the beginning of an open-ended exploration of Spirit's ongoing evolution and articulation in the world of time. And that ongoing articulation requires the freely chosen and tireless participation of individuals choosing to transcend their egos in order to reveal the as yet unborn spiritual potentials lying latent at the outer edge of human evolution. To that end, Cohen has devised an original, multi-dimensional, extraordinarily sophisticated, and spiritually potent approach to human transformation, which he refers to simply as Evolutionary Enlightenment.

And while initially on his own in this endeavor, with only his own awakened spiritual intuition to guide him, Cohen was, for years, joined by a growing number of committed students and cutting-edge thinkers. It is unfortunate that in the process of the powerful experiment that Cohen spawned and drove for nearly thirty years he seemed stubbornly unaware of the pathological aspects of his own ego, though they had been apparent to others around him, including his closest and most committed students, for years. Clearly this raises many questions about the nature and significance of enlightenment and its interplay with human drives for power, all of which need to be examined with great care.

That said, it is also clear that Evolutionary Enlightenment is best contextualized in the broader stream of Western evolutionary philosophy outlined above. In other words, it attempted a potent integration of the streams mentioned above—German idealism, American pragmatism, process philosophy, Teilhard, Aurobindo, and integral philosophy—one fueled by the living power of spiritual enlightenment.

All of which brings us to the main point of this unavoidably inadequate account, which is to highlight the fact that despite the current predominance of scientific materialism and the powerful grip this conceptual and philosophical juggernaut holds on our collective psyche, a potent undercurrent of deeply inspired, intellectually rigorous evolutionary thinking has and continues to exist in the quieter depths beneath its churning wake. And, at least in this writer's view, as our current worldviews' inability to deal with today's global realities grows and spurs our increasing dissatisfaction with it, and as our own generation is able to add its own hard won insights to the historical currents of evolutionary thinking, the promise of a coherent and integrated worldview is beginning to emerge from the outer edges of a fraying culture.

NOTES

1. Tom Huston, "A Brief History of Evolutionary Spirituality," *EnlightenNext Magazine* (January–March 2007), www.enlightennext.org/magazine/j35/evo-spirituality.asp.

2. www.alcott.net/alcott/home/champions/Schelling.html.

3. Quoted in Peter Singer's *Hegel: A Very Short Introduction* (Oxford: Oxford University Press, 1983), p. 15.

4. Will Durant, *The Story of Philosophy: The Lives and Opinions of the World's Greatest Philosophers from Plato to John Dewey* (New York: Pocket Books, 2006), p. 457.

5. Richard Tarnas, *The Passion of the Western Mind: Understanding the Ideas That Have Shaped Our World View* (New York: Ballantine Books, 1991), p. 383.

6. Durant, op. cit., p. 460.

7. Kelly Parker, "The Ascent of Soul to Noûs: Charles S. Peirce as Neoplatonist," in *Neoplatonism and Contemporary Thought: Part One*, ed. R. Baine Harris (New York: State University of New York Press, 2002), pp. 176–177.

8. Nicholas Rescher, *Process Metaphysics: An Introduction to Process Philosophy* (New York: State University of New York Press, 1996), pp. 14–16.

9. Quoted in Matthew and Doris Nitecki's *Evolutionary Ethics* (New York: State University of New York Press, 1993), p. 109.

10. Ibid.

11. Quoted in Nicholas Rescher, op. cit., pp. 17–18.

12. Quoted in Durant, op. cit., pp. 587–588.

13. The notion of an *élan vital* as being the essence of our own vitality and the force driving life forward has been by and large discredited by advances in biochemistry, which have successfully explained most aspects of our experience of a "life force." However, I would argue that the attributes Bergson ascribes to an *élan vital* are, in fact, attributes of consciousness itself when understood in the sense of an absolute principle underlying all of reality and as discovered experientially in powerful experiences of spiritual awakening.

14. Ibid., p. 589.

15. Rescher, op. cit., pp. 20–22.

16. Consider, in this context, the case of chaos theory, which studies dynamic systems, such as weather patterns, that are highly sensitive to initial starting conditions. In them small differences in initial conditions produce widely divergent outcomes, making long-term predictions essentially impossible. This is the case despite the fact that the system is subject entirely to deterministic influences, that is, the calculable impact of known events and forces. In other words, despite the fact that the system is entirely deterministic its future behavior is still radically unpredictable. The common example given to illustrate this notion is referred to as "the butterfly effect," in which the flapping of a butterfly's wings in one part of the world can have an impact on the weather systems in another part. With respect to the current discussion concerning small degrees of freedom of choice, the implication is that even within a deterministic universe, which is clearly a highly complex and dynamic system, small degrees of freedom of choice can, over time, have significant unpredictable effects thus constantly leaving open the possibility for the emergence of novelty. In the context of process philosophy this is also related to the question of "divine influence," which will be discussed shortly.

17. J. R. Hustwit, *Process Philosophy*, Internet Encyclopedia of Philosophy, originally published April 10, 2007, www.iep.utm.edu/process.

18. Ibid.

19. For an in-depth discussion of Whitehead's understanding of value see John B. Cobb, Jr.'s "Whitehead's Theory of Value" at www.religion-online.org/showarticle.asp?title=2232.

20. Rescher, op. cit. p. 22.

21. Pierre Teilhard de Chardin, *The Future of Man* (New York: Doubleday, 1959), p. 1.

Chapter 1 - The Evolution of Evolutionary Thinking

22. For an excellent introduction to Aurobindo's thought in his own words see P. B. Saint-Hilaire's *The Future Evolution of Man: The Divine Life Upon Earth* (Twin Lakes, WI: Lotus Press, 1973).

23. Ibid., opening lines of chapter 1.

24. Most simply put, epi-genetics argues and has consistently shown that environmental influences can change the way that genes are expressed and that the resulting changes in the phenotype (physical organism) can be passed on to daughter cells. In other words, genetic mutations alone do not necessarily account for the totality of the characteristics of the physical organism.

25. Specifically Baldwinian evolution.

26. See Carter Phipps, "The Real Evolution Debate," *EnlightenNext Magazine* (January–March 2007), www.enlightennext.org/magazine/j35/real-evolution-debate-intro.asp.

27. Phipps, ibid. I highly recommend reading this succinct article in which, after synthesizing an enormous amount of information, Phipps sketches out the basic positions of each of these schools, lists some of their main proponents, and suggests relevant books from each area. Very informative and a great starting point for further research.

28. Kosmos is a spelling of the more common "cosmos" that Ken Wilber likes to employ in order to distinguish his notion of a living, developing universe with both interior and exterior dimensions from the cosmos of dead matter which scientific materialism has presented to us. The word Kosmos comes to us originally from the Greeks for whom it meant "ordered world" as distinct from the disorder of chaos.

[29] I will likely explore all this in great depth in a future book dedicated to this subject.

[30] For more on both the nature and direct experience of Evolutionary Enlightenment see my book 11 Days at the Edge: One Man's Spiritual Journey into Evolutionary Enlightenment in which I chronicle my experience of being on an eleven day retreat with Cohen.

Chapter 2
The American Roots of Evolutionary Spirituality

Jeff Carreira

In the previous chapter, "The Evolution of Evolutionary Thinking," Michael Wombacher outlined some of the major figures and ideas in the historical development of what has come to be known as evolutionary spirituality. In that essay the American pragmatists are mentioned mainly for their influence on other thinkers. In this essay we will more fully explore the contribution of American Philosophy to evolutionary spirituality and especially its influence on thinkers such as Ken Wilber, Andrew Cohen, and Barbara Marx Hubbard who are carrying forward a tradition of evolutionary thought that has been at the heart of American philosophy since its inception.

Pragmatism is the name of the greatest American contribution to world philosophy and it can be seen as a characteristically American response to the evolutionary theory put forth by Charles Darwin in his 1859 publication of *On the Origin of Species*. Darwin didn't originate the concept of evolution, but he did describe a mechanism for evolution through "natural selection" that required no outside intelligence to guide it. This profound image of a self-evolving universe captured the imaginations of all of the founding pragmatists, most notably Charles Sanders Peirce, William James, and John Dewey.[1]

Both pragmatism and Darwin's theory were products of the modern age, which grew in large part out of the increasing success of the scientific method in predicting and altering the course of the future. Modernism represented a transition in human understanding from one that was bound up in a static image of the universe to one that began to see the universe in a perpetual state of developmental unfolding. The United States was itself a product of modernism and as such fashioned a system of government designed to accommodate perpetual change in the seats of power and embraced as its quintessential philosophy a progressive definition of truth that honored the significance of change and development.

Pragmatism was initially developed as a way to validate truth that was built on a profound conception of reality. The early founders of pragmatism all ascribed to an evolutionary metaphysics that explained the universe as a perpetually evolving event. Because pragmatism was fundamentally a method of inquiry and not a metaphysical theory, each of the founding pragmatists developed a somewhat different conception of the nature of our universe. Although varied in many regards, their different philosophies shared at least three essential components that still retain prominence in the present-day discussion of evolutionary spirituality. These are:

1. The Continuity of Reality: An insistence that the nature of the universe is continuous and unbroken from the inner experience of human beings to the outer forms of the physical universe.
2. The Creative Potential of Human Beings: An appreciation of the fact that human choices shape and create the reality of the future.
3. The Necessity of Evolutionary Ethics: An understanding that an evolving universe demands a new conception of goodness to guide human activity.

These foundational characteristics can be found in many of the forms of evolutionary spirituality that have grown in popularity over the past several decades. The ideas of prominent figures such as Catholic priest Thomas Berry, cosmologist Brian Swim, futurist Barbara Marx Hubbard, philosopher Ken Wilber, and spiritual teacher Andrew Cohen, all share, at heart, these underlying characteristics of American pragmatism. And like the pragmatists these present-day thinkers are constructing a spiritual philosophy designed to effectively navigate humanity through the turbulence of an evolving universe.

If we look to the history of American philosophy what we see developing through the span of about a century is the recognition that the

Chapter 2 - The American Roots of Evolutionary Spirituality

universe we inhabit is a continuous whole that grows ontogenetically in the same way that organism do. As the universe as whole evolves, the structures within the universe evolve into ever more complex and integrated systems. The evolving structures within the universe include both the outer structures of energy, matter, and life, and the inner structures of consciousness, thought, and feeling. The creative potential of the self-aware human being in this evolving universe lies in the possibility of consciously guiding the further development of evolution through human choice and activity. Although ideas put forth by the early American pragmatists have fallen out of step with some of the most recent currents of thought in both philosophy and science, many of their ideas have laid trails that contemporary luminaries of evolutionary spirituality are still following (often without realizing it). It has been my observation that many Americans who are impassioned by contemporary forms of evolutionary spirituality have little or no knowledge of the rich heritage of these ideas in the history of their nation's philosophy.

Only after spending many years studying contemporary forms of evolutionary spirituality did I discover a deep evolutionary tradition within American philosophy. Those interested in evolutionary spirituality today are more likely to be aware of some of the historical contributions outlined by Michael Wombacher in the first chapter of this book, including the German idealist George Frederick Hegel; the process theologian Alfred North Whitehead; the French evolutionary philosopher Henri Bergson and his fellow countryman, paleontologist, and Jesuit priest, Pierre Teilhard de Chardin; as well as the contributions of the Indian sage Sri Aurobindo. Comparatively little is known about the profound contributions of classical American thought to this emerging spiritual view. This paper will illustrate key aspects of the evolutionary philosophy of the American pragmatists showing their direct connection to many essential elements of evolutionary spirituality today.

Pragmatism both came out of and subsequently helped recreate a particularly American attitude toward life. That character can be seen as a dynamic tension between two opposing tendencies—an anti-intellectual, action-oriented utilitarianism on the one hand; and a passionate, utopian idealism on the other. The utilitarian side of the American character was forged through the grueling process of carving a nation out of an untamed wilderness, while the idealism inspired Europeans to believe they could build a new world, and empowered the revolutionary generation to a bold and daring attempt to build a nation out of the ideas that had come from the European Enlightenment.

The Evolutionary Truth of Pragmatism

In order to understand pragmatism and its contribution to evolutionary spirituality we should first examine it as it was originally conceived—as a theory of truth that was congruent with the demands of an evolving universe. The official public birth of pragmatism occurred during the last decade of the nineteenth century, although it had been germinating in conversations and writings within a circle of intellectuals over the course of a few decades prior to that. To limit the birth of pragmatism to its moment of public recognition or even to the decades during which it was incubated does discredit to the fact that its ideas are at least as old as the American character, and were certainly reflected in the thinking of Thomas Jefferson, Benjamin Franklin, John Adams, and virtually all of the American founders. William James recognized that there was little true novelty in the initial conception of pragmatism when he called it "a new name for some old ways of thinking."[2]

Pragmatism grew through impassioned conversations among a small group of individuals in the 1870s. Most of these individuals were connected to Harvard University in Cambridge, Massachusetts, and they met regularly to talk about the relationship between science, evolution, religion, and philosophy. They formed a group they called the Metaphysical Club and they were particularly eager to explore the implications of the conception of evolution by natural selection that Charles Darwin had shared with the world. Among these individuals were Charles Sanders Peirce, William James, Oliver Wendell Homes Jr., and Chauncey Wright. In their meetings a simple and magnificent idea was developed that would later be popularized by William James as the philosophy of pragmatism.[3]

The original conception of pragmatism, however, should be credited to Charles Sanders Peirce. Peirce was a trained scientist and arguably the most brilliant thinker in America's history. Among his many scientific achievements was the discovery that length measurements could best be standardized in wavelengths of light. He was the first American

Chapter 2 - The American Roots of Evolutionary Spirituality

ever inducted into the French Academy of Sciences. His philosophy has been credited as one of the influences that inspired Heisenberg's uncertainty principle and Ken Wilber has credited Peirce with an early formulation of his four-quadrant model. In spite of his many gifts Peirce's dearest passion was for the study of logic. He, along with the other members of the Metaphysical Club, had little patience for classical philosophy, which they saw as entrenched in metaphysical arguments that could not ultimately be resolved. In an effort to rectify this situation Peirce conceived of the pragmatic maxim.

The pragmatic maxim states that the truth of an idea can only be found by looking directly at the consequences that result when that idea is put into action. By contrast, classical definitions of truth tended to rest on validation through "first principles." An idea is held to be true if it is built from first principles that can themselves be shown to be true. In this way, the truth of an idea was seen as being constructed securely on the bedrock of earlier truths, independent of any connection between that idea and its result when put into action. The pragmatists did not accept this separation of truth from its real-world consequences.[4]

The American propensity for utilitarianism and action are obviously reflected in the pragmatic maxim, but if we look to the motives of the early pragmatists we will also find the spirit of utopianism in it. The pragmatists felt strongly that philosophy should be useful in the effort to create a better world, and therefore philosophers must hold a conception of truth that allows them to avoid the mire of unending argument and debate. In pragmatism, an idea must prove its worth in action before it can be accepted as true; if any two or more ideas do not result in any measurable difference in result, they have to be considered, for all practical purposes, equivalent. In this way, the pragmatists hoped to find final solutions to philosophy's most challenging arguments and conflicts, so that philosophers could begin to put philosophy to work creating a better future.

The pragmatic conception of truth was deeply influenced by the American character, but it was also a direct response to Darwin's evolutionary ideas. The truth they envisioned was an evolving truth—not a fixed truth rooted in first principles from the past but a developing truth in which only the fittest ideas would survive. If the universe were evolving through a process of natural selection, so too, should our ideas. The major pragmatists, Charles Peirce, William James, and later John Dewey, were impassioned by the creative power of an evolutionary worldview, and formulated a definition of truth that mirrored it.

Ralph Waldo Emerson's Conception of Nature and Self-Reliance

To uncover the roots of the metaphysical assumptions that are the ground under pragmatism's feet we need only look one generation earlier into the mind of Ralph Waldo Emerson. Emerson lived most of his life in Concord, Massachusetts where he gathered one of the most remarkable intellectual circles in American history. Henry David Thoreau, Nathanial Hawthorne, Margret Fuller, Henry Wadsworth Longfellow, and many others could all be found orbiting in concentric paths around this towering figure of American letters. During the decades of the early and mid-eighteenth century, Emerson inspired the birth of American culture, and his influence on the development of the American mind cannot be overestimated. The twentieth century literary critic Harold Bloom has often been cited as saying, "The mind of Emerson is the mind of America."

Emerson's Transcendentalism, which recognizes intuition and not logic as the ultimate source of wisdom, stands in opposition to many core pragmatic values. At the same time, central to Emerson's thinking are two ideas that would become foundational to the later metaphysics of the pragmatists. The first is his belief that the inner reality of consciousness has to be continuous with, and nonseparate from, the external reality of the world of the senses. The second is his conviction that individuals have the freedom to make choices that will control their destiny and unleash their true creative potential.

The connection between the early pragmatists and Emerson was deep and intimate. Of the three most significant originators of American pragmatism, two had fathers who were close associates of Emerson. Charles Peirce's father, Benjamin Peirce, a professor at Harvard's Lawrence Scientific School; and William James's father, Henry James Sr., a converted Swedenborgian and a self-styled devotee of Emerson, were both part of Emerson's inner circles. Emerson was a frequent guest at the homes of both Peirce and James in their youth. Emerson was William

Chapter 2 - The American Roots of Evolutionary Spirituality

James's godfather and the James children went on summer holiday with Emerson's children. Emerson was said to have visited the James home so often that a room in the house was affectionately referred to as Mr. Emerson's room.

To consider Emerson's metaphysical contribution to pragmatism we should go to 1836, when he published his first book, *Nature*. In it he described, in his uniquely poetic fashion, an integrated view of man and nature. The word "nature," as Emerson used it, did not refer to the outside world of animals, plants, and landscapes, in the way it is most commonly used today. He used it with a connotation more common during his time, to refer to the fundamental essence of things. And in his book he describes his firm belief that the nature or essence of man and the nature of the outside world are one and the same. In the first chapter of *Nature*, Emerson writes:

> Standing on the bare ground,—my head bathed by the blithe air, and uplifted into infinite space,—all mean egotism vanishes. I become a transparent eye-ball; I am nothing; I see all; the currents of the Universal Being circulate through me; I am part or particle of God.[5]

Emerson, in moments of deepest revelation, saw the boundary between inner and outer dissolve and become transparent, revealing a deeper unity between the inner life of human beings and the outer manifestation of the physical world. This is Emerson's expression of the continuity of reality that was to become central to the evolutionary metaphysics of the pragmatists. Emerson expressed the same sentiment in his famous American Scholar Address when he wrote:

He shall see, that nature is the opposite of the soul, answering to it part for part. One is seal, and one is print. Its beauty is the beauty of his own mind. Its laws are the laws of his own mind. Nature then becomes to him the measure of his attainments. So much of nature as he is ignorant of, so much of his own mind does he not yet possess. And, in fine, the ancient precept, "Know thyself," and the modern precept, "Study nature," become at last one maxim.[6]

The second strain of thought that can be traced from Emerson to the pragmatists is sanctification of the creative power of the individual. Emerson was a strong voice for the revitalization and liberalization of religion and a relentless voice calling for the birth of the American intellect. In both spirit and intellect Emerson demanded a bold individual autonomy. In his essays and addresses he sanctified the creative power of the individual and preached a doctrine of "self-reliance" designed to release the deeper creative genius of individuals. By insisting on both the fundamental continuity of the universe and the inherent creative power of the individual, Emerson was setting the stage for the pragmatic revolution that was to follow.[7]

Continuity and Evolutionary Metaphysics

One of the primary concerns of the early pragmatists was the age old split between mind and matter. In their vision of a continuous universe no such split could exist and each of the pragmatists worked out their own understanding of how mind and matter could be shown to be ultimately part of one integrated larger whole.

The division of mind and matter is an unconscious assumption in human perception. In philosophy it tends to divide thinkers between idealists who see the realm of mind and ideas as primary over the material world of the senses, and empiricists who place the material world first and see ideas as a secondary manifestation of matter. Of all the American pragmatists it was Charles Sanders Peirce who held the most comprehensive integral understanding of reality in which he simultaneously acknowledged the existence of different realms of being while insisting that all were equally real. Peirce's conception was fundamentally adopted by all of the early pragmatists and was influential in Ken Wilber's articulation of the Four Quadrants of Integral Theory. Readers familiar with Wilber's popular writings will know that he uses the first, second, and third person perspectives as the starting point upon which to develop his conception of the Four Quadrants.[8] Peirce began his thinking from the same starting point.

A century before Wilber, Peirce claimed that reality was made up of three fundamental modes of being that he called "firstness," "secondness," and "thirdness," which correspond to first, second, and

Chapter 2 - The American Roots of Evolutionary Spirituality

third person perspectives. Firstness is the quality or character of things in themselves. It is the "redness" of red, the "hardness" of hard, or the "coldness" of cold. Secondness is the brute impact of direct contact with things. It is the event of experiencing the quality of firstness. It is the seeing of redness, the feeling of hardness, or the sensation of coldness. Thirdness is the laws and habits of mind that allow us to understand how "firsts" connect to "seconds," or more simply how things connect to their experienced qualities. It is the understanding that something is red, something else is hard, and a third thing is cold.

To understand Peirce's integrated view of reality from mind to matter it is critical to see that to him thirdness was not an understanding of some external reality, but rather an independent and equally real part of reality. Ideas are not simply ideas about the "real world." To Peirce they were just as real as anything else. Peirce in his lifetime articulated to greater and greater depth a vision of how the universe as we know it could be built from the basic building blocks of "firstness," "secondness," and "thirdness." It was in the third domain of reality where Peirce saw human beings directly participating in the evolution of the universe because, as he understood it, our growth in knowledge about the universe is part of the growth of the universe itself. The fate of the universe would be determined by what Peirce imagined as an ever-expanding and ultimately unlimited community of investigators. These investigators, through their shared inquiry into the nature of reality, would slowly converge toward a final agreement about what was true and the final encounter with that ultimate truth would become the concluding state of the universe.[9]

Peirce's evolutionary philosophy, to a much greater extent than that of the other early pragmatists, included a vast and sweeping view of cosmic evolution. In his cosmology he envisioned a universal play of two fundamental forces at work. One of these forces was the pull toward continuity, the inclination toward habit formation. This force gave the universe its tendency to remain fixed, static, and whole. It is the force that holds everything together. This force was countered by a second tendency toward spontaneity. Spontaneity is the element of chance and novelty in the universe that ensures the ongoing flow of creation. Peirce called the tendency toward continuity "synechism," and that towards spontaneity "tychism."[10]

Our evolving universe represents a perfect balance of these two tendencies. If the force of tychism were too strong, the universe would explode into the chaos of unmitigated change. If synechism were too strong, the universe would slow down to a dead stop. The universe that the pragmatists pictured was one of dynamic equilibrium; in which the potential for change kept things moving, and the tendency toward wholeness kept that change from getting out of control. This was the basis for their evolutionary metaphysics, and each of the three founders took this fundamental notion in different directions and addressed different implications.

Peirce imagined that the universe was initially in a state of absolute tychism, pure chance and possibility, or to use his language, absolute firstness. The universe then entered into a process of growth in which chance spurts of emergent form leapt out of the infinite sea of pure possibility. Because of the force of synechism these chance spurts would tend to occur again and again and the universe would come into being through the alternating interaction of chance and habit. This cosmological vision is powerfully reminiscent of the cosmological philosophy currently being taught by spiritual teacher and cultural critic Andrew Cohen. Cohen similarly sees the universe as arising from pure potentiality and evolving as a continuous whole into its current form. He writes:

> Before time and space, before the universe was born, there was nothing. Then suddenly from nothing came something. There was an explosion, and what we all are right now—including you and me—is that explosion in motion. That explosion in motion is one radiant being—conscious, whole and undivided.[11]

William James was Peirce's lifelong friend and intellectual compatriot. James was born in Upstate New York to a wealthy family. He is the brother of the famous novelist Henry and both spent their childhoods living between the United States and Europe. Because of the unending travel William James was never in any place long enough to successfully complete an educational program, and the first diploma he earned was his medical degree from Harvard University.

James like Peirce was a wildly original thinker who vehemently opposed the notion that reality could consist of two distinct substances, one called mind and the other matter. James rectified the division of mind and matter by envisioning a world made up of only one substance—"pure

Chapter 2 - The American Roots of Evolutionary Spirituality

experience." To James, everything, from the inner experience of mind to the outer experience of the physical world, was continuous because it was all fundamentally made of the same "stuff." That stuff was experience itself, and to him reality was an ever-expanding accumulation of bits of pure experience, in which each moment grows out of the one before in an unending stream of consciousness.

James, like Peirce, saw human interaction as central to the process of universal unfolding. Each human being was viewed as a train of experience moving relentlessly forward and, at times, colliding with the experience of another. In these collisions of experience, two or more human beings temporarily merge into a shared experience and then separate again. Each person was enriched through the encounter and, on the whole, James believed that the universe was becoming more unified through this continuous exchange of experience. In his essay "A World of Pure Experience" he writes:

> . . . trains of experience, once separate, run into one another; and that is why I said . . . that the unity of the world is on the whole undergoing increase. The universe continually grows in quantity by new experiences that graft themselves upon the older mass; but these very new experiences often help the mass to a more consolidated form.[12]

John Dewey was the third major pragmatist, although he was still an adolescent when the Metaphysical Club was meeting in Cambridge. Dewey was born in Burlington, Vermont and was initially educated as an undergraduate at the University of Vermont, in a philosophy department that had been founded decades before by a Transcendentalist named James Marsh. By the time Dewey arrived at the university, the philosophy department had shifted to become strictly Hegelian, and Dewey would be a Hegelian thinker himself until reading William James's *The Principles of Psychology*. From that time on, Dewey became the third leg of the classical stool of American pragmatism. Over Dewey's long career as a philosopher he wrote widely, bringing his unique form of pragmatism to the study of logic, ethics, democracy, and most famously, education.

Dewey, like Peirce, James, and many modern adherents of evolutionary spirituality, also described a world that was continuous from inner to outer. In an early paper entitled *The Reflex Arc Concept in Psychology* he articulates his fundamental conception of reality as a process in a constant state of stabilizing flux from inner experience to outer manifestation. The subject of the paper was a critique of the then popular "stimulus and response" model for human behavior, and looking at it for a moment will give a powerful sense of Dewey's conception of a continuous universe. The classic stimulus/response scenario involves an object that stimulates a person to act. For instance, a lion is a stimulus that results in a person running in fear. Using an example like this, Dewey saw that the hard separation of stimulus and response was overly simplistic and didn't include the setting in which the lion was encountered or the ideas held by the person seeing the lion and how those affect the result of the interaction. In a zoo, for instance, we have the same stimulus, a lion, but the environment in which we see it changes the response. In the wild, if we are hunting for lions, the same stimulus will create a third response. The stimulus, Dewey realized, cannot be entirety separated from the physical and mental environment in which it arises.

Dewey recognized that the stimulus and the response do not independently exist. They are mental labels that separate out different aspects of a single intricate set of physical and mental processes. The stimulus is not "the lion." It is the set of visual images, sights, sounds, mental images, thoughts, understandings, motivations, memories, emotional sensations, physical sensations, muscular movements, etc., that make up the experience of seeing that particular lion at that particular moment. Similarly, the response is the set of visual images, sights, sounds, mental images, thoughts, understandings, motivations, memories, emotional sensations, physical sensations, muscular movements, etc., that culminating in the act of running in fear.

The so-called stimulus and the so-called response are actually made up of exactly the same "stuff," to use James's language. This process-oriented view of reality envisions all of reality as a constant self-adjusting dance of visual images, sights, sounds, mental images, thoughts, understandings, motivations, memories, emotional sensations, physical sensations, muscular movements, etc. In some ways it is a more nuanced version of James's world of pure experience. This vision was the foundation of Dewey's metaphysics and his immensely influential body of work. In Dewey's eyes, the universe was one continuous, unfolding, intricate set of processes going through continuous cycles of disruption and stabilization.[13]

Chapter 2 - The American Roots of Evolutionary Spirituality

Because pragmatism was originally a definition of truth and not a metaphysical philosophy, it allowed each of the founding pragmatists to develop along different metaphysical lines. However, their metaphysical notions all rested on similar conceptions of a fluid reality in which the seemingly hard boundaries that separated inner and outer were in a state of constant flux in the swirling currents of a growing universe. And, as we will explore in the next section, their efforts at philosophy, not unlike those adherents of evolutionary spirituality today, were an attempt to understand and control the future development of the universe.

Human Choice and Evolutionary Ethics

When the boundaries between self and other, individual and society, inner and outer, begin to dissolve into a single universe of continuous unbroken reality, it becomes obvious to some that our choices take on new evolutionary implications that open into inherently moral questions. If the inner and the outer are truly one continuous event, then our consciousness inevitably leads to actions that result in what the world becomes. We are responsible for the future. For the pragmatists, as for Emerson before them, human choice was the defining and foundational characteristic of being human. It was choice that allowed human beings to participate in the creation of the future; choice liberated the world from the more fatalistic view of determinism. For this reason, Emerson defined human beings as a "selecting principle."[14] And William James, in his essay "Are We Automata?," defined the mind as "an organ of selection."[15]

As with their metaphysics, the three original pragmatists each went their own way in defining an evolutionary ethics that human behavior could be based on. What they all shared was the conviction that an evolutionary universe demanded a different ethics than a static universe. In James's essay, "The Will to Believe," he outlines the foundations of his view on human life and ethics.[16] James, the most psychologically oriented of the early pragmatists, recognized that the beliefs we hold to be true dictate our actions; yet, he also believed that we ultimately choose which ideas we believe in. To him our greatest ethical responsibility was in deciding which ideas to adhere to, and therefore which ideas would guide our actions in the world.

All of the pragmatists felt that the newly emerging conception of our evolving universe required the development of a new evolutionary ethic to guide human activity. Charles Peirce, for his part, would eventually propose a third fundamental drive in addition to tychism and synechism that could guide the evolution of the universe. That force he called "agapism," or "evolutionary love." He recognized that the universe contained an almost magnetic pull towards that which is growing and evolving. The original forces of continuity and spontaneity kept the universe moving, but it was evolutionary love that pulled the universe forward. To Peirce, a Christian, this force of agapism was the tug of the love of God described in the Bible, and it was the force that could compel us to sacrifice for the sake of another's growth. Sacrifice for the sake of evolution was the heart of Pierce's evolutionary ethics.[17]

Dewey felt that in an evolving universe our notion of goodness must also continuously evolve. Our understanding of evolution had matured beyond static ideals and fixed notions of goodness. Goodness was now a moving target, and our assessment of what is good must continually change to keep up with the pace of evolution. Dewey, in his book *Human Nature and Conduct*, describes morality as a "continuous process not a fixed achievement." He explains that evolutionary ethics is often misinterpreted simply to mean projecting fixed goals into the future and then acting toward them. In Dewey's opinion, this did not represent useful evolutionary ethics because it was still fundamentally aimed at static ideals. He felt that in an evolving universe our ethical goals and ideals would need to be continuously evolving and that any fixed notion of goodness to be achieved in the future would ultimately lead to despair. The nature of evolution, Dewey realized, is such that its forward progress creates greater unity and harmony and simultaneously new and greater chaos to be dealt with. If we imagine any static point where we achieve our goals and our challenges come to an end, we will be perpetually disappointed to find new and greater challenges behind each of our victories. Dewey writes:

There is something pitifully juvenile in the idea that "evolution," progress, means a definite sum of accomplishment which will forever stay done, and which by an exact amount lessens the amount still to be done, disposing once and for all of just so many perplexities and advancing us just so far on our road to a final stable and unperplexed goal.[18]

Chapter 2 - The American Roots of Evolutionary Spirituality

Any notion of some future static goodness must be replaced by an evolutionary sense of goodness—a goodness that is best understood as the "process of perfecting" and the "experience of growing." In an evolving universe there will never been an end to growth, Dewey realized, because the only thing that the process of evolution rewards is the opportunity for more growth. Any developmental line that comes to a point where no more growth is possible dies out. For Dewey the process of growing was itself the only useful definition of goodness that could be used as an ethical guide to follow. In his long and fruitful career as a philosopher, Dewey envisioned systems of democracy and education that maximized the growth potential of all of the individuals involved.

Evolutionary Spirituality and American Philosophy

The contemporary forms of evolutionary spirituality share elements of an evolutionary metaphysics that sees the universe as one continuous event, with human beings both growing out of that event and affecting its further development. They are all also involved with essential ethical questions about how our recognition of the evolutionary process and our place in it changes the way we should live. Many of those who are enamored with present-day forms of evolutionary spirituality might be surprised to find the ideas they cherish and the questions that confront them alive and well in the evolutionary metaphysics of the early pragmatists.

As an example, take the influential philosopher Ken Wilber. In his writings he describes the evolution of the interior and the exterior of the universe as always occurring simultaneously; the interior of the universe is consciousness and the exterior is the physical world of the senses. The physical universe we know evolves with the emergence of successive new forms—atoms become molecules, which become cells, which become organisms. With every newly emergent external form that arises in the universe, Wilber insists that there must be a corresponding new depth of consciousness being plumbed. Wilber reintroduced the Greek spelling of Kosmos, using a "K" in his writings because he felt that the word "cosmos," as it was generally used, was limited to only the physical part of the universe, and left out the interior dimension of consciousness. Wilber's conception of an integrated and unified Kosmos that evolves simultaneously internally and externally is clearly aligned with the work of the early pragmatists.[19]

Another example where this inner and outer continuity resurfaces in contemporary evolutionary spirituality is in Andrew Cohen's conception of Evolutionary Enlightenment.[20] Cohen initially upheld the unity of inner and outer in his teaching by insisting that what we believe to be true is always most clearly expressed through how we act. Cohen began his career teaching a traditional form of Eastern spirituality, but broke with that tradition on pragmatic grounds. Cohen insisted, in opposition to his own teacher, the Indian sage H. W. L. Poonja, that if the Eastern notion of enlightenment was to mean anything, it could not be merely an inner experience of peace, bliss, and detachment. Enlightenment, whatever it was internally, had to manifest as enlightened action in the world.[21] Cohen, like Emerson and James before him, held that the human ability to choose and act was the defining characteristic of being human. He describes the human being as a "choosing faculty" and maintains that the conscious choice to evolve is the most appropriate definition of goodness in an evolving universe—and that the refusal to evolve is the fittest description of evil.

Barbara Marx Hubbard, whose book *Conscious Evolution* is one of the seminal works in the modern movement of evolutionary spirituality, also describes an integrated evolution towards greater unity reminiscent of the earlier works of Peirce, James, and Dewey.[22] Her vision of our evolutionary future involves a global merging of individual human beings into a greater societal whole. In her book she writes:

> We see the Earth herself as a whole system. We are being integrated into one interactive, interfeeling body by the same force of evolution that drew atom to atom and cell to cell. Every tendency in us toward greater wholeness, unity and connectedness is reinforced by nature's tendency toward holism. Integration is inherent in the process of evolution.[23]

If we examine the writings of other modern leaders in the evolutionary spirituality movement we will find many elements of classical American philosophy coming to light in new expressions. Why is it then that the tradition of American philosophy appears to have garnered so little recognition for its part in formulating these ideas? One reason is that

Chapter 2 - The American Roots of Evolutionary Spirituality

the cultural shifts that occurred in the middle of the twentieth century effectively banished pragmatism from the public eye.

Pragmatism was a powerful force in world philosophy during the early decades of the twentieth century. Then the First World War erupted, followed by the Great Depression, and later the horror of the Second World War. The modernist assumption that progress was always toward the good became more difficult to support. In fact, many began to believe that modernism's obsession with progress had resulted in a disconnection from the deeper values held in the storehouse of human history. Dewey eventually headed the philosophy department at Columbia University and found himself intellectually opposed by traditionalists like Mortimer Adler and Mark Van Doran, who were teaching their students to look toward the great literary works of the past to rediscover deep truths and spiritual values.

Mark Van Doran in particular had a unique ability to inspire in his students a love for the human spirit as it is found in the great writings of humanity. And in an interesting twist of fate three of his students would go on to play significant roles in creating the cultural movement that would usurp modernism's dominance in American life. These three students were Thomas Merton, Allen Ginsberg, and Jack Kerouac. Merton would pursue spirit as a Catholic monk, and gain fame as an enormously popular author and pioneer of interfaith dialogue through historic meetings with Asian spiritual masters. Ginsberg and Kerouac sought spirit in poetry, prose, drugs, alcohol, and Buddhism. They ignited the Beat Movement of the 1950s, which in turn catalyzed the counterculture of the 1960s, ultimately giving birth to the human potential movement and New Age spiritualities of the 1970s and '80s.

This new cultural mood is part of what is generally called postmodernism and it is best understood, despite its liberal elements, to be a conservative backlash against the progressive mood of modernism. Recognizing this allows us to see that what we currently see as postmodernism should equally include the rise of religious and scientific fundamentalism, which also arose as conservative responses to the excesses of modernism. The uproar and sensation around the Scopes Monkey Trial of the 1920s, which challenged Tennessee's right to block the teaching of evolution in schools, galvanized the spirit of both religious and scientific conservatives while at the same time polarizing these two groups. John Dewey was the only original pragmatist who lived long enough to witness the decline of modernism. He was the great progressive educational reformer who found himself the recipient of a barrage of criticism from religious conservatives who held him personally responsible for ripping the soul out of the school system. On the other side, his philosophy was attacked by scientific conservatives who felt that only a strictly materialistic and deterministic interpretation of reality could be considered scientifically valid. The philosophy of the pragmatists yielded to an influx of analytic approaches to philosophy that shied away from metaphysics altogether and the more scientifically palatable psychology of behaviorism.

Towards the end of the twentieth century, the liberalism of the counterculture became the self-infatuation of the "Me Generation." The spiritual pursuits of the New Age seemed to abandon reason altogether. And the rigidity of religious fundamentalism and scientific materialism came under increasing scrutiny. This trend has rekindling a progressive mood in America, a mood that the great excitement around Barack Obama's presidential victory gave evidence. In American philosophy this emerging progressive atmosphere spurred philosophers like Richard Rorty, Hillary Putnam, Cornell West, and others to revisit pragmatism in search of gems among the rubble. The surging interest in popular forms of evolutionary spirituality today might also be seen as part of a general renewal of interest in the progressive spirit that has long been the heart of American philosophy.

Conclusion

The volume at hand contains voices from a new generation of integrally informed and evolutionarily awakened thinkers. The continuation of any lineage must always include the honoring of the predecessors upon whose shoulders it stands. The journey of discovery that trails up to our own backs includes our teachers and their teachers, and their teacher's teachers. It continues back to some magnificent minds of ancient Greece, a brilliant cadre of thinkers in Germany, and many other eruptions of individual and collective genius across time and around the world. As the lineage of evolutionary spirituality grows, its past as well as its future will be created by those of us who have dedicated our lives to its unfolding.

Chapter 2 - The American Roots of Evolutionary Spirituality

In this paper we have explored the contribution to evolutionary spirituality that erupted in America in the wake of its civil war. At that time a group of friends, mostly in their twenties and fresh out of college, set out to change the world through the fruits of spirited discussion. Their goal was to create a new vision of reality that could guide humanity forward in accordance with the dictates of how evolution unfolds. Darwin had left too much of reality out of his evolutionary musings, and so the members of the Metaphysical Club envisioned a universe that evolved as a continuous whole from the deepest spiritual yearnings of the human heart all the way to the outer edges of the cosmos. A universe in which mind and matter, thoughts and things, life and nonlife, were all intimately connected aspects of one relentless act of creation that was propelled forward through bursts of novelty, and then arranged into harmonious union through the power of habit. In the midst of this miraculous unfolding the human species awakened to the truth that it was itself a transitional creation in this cosmic process. Those of us who have awakened to our own evolutionary heritage are faced with many of the same questions and concerns that were discussed, often into the early hours of the morning, by the members of the original Metaphysical Club many years ago.

Notes

1. Philip Wiener gives an overview of how the concept of evolution influenced the early pragmatists in his book, *Evolution and the Founders of Pragmatism* (Cambridge: Harvard University Press, 1949).

2. William James used this as the subtitle of his book, *Pragmatism* (New York: Longman, Greens and Co., 1912).

3. Louis Menand describes the workings of the Metaphysical Club in his Pulitzer Prize–winning book, *The Metaphysical Club* (New York: Farrar, Straus and Giroux, 2002).

4. Charles Sanders Peirce presented the ideas behind the pragmatic maxim in a paper entitled "How to Make Our Ideas Clear," published in *Popular Science Monthly* (January, 1878): pp. 286–302.

5. Ralph Waldo Emerson, *The Complete Works of Ralph Waldo Emerson* (Cambridge: Houghton, Mifflin and Company, 1904), p. 10.

6. Ibid., p. 87.

7. Philip Gura gives a thorough description of the development of transcendentalism in New England in his book, *American Transcendentalism: A History* (New York: Hill and Wang, 2007).

8. Ken Wilber's views on the holistic nature of reality are expressed in his book *Sex, Ecology, and Spirituality* (Boston: Shambhala Publications, 1995).

9. Karl-Otto Apel offers an excellent overview of the development of the work of Charles Sanders Peirce in his book *From Pragmatism to Pragmaticism* (Amherst: University of Massachusetts Press, 1981).

10. Carl R. Hausman gives a thoughtful account of Peirce's cosmological vision in his book, *The Evolutionary Philosophy of Charles Sanders Peirce* (Cambridge: Cambridge University Press, 1993).

11. Andrew Cohen, *Embracing Heaven and Earth* (Moksha Press: 2000).

12. Ralph Waldo Emerson, *The Complete Works of Ralph Waldo Emerson* (Cambridge: Houghton, Mifflin and Company, 1904), p. 144.

Chapter 2 - The American Roots of Evolutionary Spirituality

13. William James, "A World of Pure Experience," *Journal of Philosophy, Psychology, and Scientific Methods* 1 (1904): pp. 533–543, 561–570.

14. John Dewey, "The Reflex Arc Concept in Psychology," *Psychological Review* 3 (1896): pp. 357–370.

15. William James, "Are We Automata?" *Mind* 4 (1879): 1–22.

16. William James, *The Will to Believe and Other Essays in Popular Philosophy, and Human Immortality* (New York: Longmans, Green and Company, 1907).

17. Charles Sanders Peirce, "Evolutionary Love," *The Monist* 3 (1893): pp. 176–200.

18. John Dewey, *Human Nature and Conduct* (New York: The Modern Library, 1950) p. 285.

19. Ken Wilber explains his preference for the original spelling of "Kosmos" in his book *Sex, Ecology, and Spirituality* (Boston: Shambhala Publications, 1995).

20. Andrew Cohen, *Evolutionary Enlightenment* (New York: Select Books Inc., 2011).

21. It is interesting here to note that in his autobiography Cohen states that after his first life-altering spiritual experience as a teenager, it was only reading William James's classic text *The Varieties of Religious Experience* that gave him any understanding of what had happened to him. That text revolves around the pragmatic position that the value of any religious experience can only be determined based on its effect on the life of the person who has it.

22. To my knowledge the ideas of American pragmatism did not directly influence Barbara Marx Hubbard. She was, however, influenced by two other prominent thinkers who would undoubtedly themselves have been influenced by the development of American philosophy. These two thinkers were the psychologist Abraham Maslow and the scientist Jonas Salk.

23. Barbara Marx Hubbard, *Conscious Evolution* (Novato, CA: New World Library, 1998), p. 48.

Part 2: Transformation

Chapter 3
Wake Up, Grow Up, Clean Up, Show Up

Dustin DiPerna

There is much reason for celebration. A bright alliance of *awake* human beings is beginning to form. Like a bolt of lightning flashing forth in the night, these exemplars of human potential are radiating their light in the darkest corners of the globe.

As more and more of us begin to find ourselves surfing the coming waves of Integral consciousness, the patterns that connect us and the Kosmic laws that govern our interactions are being revealed. Although it would be presumptuous to assume a position of representation for this group, I do feel that I can speak to some of the guiding realizations that move our hearts and in doing so, I am provided with an opportunity to point to the motivating framework that lead me to gather the authors in this book.

For many of us, it has become clear that the self-organizing force of Reality is clustering us together in unstoppable proportions. Synchronicity has become the drumbeat of our inter-generational coordination. We trust in the guidance of the Kosmos as each new step is revealed. No matter how full of hubris it might sound, we know that as we manifest the unified force of our will together, we will bring a massive stream of goodness and healing to our Earth. For all of these reasons, there is a sense that we already stand in the future and we know that it is bright.

As the light of this new dawn breaks, we give thanks for the flourishing of each living stream of wisdom carried forward by the world's great spiritual traditions. Through the distribution channels enabled by the Internet, new media, and social networking, these streams of truth are readily accessible to nearly all of humanity. Our world's great lineages teach us not only of the true nature of Reality but also how to stabilize the recognition of this true nature persistently from moment to moment without end. How incredible! We pay homage to all of the great masters that have come before and know that the work that we are here to do is only possible through the humble recognition that we stand on the shoulders of giants.

In this time of spiritual growth and awakening on Earth, it is helpful to have a framework that can orient our practice and our progress. For this purpose, a few years ago, I introduced a frame into the Integral lexicon called "wake up, grow up, clean up, show up". I am pleased to say that the frame has gone viral. And although it is now being used in ways that are not totally aligned with my original intention, I am delighted that so many (both teachers and students alike) have benefited from its use. It is with this frame that I set the context for this book, and it is the unpacking of this frame that I explain in brief in the following pages.

Wake Up

Whether conscious of it or not, all members of humanity have the heart-desire to return Home; to return to the glorious abode of Ultimate Reality. All human beings have an intrinsic desire to know the single, indivisible, Great Sphere of Love from which, into which, and as which all of existence shines forth. All human beings have the desire and opportunity to "wake up" and realize that their very own awareness is none other than the single Bright Sphere that is Reality-Itself.

Within the context of Integral Theory, we speak about "waking up" as it relates to various state-stages of consciousness. As one awakens, one's exclusive identification with gross, subtle, and causal layers of reality is dismantled. One moves beyond an exclusive identification with thought (gross), beyond an exclusive identification with personal identity (subtle), beyond an exclusive identification with the coming and going of time and space (causal), and even beyond an exclusive identification with individual consciousness (witness). With all the layers of obscuration removed, one can affirm what remains -- the non-dual base of awareness; a base that naturally and spontaneously manifests as all relative form.

Chapter 3 - Wake Up, Grow Up, Clean Up, Show Up

Waking up to this base awareness is fundamental to the New Civilization now emerging on Earth. Waking up to this single sphere, always already perfect exactly as it is, must be our most prominent priority.

Grow Up

With all that said, let it be clear that waking up to the true nature of Reality is only part of our duty. The single abode of Awakened Awareness, intrinsically good by its very nature, shines forth and refracts through manifold aspects of Itself. This refraction of perfect light forms seemingly individual constellations of consciousness. We commonly call these relative vortices of consciousness "selves". We give them names, social status, and roles. In Integral circles, we even say that each self has Four Quadrants, with various degrees of developmental capacity and a whole matrix of qualities. Each unique expression deserves our recognition. Each unique expression deserves dignity and respect. At the same time, it is also true that each of these selves, whether we speak of you, me, your mother, your father, your son, or your daughter, is simply an expression of the very same base. Each refraction of light is part of one occurrence; the single gesture of Life-Itself.

From the Absolute perspective, Reality is in perfect coherence with Itself unconditionally. Simultaneously, it is also true that all of the entities and individuals that we conventionally call relative selves create the contours through which Ultimate Reality can play, dance, and create with Itself. The natural state of Reality, can only use what it has available in each unique constellation of consciousness to interact and communicate its message with other beings in relative time. The non-dual base of all, can only use what the relative self has at its disposal to breathe its blessings into the dimensions of time and space. From this relative perspective, you and I are simply sacred instruments Divinity uses to play the symphony of life. As such, it matters how finely tuned we are as instruments.

All of this means that no matter how awake you are, your individual development and psychological health make a difference. Everything you are, and everything you do, either enhances or dampens the potential of Reality to express itself through you, as you, for the benefit of the whole. So even if Reality needs no affirmation to Itself, relative selves who are not awake to Reality need you to be as healthy and as developed as possible. Other relative selves depend upon you as a portal to access the single Great Sphere.

The more we "grow up" through varying structures of consciousness (from red to amber to orange to green to teal to turquoise, etc.) the more perspectives we can take, the more complexity we can hold, and the more care we can release in the world. Reality can flash forth even more effectively in the world as it comes through more developed structures of mind and more developed sensitivities of the heart. A commitment to "growing up", in all dimensions of life, becomes a sacred vow one takes to allow Reality to incarnate through us to the fullest degree possible.

Clean Up

In a similar way, the more integrated each of us is, the more whole and psychologically healthy we are, the less dusty the glass is in our stained glass window of life. The less dusty our window, the more brightly the Light of Reality can shine. This means we all have a responsibility to "clean up" anything that might be clouding our transmission. If the process of "growing up" helps to provide more tools in the toolkit of life, "cleaning up" gives us more refined skills and more potent energy for how we actually use those tools. At a certain point in practice, we no longer do psychological work for our own benefit. Rather, because we know that Reality can touch more people through us the cleaner we are, we clean up to be of deeper service. Cleaning up shadows and integrating all relative dimensions of self allows us to purify the signal from Source as it broadcasts out into the world.

Show Up

Finally, all of this, whether we speak of waking up, growing up, or cleaning up, is used in service of the whole. The entire frame is just a skillful way to catalyze your maximum potential to "show up" in all of your glory, as a true emanation of Source. As we move beyond individual paradigms of isolation and separation, humanity will more fully discover the power and potential of shared unified intention. Then with this

Chapter 3 - *Wake Up, Grow Up, Clean Up, Show Up*

understanding at heart and with each of us exemplifying a unique expression of intrinsic unity, "We" can, together, rain-down the blessings on the Earth that we have come here to give. May this be an invitation and activation of all that is necessary for us to show up together as the single unified force of Reality that we truly are.

And with that, a simple outline is offered: Wake up. Grow up. Clean up. Show up. We explore each of these concepts in detail in the following four chapters.

Chapter 4
Waking Up: The Path of Spiritual Awakening

John Churchill

For a new future, and new integral culture, to be born we need to appreciate that the recognition of our innate nondual wisdom awareness is essential. As "Human Beings," we have both the capacity for Becoming and Being. Many of you reading this article see the integral paradigm as the next step in our evolutionary process of Becoming. Integral Theory heavily emphasizes the importance of structural development and the capacity for increased perspective taking. However, from a more fundamental perspective, another next step is for more of us, no matter what level of structural development we operate at, to rediscover, to remember, and recognize what is already here—the nondual ground of Being. Without this recognition the human mind is forever caught in the reactivity of seeking contentment within Becoming and within time. Without this recognition we are bound to the frustration and dissatisfaction of being separated from who and what we really are. This resolution of existential discontent is simply impossible to be resolved within the never-ending process of becoming and evolving in time. The recognition and nondual integration of Being can embrace and contain Becoming, but not the other way round.

It could also be easily said that to fully operationalize the potential indicated through Integral Theory that awakening to the nondual ground of being is necessary. Without awakening to the nondual, clear light mind of the open ground, which is beyond all perspectives, our true nature is identified within the realm of structure and we are unable to fully operate on integral perspectives. We remain caught in reactivity and unable to fully actualize the inherent positivity of our essential nature. This does not mean that Integral Theory is not useful before realization, only that it can easily trap our true nature in the increased complexities of mind if not operated on from a nondual awareness. To fully actualize and stabilize the next levels in structural development it is necessary for us to awaken and learn to function from the essence of awareness itself—the open, spacious, nondual wisdom nature. It is particularly important that this is taken to heart: a little experience and too much conceptual knowledge can give the integral practitioner a sense that they know the territory which the map is pointing to. This hubris can easily conceptualize awakening and make authentic contemplative development difficult.

In this piece of writing I am using the term "nonduality" to include the resolution of a number of apparent dualisms. There is the primary dualism of separation between subject and object, between awareness and the prima materia, the primal ground of being that experience arises from. It is this split that leads to the experience of separation and alienation from reality that is the deepest source of human disease and stress. As energetic flow and interdependence between self and other is blocked the psychic and bio-energy of the individual stagnates, leading to further emotional and eventually physical disharmony. We also split our experience into the dualism of whole and part, breaking up our experience into its parts rather than experiencing the whole. For instance, rather than experiencing our embodiment as a whole field of sensation, we experience the body as parts, and then locate ourselves in one part rather than another. This then leads to the dual split between the ego as the "conscious" identified part of the body-mind and the rest of the body-mind as the "unconscious" parts. Then there is the further dualistic split between mind and body. The ego/subject, threatened by the apparent chaos of the body, retracts away from embodiment and subtly disassociates, creating a cerebral mental identity. In the view of this identify, the body is not to be trusted, and the ego contains this anxiety through psychological defense mechanisms and through somatic armoring and collapse. In order for the recognition of nonduality to be complete, we need to fundamentally address these basic splits.

There are numerous contemplative approaches to nondual recognition, from the poetic koans of Zen to the samadhis of raja yoga,

Chapter 4 - Waking Up: The Path of Spiritual Awakening

from the completion stage alchemical practices of Vajrayana to the directness of Advaita, from the prayer of the Christian heart to the simplicity of Mahamudra. However, for this compilation on the next generation of integral, I decided to write a guided meditation outside the traditions, and in the spirit of future trans-lineage practice that many integral students are drawn to. So any limitations in my guidance and precision of these instructions is mine, and should not reflect on traditional lineage approaches that are more thorough and rooted in a student/teacher relationship.

The practice is offered in the spirit of a liberal arts overview of nondual recognition. It is a stage-by-stage practice leading to a recognition of the clear light, nondual, open ground of reality. It should be practiced sequentially over weeks and months, but eventually could be practiced in a single sitting. My hesitation in offering instructions such as these openly, is that without being followed by a competent guide interested people might easily conceptualize awakening which is deeply damaging to their further development. However, offerings such a this can give people a glimpse of the value of contemplative practice and therefore act as a catalyst for those interested to seek further instruction within an established lineage system of practice. What is most important is that you practice up to the level at which your direct experience matches the instructions. It is better to stay and work where you are at in your practice rather than trying to mentally represent an experience due to a narcissistic need to see oneself as being developed. Such inauthenticity and spiritual dishonesty is deeply harmful for growth.

That being said, I suggest first reading the text and the short commentary to get an overall sense of the meditation's progression and the deeper contemplative pedagogical structure underlying it. Contemplative practice is always a fine balance between cognitive and non-cognitive direct knowing. You need to know the perspective you are going to be adopting in the meditative practice. That perspective or view is informed by discriminating intelligence, and then actualized through the process of meditation. The more precise the cognitive understanding, the clearer the meditative experience can be.

A recording of this guided meditation is available for download at the book's website.

Motivation

The foundation of practice is always your motivation. It is the quality of the motivation that activates and shifts your psychology, anatomy, and energy system from its dualistic functioning towards that which already approximates the motivation of a bodhisattva—an awakening being who ceaseless works for the alleviation of suffering and evolution of human consciousness, culture, and the cosmos.

As part of setting the motivation it is important to recognize the precious interdependence of your human body and mind with the entire evolutionary process. By shifting out of a reified and bounded sense of self, and recognizing our weavings in the deep time of the cosmos, we can recognize the preciousness of the present and relax the self-grasping that so easily obscures our wisdom nature.

The posture of the body is important. Our bodies reflect the evolutionary journey that we are participating in. Over the last few million years, as we have evolved from the trees, we have become more and more vertical. As our posture becomes more vertical we have simultaneously evolved in consciousness. So the upright expression of the posture, the crown reaching for the sky, is an expression of the reaching of Eros, the evolutionary strive to become. Physically, when we align ourselves with the gravitational force of the earth, we are structurally aligning ourselves with the deep structure of the cosmos. We are aligning ourselves in a very direct way with the larger world system and then completely surrendering into the embrace of that whole. The relaxation of the upright posture into the release of gravity, without collapsing our sense of uprightness, is the open embrace of unconditional love, Agape, the release into pure being. Here in the very structure of our body we can meet these two forces that seem so different, and yet under close examination we can directly experience the "sweet spot" when both Being and Becoming co-arise simultaneously.

We begin by recognizing the preciousness of our human experience. It has taken 14 billion years for this physical body to be able to sit here. Contemplating that 14-billion-year process that is embodied in our very structure. The Hydrogen of our body created moments after the big bang, the iron generated within dying red dwarf stars, our whole physical body carries the information of its cosmic evolution from the big bang to this very moment. Now.

Chapter 4 - Waking Up: The Path of Spiritual Awakening

Culturally, recognize the ancestral influences that make up your physical and psychological code; the generations of ancestors that helped in the development of the human race, the family system within which we matured and were psychologically born. These influences of culture and evolution from prehistory to post-modernity are all here in this very moment. Now.

Like the sprout reaching up towards the sky, allow the spine to naturally lengthen and evolve. Let the crown be drawn by a magnetic pull upwards as we reach up towards the light of the sun. Now, without collapsing, relax into gravity and into contact with the ground. Consciously align yourself with gravity and the larger world system.

Sense the "sweet spot" between being upright and letting go. Between the creative tension of Becoming and the sweet release of Being.

Once you can balance the two forces, then expand your awareness and sense the whole kinesthetic field. Beyond the body image of age, gender, and shape, experience yourself as a subtle and very subtle nexus of interdependent threads of energy and relationship extending from the symbiosis of breathing to the radiant subtle body and beyond to the fine weave of very subtle energy that connects you to the planetary system and beyond.

1. Recognizing the Fields of Sensory Experience

To begin the process of recognition we want to shift from the activity of thought to attention to awareness. Hopefully, those of you who are reading this writing have done enough training of the mind that you can shift from thought to attention by directing your interest to the subject at hand, in this case the different fields of sensory experience. We shift out of our attention mode to awareness by directing our interest away from the specific objects in the sensory field (specific sensations, sounds, etc.), which is the habitual action of attention, to the whole field itself, the action of awareness. For instance, rather than focusing on the sensations of particular parts of the body, we become interested in the whole gestalt of the sensory field. In this practice we will move through the different fields of sensation, sound, and vision, taking in the whole field in each case and allowing our recognition to align with awareness. At the end of this stage we open to all our senses and recognize a moment-by-moment bare awareness of all the sensory fields.

We address the sensory field first to begin the process of resolving the dualistic mind-body split. The more we become aware of the whole field of sensation we release the dualistic tendency to split the mind from the body. Awareness is opened to the sensory field allowing the information flow to wash our mind and brain. Rather than trying to be attentive to the sensations of the body as if they were separate from you, allow your awareness to become more and more sensitive to the sensory information that is already arising naturally in your experience. Working with the whole field of sensation is also an easy way to help resolve the split between whole and part. As you continually allow the whole field of sensation to arise within your awareness, the mind will naturally shift back from being aware of parts of the field to the whole field, just as your mind shifts from the splitting activity of attention to the capacity of awareness to receive the whole.

This guided meditation does not work specifically with taste and smell as they are not so prominent in most people's moment-to-moment experience. However, once the meditation is practiced, understood, and realized, the practitioner should have no problem extending the realization to smell and taste. Also, more experienced practitioners will notice that I am not addressing any approaches to work with the nature of thought. In a more extensive contemplative education there are many insights into inner experience that need to be integrated. For the sake of simplicity and directness I have here offered a particular route up the mountain that bypasses working with thought. But in the long run I would suggest that those interested should apprentice themselves to further contemplative training in a relationship with a teacher who can closely follow their progress all around the mountain.

A) Whole Field of Sensations

Allowing the spine to be upright and dignified, let awareness open to the whole kinesthetic field of sensation. Let awareness receive the sensory information. The sensation of the face, jaw, neck, arms, torso, belly, pelvic bowl, thighs, legs, and feet. Receive the information of the whole field. Let your awareness open to the core of the body, opening and saturating in the radiance along the front of the spine. Let your

Chapter 4 - Waking Up: The Path of Spiritual Awakening

awareness rest deep into the body-mind, deep within the core of your experience, and take in the whole field of sensation as a field of ceaseless subtle movement. The more you relax the mind the more sensitive and open your awareness becomes receiving all the sensory information.

B) Whole Field of Sound

Allow awareness to open itself to listen closely to the whole auditory field of sound. Like an owl sitting in a winter forest listening to the sounds of the night. Let awareness immediately receive all the sounds as they arise. Listening so closely that the sounds are not distinguished as concepts, but as just the pure texture of sound. Listen to the whole unbounded field of sound, allowing the sensitivity of awareness to receive everything. The more you relax the mind the more sensitive and open your awareness becomes receiving all the auditory information.

C) Whole Field of Vision

Open the eyes. Let awareness open to the whole visual field of color and light. Let your awareness take in all the visual details. Appreciate the saturation of colors, geometry, angles, and lines of the visual experience. Like an infant, look without the construction of depth perception; just see color, shape, angles, and lines. The more you relax the mind the more sensitive and open your awareness becomes receiving all the visual information.

D) All Fields

Now open all your senses fully. Sensation, Sound, and Vision. Your clear awareness recognizes the immediate arisings through all fields of sensation, sound, and vision. Practice a continuous moment-to-moment awareness of your ongoing experience. In each moment, arising awareness is immediately aware of what is arising within it— a sound, sensation, brief thought, and color. The more you relax the mind the more sensitive and open your awareness becomes receiving all the sensory, auditory, and visual information.

Continue practicing with full open interest until you have a continuous awareness tracking whatever is arising in the fields of sensation, sound, and vision.

2. Recognizing the Base of the Sensory Fields

By establishing a continuous awareness of sensation, sound, and vision the mind can shift from thought to attention, and then to consciously operating from awareness. You will know if your recognition is operating at awareness as there will be next to no thought and you will experience the speed of being simultaneously aware of all information coming in from the senses without having to conceptualize about it.

In this process of recognizing nonduality we will now examine the bases of each of the three main senses. In the contemplative sciences it is understood that everything we experience, every sound, sight, sensation, smell, and taste is experienced in awareness. This means that our experience is complete, it all arises within our experience. We do not experience a world "out there," we do not experience a world "in here," we experience a body-mind projection of the world. There might be a world but phenomenologically speaking we can never experience it, as we can only experience our experience.

We project our experience onto a screen, and in normal day-to-day activity we are not aware of the nature of this screen and what is being projected onto it. However, to recognize nonduality we have to first be aware of the nonduality of projection (sensation, sound, vision) and the projection screen. Then we can recognize the nonduality of object (projection and projection screen) and subject (the projecting body-mind). The screen or base of the sensory fields is formless and as such is easy to miss. It is best recognized in contrast to the nature of the specific sensory information. Thus, stillness is recognized in relationship to movement, silence to sound, and space to vision.

The advantage of working first with stillness/sensation is that we can use the influence of gravity as a scaffold to help us release into stillness. Typically the resistance of the self-contracted ego separates itself from interdependence with the world system. It does this structurally by not fully releasing the body-mind into gravity. As such, releasing into gravity is an easy feedback mechanism to support releasing self-contraction. Experientially gravity pulls the body-mind into the still ground beneath us and from the perspective of the nonduality this still ground beneath us is also the stillness of awareness. The stillness is said to be unbounded because under closer inspection it has no boundaries! The stillness, silence, and space are all unbounded experiences of infinite openness. Once supported by continually releasing into the unbound field of stillness, through the support of gravity, we then continue to recognize the fields of silence and space.

A) Unbounded Field of Still Awareness

Close back down your eyes and come back to the sensory field and the alignment of the body. Allow the spine to lengthen. Once the spine is fully upright then rest into the field of gravity. Allow gravity to flow through the body and down through the sitting bones and feet. Without collapsing, enter into a continuous flow of letting go. In each moment letting the body completely go. Recognize that you are completely letting the body go into an unbounded stillness. Gravity pulls the body-mind into stillness, into an unbounded still awareness. Continue to ceaselessly and naturally release self-contraction into the still awareness. Rest completely into the stillness, that is simultaneously the stillness of awareness.

B) Unbounded Field of Silent Awareness

Open your awareness to the auditory field and recognize the background silence within which all the sounds are arising. Listen to the roar of the silence, an unbounded silence. Continue to ceaselessly and naturally release into this silence. Resting completely into the silence around that is simultaneously the silence of awareness.

C) Unbounded Field of Spacious Awareness

Open your awareness to the visual field. Like an infant unable to conceptually differentiate what she sees, just take in the whole field as a single kaleidoscope, a single intricate stained glass window, a window of wondrous beauty. Relax your gaze as you look at the whole window and recognize the clear light that shines through, an unbounded field of clear light space illuminating everything, shining through everything you see. Rest completely into the unbounded field of clear light space that is simultaneously the spaciousness of awareness.

3. Nonduality of the Base and Sensory Experience

Once we have recognized the ground of the senses as an unbounded still silent space, we now continue to recognize the integration of sensory experiences back into the sensory base. Just as under examination a television image is not separate from the screen, if we deeply examine our direct experience to see if we can find the separateness of movement, sound, and vision from the still, silent, spacious base, we will not be able to find the boundary. The construct of a boundary depends upon distinct separation and under examination the apparent boundaries reveal themselves to be open, unlocatable, and unfindable.

Examine your direct experience and see if you can find a boundary between stillness and the movement within stillness.

Continue until the boundary is clearly unlocatable and unknowable, and rest into the indivisible field of stillness and movement.

Examine your direct experience and see if you can find a boundary between silence and the sounds within the silence.

Continue until the boundary is clearly unlocatable and unknowable, and rest into the indivisible field of silence and sound.

Examine your direct experience and see if you can find a boundary between clarity and the visual forms that arise within clarity.

Continue until the boundary is clearly unlocatable and unknowable, and rest into the indivisible field of clarity and vision.

4. Unbounded Spherical Mandala of the Senses

We have now established the inseparability of the sensory base and the sensory information that arises from the sensory base. However, there is a tendency for there to be a residue of conceptual separation between the different senses which needs to be cleared so that the nondual field of the sensory base and its expression can be recognized seamlessly through all sense doors. Under direct investigation one cannot find the boundary between seeing and listening, and even though the task sounds futile and pointless, the activity of investigation clears a subtle dualistic tendency in experience.

Chapter 4 - Waking Up: The Path of Spiritual Awakening

Examine your direct experience and search to find where the field of auditory awareness ends and the field of visual awareness begins. Can you find the boundary between auditory, sensory, and visual awareness? Continue until the boundaries are clearly unlocatable and unknowable. Allow the senses to be a seamless field, an open sphere, a whole unbounded kaleidoscopic mandala of the senses. A still, silent, spacious sphere full of creativity and expression as movement, sounds, and vision.

5. Nonduality of Subject and Object

Once we have opened the field of the sensory base and its creative expression through the doors of sensation, sound, and vision, we now want to examine the dualistic construction of subject and object. Nondual perception is not something that can be created. Our minds are always already perceiving their constructions nondualistically. The issue is that we simply do not realize this to be the case. In this exercise we simply investigate to see whether we can find the boundary between our apparent subjective awareness and the objective experience of the senses. With investigation we are unable to find the boundary between subject and object and this naturally reveals the inherent nonduality of our ordinary natural experience.

Now, carefully examine your direct experience. Can you find the boundary between the sensory field of stillness/movement and awareness? Where is the boundary between body and awareness? Carefully investigate until it is apparent and clear that there is no such boundary, and recognize the inherent nonduality of stillness/movement and awareness.

Can you find the boundary between the sensory field of silence/sound and awareness? Where is the boundary? Carefully investigate your direct experience until it is apparent and clear that there is no boundary, and recognize the inherent nonduality of silence/sound and awareness.

Can you find the boundary between the sensory field of space/vision and awareness? Where is the boundary? Carefully investigate your direct experience until it is apparent and clear that there is no boundary, and recognize the inherent nonduality of space/vision and awareness.

6. Not-Knowing

Up to this point we have established the nondual perception of subject and object. However there is still a construct of subject and object, even though it is now nondual. To recognize primordial awareness we need to recognize an awareness that is prior to any subject/object, even if that subject object is nondual. We need to recognize an awareness that has never tasted duality, never known the suffering of ignorance, an awareness that has never known anything: a complete open innocence, or as the 9th-century Zen master Dizan put it, "A most intimate not-knowing."

In the Hindu yogic systems this shift is recognized as releasing the subtle knot or granthi at the third eye which allows the unimpeded energy to flow through the head and out/in at the crown. As long as we are trying to gain knowledge of something, no matter how subtle, we will be engaged in an activity that will keep the energy from flowing through the central channel, which stops us from recognizing what is beyond activity, beyond knowing, beyond all perspectives.

Close the eyes. Begin by recognizing the energetic activity and tension between the eyebrows. Relax the face, allow the space between the eyebrows to soften and release. Releasing the subtle tension to seek for fulfillment in the future, the subtle tension caused by waiting for something else. Just like an infant let the mind be free from knowing anything. Recognize the natural innocence of mind. Innocent like an infant. This innocence is similar to the gentle light of the moon—soft and comforting. Rest into that deep intimate not-knowing, that direct knowing that has no object.

This open knowing is like a flower that is ceaseless opening itself, a flower that is rooted in the warm radiance of the heart.

7. True Nonduality

Now to recognize the whole, the true nondual clear light wisdom mind, the primordial nondual awareness, we need to let the innocent not-knowing of awareness receive the whole unbounded still, silent, spacious sphere of movement, sound, and vision.

Chapter 4 - Waking Up: The Path of Spiritual Awakening

> *Allow the heart flower of this moonlike innocent awareness to open itself completely to the unbounded still, silent, space of the open sense sphere and recognize the indivisibility of awareness and the unbounded field. Nondual.*

If this practice has stimulated your interest in further contemplative development, I would encourage you to find a teacher who has been trained in a traditional lineage. Although the very nature of a tradition is to be conservative, it does have advantages in terms of training. The traditions have mapped out much of where you can get stuck in your development. A good teacher who has gone through a traditional training will have hopefully been followed by others concerned for the teacher's personal development and teaching capacity. Self-proclaimed teachers who have become awakened through their own inner exploration and then teach their own meditative practices often do not have the pedagogical insight or practices to address all the necessary stages for stable recognition and integration into nonduality. Being contemplatively gifted in your own practice does not mean you will be able to understand all the possible places other less gifted minds might get stuck.

It is also not necessary that your contemplative teacher be informed by Integral Theory, or even operate structurally at integral. That would be a bonus, but what is much more important is the character, training, realization, and the capacity of the teacher to teach. I believe it is a mistake for students of integral self-development to try and find all the answers in a single teacher. Teaching contemplative practice is a specialty that differs from evolutionary alignment, "we" practices, or psychological integration. These are all necessary components of an integral approach; however, at university you would not expect a professor of ethics to be also a professor of psychology, sociology, and evolutionary theory! Maybe two disciplines, but not everything. In your search for a teacher I encourage you to find somebody who has been trained in the traditional lineage systems such as Zen, Sufism, Mahamudra, Theravada Vipassana, Shaivism, Advaita, Dzogchen, etc. When you have a good grounding in a particular system you can then also expand your study with other teachers.

Chapter 5
Growing Up: Your Capacity for Developmental Growth

Clint Fuhs

Contemplate for a moment what it means to grow up. What does this notion bring to mind for you? Remember back to when you were a teenager—all awkward and striving but so self-assured. How did you think? What did you believe? How did you behave? Of course each of us was different, but there are surely some common experiences, right? Always thinking you were right, that you knew better than your parents, friends, and teachers. Sure we expressed this in different ways, but as your sense of individuality began emerging you struggled to defend it, protect it, ensure and express its sense of rightness . . . right? And then think back to your behavior—doing what you wanted and justifying your intentions regardless of outcomes. Now, take a moment and reflect on how all of this has changed—how your beliefs, values, and way of thinking have shifted —hopefully towards more mature expressions. Bring to mind a few things that are clearly different now as compared to back then.

Consider next something non-human, maybe an oak tree, one that is 200 years old, but started out as a simple acorn. Clearly there is a difference between those two phases—being an acorn and an oak tree, that is. Next, consider your children, and how they have learned language. Starting out struggling to make a few noises to represent their parents or the family pet, and then, all of a sudden, an explosion of phrases and then sentences—all as if it were some string of magical emergents from one day to the next. Finally, consider your nation's culture—at some point in the probably not-too-distant past, it was likely enslaving other humans. Of course, this horrible practice isn't entirely eradicated but surely its prevalence has diminished, and surely not as many cultures are presently involved in such practices compared to the extent in which they were in the past.

Each of these scenarios—from yourself to oak trees to children to your culture—have one thing in common. They've all grown up. Or, as we often prefer to say, they've all undergone development. In each of these instances, the entity under consideration started out with less complexity and then, over time, developed, grew, and expanded into greater complexity or skill. Regardless of whether we are speaking of social practices, the physical properties of organisms, or the values and beliefs of individuals and groups—each of these show a universal and mysterious drive towards more complex development over time. So what is development? And how does it operate? These very questions are the topic of this chapter.

By virtue of the fact that you have developed—most likely through at least four or five major levels or waves of unfolding—you possess a fairly refined intuition for recognizing development in both yourself and particularly in others. This is to say that you already possess a fairly robust ability to gauge more or less developmental complexity. And I'm not just talking about higher or lower complexity in exteriors—surely you can tell the difference between an acorn and an oak—I'm talking more so about the differences in interior development—say between someone who is egocentric and only cares about their needs and someone who is worldcentric and cares about the needs of all human beings. We access this intuition of developmental complexity in two primary ways: from remembering our own life history and through our communicative experiences with others. As you saw before, you remember your past and you have a keen intuition about the nature of our developmental changes. These intuitions are also present in regards to the growth of others. Let's say you were talking to a six-year-old about gravity. Would you say (1) gravity holds us to the earth—it is what makes something fall when dropped; or (2) gravity is a natural phenomenon by which objects with mass attract one another and it is a consequence of the curvature of space-time which governs the motion of inertial objects? Obviously, you'd choose the first option, but why? Well, because you know a child's way of understanding is less complex or less developed and therefore the second option would be too confusing, literally over their heads, as it were. You

Chapter 5 - Growing Up: Your Capacity for Developmental Growth

already have an intuition of development and you most likely acquired it without a chapter on development—so what then is such a chapter good for?

Learning about development helps us to refine our intuition, to raise it to new and more effective heights. Exactly how it does this is something you'll see as we proceed. Through the process of coming to understand levels of development in a more sophisticated way, you will uncover a deeper and more robust experience of who you really are and how your strengths, weaknesses, capacities, skills, beliefs, values, and behaviors all came to be exactly how they now are—and, you'll learn how they can continue to develop into wider, more encompassing, more compassionate expressions of your true nature. But that's not all. You'll also become more effective with others, you'll gain a deeper understanding of why people do the beautiful and terrible things they do; and you'll discover how to communicate with them more effectively—and not just folks like you, but particularly people who aren't like you—maybe even people you don't really like. How about a few more benefits of learning about levels? First, you learn about how we learn, how we grow, and how we can actively participate in our own unfolding—in this sense, levels are the vehicle for your own self-transcendence. In the end, to put it quite simply and kind of crudely: Understanding levels can help make you less of an asshole. Not that you are one, of course. But, as an antidote to those rare moments when you slip into your "lower" self, an understanding of levels of development as the path to ultimate fullness—fullness of perspective, of care, of concern—is the first step in consciously walking the path toward your most beautiful expression.

These benefits don't come without their challenges. As compared to the other chapters in this book, levels come with incredible rewards and greater risk. On the path to becoming more consciously engaged in your own growth and development, you may encounter some interesting challenges: Levels can be a tricky and tender issue to work with outside a developmentally-informed community because many people are resistant to the very idea of levels—particularly when talking about levels in individuals. Why? Well as we will see, the determination of higher and lower—which really just means more or less complex—can and has been used against people. It can look a lot like discrimination, stereotyping, or unnatural and oppressive ranking. I mention this now, so you can track possible solutions as we proceed carefully, compassionately, and comprehensively through this discussion. Along the way, I'll make sure to identify clearly what levels are and what they aren't—along with how to use them in a manner that promotes inclusion rather than exclusion.

Developmental Lines

Let's start with a simple question: What is your greatest gift, your most natural talent or capacity? Think about it for a moment . . . but don't think too hard, go with the first thing that comes to mind, even if you feel the inclination to qualify or judge your answer. What are you really good at? Now, on the flip side, what is your most prominent weakness? Where could you use a bit of work, or where do you not measure up as compared to the skills of others whom you really respect or maybe even envy a little bit? Then, think of someone you know—maybe a family member, a boss, or a past partner—someone who is profoundly skilled in one area but quite abysmal in another. Ever had a manager who was great with strategy and numbers but when it came to interpersonal relationships couldn't acknowledge that other people didn't always feel the same way that they did? Or maybe an ex-partner who was really good at telling you what you should do with your life, but couldn't find their own direction?

At this point, you are probably wondering why we are tracing this particularly personal line of inquiry. Each of us has different capacities, skills, or intelligences and all of us are rather unevenly and differently developed in each capacity as compared to others. The capacities are called lines of development and they are the skills that unfold through the levels or stages spoken about earlier. Lines offer tremendous insight into why people are so different—that is, why we are all so differently skilled and unevenly developed. Research has identified some two dozen distinct developmental capacities in humans and almost everyone is developed to greater degrees in some as compared to others. This alone does quite a lot in explaining the differences you perceive to exist between individuals. By understanding how these capacities arise in ourselves, first, and in others, second, we can identify the source of our greatest strengths, as well as the source of our weaknesses. This leads to a more authentic understanding of our uniqueness and it allows us to target developmental work at our underdeveloped or problematic capacities. Lines also provide insight into how we can work together—in everything from intimate relationships to workplace collaborations. Finally, lines can act as a partial cure for your desires for perfection—they show you that no one is highly skilled in every area, and that everyone is unequal in their developmental expression. They also show us that being unevenly developed is more than okay—it's actually part of being human.

From Multiple Intelligences to Lines

In the 1980s Howard Gardner's (1983) work on cognitive information processing popularized the concept of multiple intelligences —which serves as a good metaphor for lines. It suggests that humans have different kinds of minds and therefore learn, remember, perform, and understand the world in different ways. The intelligences he identified include: visual-spatial, bodily-kinesthetic, intrapersonal, interpersonal, musical, linguistic, and logical-mathematical. Again, the key here is that each of us has the capacity to learn through each of these seven intelligences, but that we typically show strengths in some more than others. The theory of developmental lines functions in a similar way, but instead of only focusing on learning styles or intelligences, we'll use lines in a manner that includes all functions, aspects, and capacities of ourselves that show growth and development.

Lines are present in all domains of existence—biological, cultural, and social—but, like Gardner, I'll focus on lines that model the interior development of individuals. These lines concern our most intimate and personal capacities, and they are the easiest to connect with and are in some ways the most exciting. It is relatively easy to tap into an intuitive sense of these individual developmental lines through a bit of guided inquiry. Wilber (2000, 2007) has pointed out that the unique capacity described by each line can be understood metaphorically as emerging to answer one of life's important questions. Questions which we all encounter, and questions which we each have some answer for. As you review these questions, see what answers emerge for you. Don't worry about getting them right, there is no such thing—just open to each question and touch in with the essence of each line as an aspect of your being.

- What is arising in the world in this very moment; what are you aware of? This question gets to the heart of your cognitive line. (see: Piaget, 1926; Commons, Richards, Armon, 1984; Aurobindo, 1985)

- Who are you? This taps in to your self-identity or ego development line. (see: Loevinger, 1987; Cook-Greuter, 1999)
- What do you find significant? This is your values line. (see: Graves, Cowan, and Todorovic, 2005; Beck and Cowan, 1996)
- What is of ultimate concern? This is your spiritual or faith line. (see: Fowler, 1981)
- How should you interact with others? This is your interpersonal line. (see: Selman, 1980)
- What should you do in your life? This is your moral line. (see: Kohlberg, 1984; Gilligan, 1982; Armon, 1984)
- How do you feel? This is your emotional line. (see: Goleman, 1998)
- What is attractive to you? This is your aesthetic line. (see: Housen, 1983)
- What do you need? This is your needs lines. (see: Maslow, 1969)

Taken in the abstract or removed from a particular context, answers to some of these questions can seem quite vague. But, that aside, did you recognize that you have encountered each of these questions before? At some point in your life, questions such as these have arisen and demanded some type of answer. Second, do you recognize that despite the lack of context, you had something to say or some thoughts that arose in response to each question? If either of these were true for you, it is because lines are very real and important dimensions of your experience.

Principles and Properties of Lines

Let's refine and extend your initial sense of this by reviewing a few important principles and properties about the nature and function of lines. First, lines generally fall into three groups of categories: cognitive, self-related, and talents. Lines falling into the cognitive group variously chart your ability to register or "see" phenomena (Wilber, 2007). At higher levels, this is sometimes referred to as your ability to take perspectives. In general, cognitive lines recognize your awareness of what is, and this is not just confined to the gross, waking state. Our second grouping, called self-related lines, includes many developmental capacities that directly affect or constitute the self. These include the self-identity, moral, needs, values, emotional, and interpersonal lines as well as lines of defense mechanisms and object relations. Lines in the self-related group tend to be developed

Chapter 5 - *Growing Up: Your Capacity for Developmental Growth*

within a certain range of each other. Talent or skill lines make up the final group. These include lines that can be developed across a wide range, which, for many of us, means not developed at all. Also, these lines show very little relation to each other. Included here are logico-mathematical, drawing, visual-spatial, kinesthetic, symbolic-play, aesthetic, linguistic, narrative, creative, and musical capacities.

Second, some lines describe very defined and specific capacities, like logico-mathematical or musical, while others, like cognition, self-sense, and morality, describe groups of similar capacities that actually pull in a number of interrelated functions. For example, your moral capacity calls on several distinct but related skills such as reflective judgment, perspective or role taking, and moral reasoning. Each of these can be understood or researched independently, and all of them combine in effect to create your moral line capacity.

Third, lines are relatively independent—meaning, as we have seen, we can be generally more or less developed in each. And fourth, there are some important relationships between some lines. These interconnections are described as necessary but not sufficient relationships, which means that you need something before you can get something else —but that having the first thing does not necessarily grant the second. Consider cognition: cognitive development is necessary but not sufficient for development in most other lines, since you must be aware of or able to register other phenomena before you can then act on them, feel them, need them, or value them (Wilber, 2006). Other relations between lines follow this general scheme: cognitive development is necessary but not sufficient for self-development, which is necessary but not sufficient for interpersonal development, which is necessary but not sufficient for moral development, which is necessary but not sufficient for ideas of the good life.

Psychograph

Each of the principles—from the uneven nature of development to the relationship between lines—is elegantly captured in a representational diagram called the integral psychograph (Wilber, 2000, 2006). This is the great thing about maps and diagrams as representations of some real territory—they are capable of holding a great deal of complexity in a relatively simple manner. The integral psychograph, shown in Figure 1, is a snapshot in developmental time. It shows several lines—cognition, self-identity, values, morality, faith, and kinesthetic. Of course, it could show more or less but this is enough to get us started.

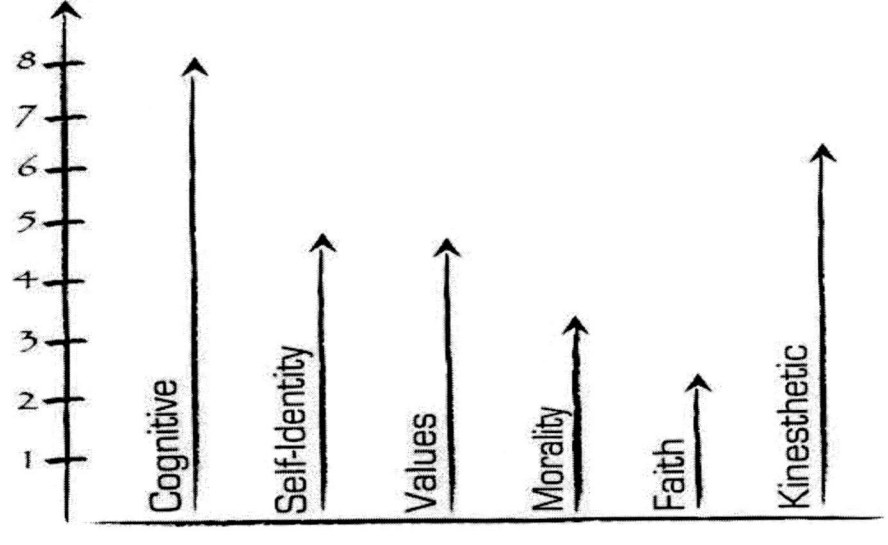

Figure 1: Integral Psychograph

Each of these lines run vertically from the bottom to a certain point up the numbered scale on the left. This numbered scale will represent our degrees of development—at least until we get to the topic of developmental altitude. As you can clearly see, development is uneven and the relationships we spoke of earlier are still holding true. Kinesthetic development, in this case, is shown as higher than most other lines because it is independent of needs, values, morals, and self-sense. Again, the point to remember here is that the vast variability in human development generally produces a psychograph with relatively uneven development.

What if we were to consider your psychograph? What would your unique developmental make-up look like across these lines? How would your uneven development show up? To be integrally developed does not mean that you have to excel in all the known intelligences, or that all of your lines have to be at the highest level. But, it does mean that you develop a very good sense of what your own psychograph is actually like so that, with an integral self-image, you can guide your future development.

Lines and Levels

So what is this common scale or ruler of development? The numbered scale on the left of the psychograph diagram is called developmental altitude and it serves as a common measure of development across any line. The numbered scale represents the general sequence of stages or levels that each lines progresses through. The higher the number, the more consciousness or complexity present in the line. A scale such as this is particularly helpful when working with psychographs, because we can't use the levels in one line to refer to the levels in another. So, this relatively neutral scale serves as a cross-line tool. Each line progresses through a series of its own distinct levels, but they can be understood using a content-neutral concept Wilber (2006) developed called altitude, which I'll get to in just a moment.

From Intuition to a Theory of Levels

Just like our sense of the different capacities described by lines, we have an intuitive sense of the levels that lines progress through. But this raises the question: How many stages are there between, say, when you were a teenager and now? How many steps did it take for your self-sense to develop from where it was as a teen to the different more self-reflective place you now embody? You might see three distinct shifts but someone else may be tracking seven. So, who's right? The problem is that our intuitive or felt experience of levels is not specific or consistent enough to answer this question. This is why we would get as many answers to this question as people we asked. Our intuition alone is just not fine-tuned enough. You remember being different in the past, but how exactly was that the case? And what has really changed? You can calibrate our language for children versus adults, but the large spectrum of adulthood is harder to grasp. Finally, what characteristics or properties are the most important ones to consider as indicators of developmental progress? Is it vocabulary? Grammar? The concepts chosen? The perspectives taken?

And so on. The fact of the matter is, intuition alone is messy. This is why we turn to science for assistance—developmental science to be precise....

Enter developmental structuralism: Pose a series of questions to large groups of people. See if their responses fall into any classes or categories. If so, follow those classes over time and see if they emerge in a sequential order of stages. If they do, you then attempt to determine the structure or makeup of those stages. How about an example. When Carol Gilligan (1977) refined Lawrence Kohlberg's (1969) moral spectrum through studies which specifically focused on women, she saw an emphasis on relationality and came to describe her stages in those terms: selfish, care, universal care, and integrated.

Levels Defined

If levels are determined by science and not your intuition, what are they exactly? In a strictly theoretical and precise sense, levels are defined as qualitatively distinct degrees of organization within a nested holarchy that have enduring holistic patterns of whole/ partness, which are fluid and not rigidly separated, and which occur or unfold in a sequence (Wilber, 1995). Damn, bet you can't say that three times fast. In light of this technical definition maybe you are now leaning back towards your intuitive sense. So, what does all of this mean? Good question. In this section, we work slowly through each of these points. For now, consider it like this: Levels are the stops along the developmental path towards greater complexity and consciousness in every line.

Developmental Altitude

Let's ease into this by taking a step back to something familiar as we transition to an elegantly simple and accessible way to understand development—a concept called developmental altitude. Let's go back to the integral psychograph. Figure 2 should look familiar, but this time around I've replaced the numbered scale with a colorful spectrum. In the simplest sense, the vertical scale represents the degree of complexity or

Chapter 5 - Growing Up: Your Capacity for Developmental Growth

consciousness per se, through which any line has progressed. Rather than a scale of numbers, lets conceive of the vertical axis as a spectrum of developmental altitude.

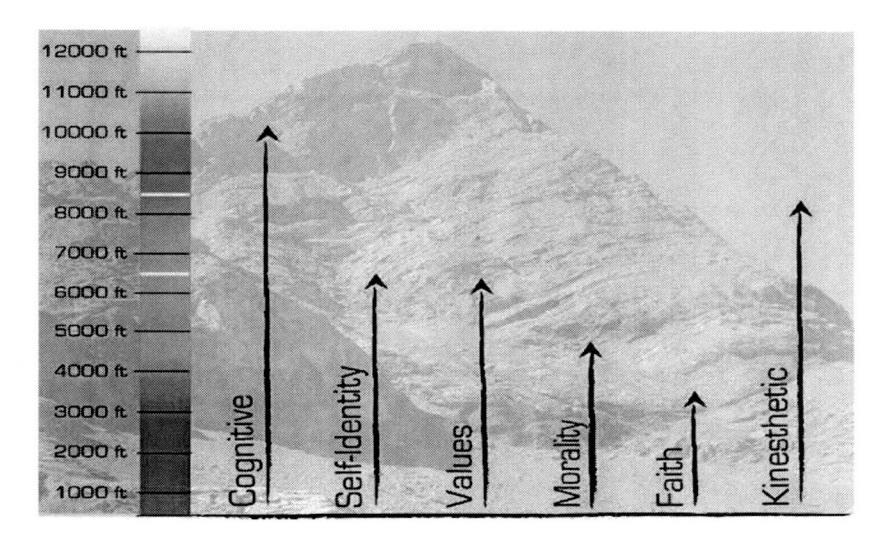

Figure 2: Developmental Altitude

Imagine that each line is a different path or route up the same mountain. Each path starts at 0 ft. and travels to the top at 12,000 ft. Each path takes a very different route up the mountain, but at some point every path passes through 2000 ft., 3000 ft., 4000 ft., and so on. The actual territory on each path at say 5000 ft. is incredibly varied and diverse. On one path, at 5000 ft., it could be a relatively easy hike while on another at the same altitude it could be a nearly vertical cliff face. The same is true for each line. At 5000 ft. of developmental altitude the territory in one line, say ego development, is quite different than the territory in the needs line. Both have the same degree of altitude or development, but one talks of self-sense and the other of needs—two different capacities indeed! This is why we can't use the name of levels in one line to refer to levels in another line. We can, however, use this content-less or content-neutral altitude spectrum—denoting the general degree of consciousness, complexity, or altitude—to refer to development in any line.

The Coming Waves

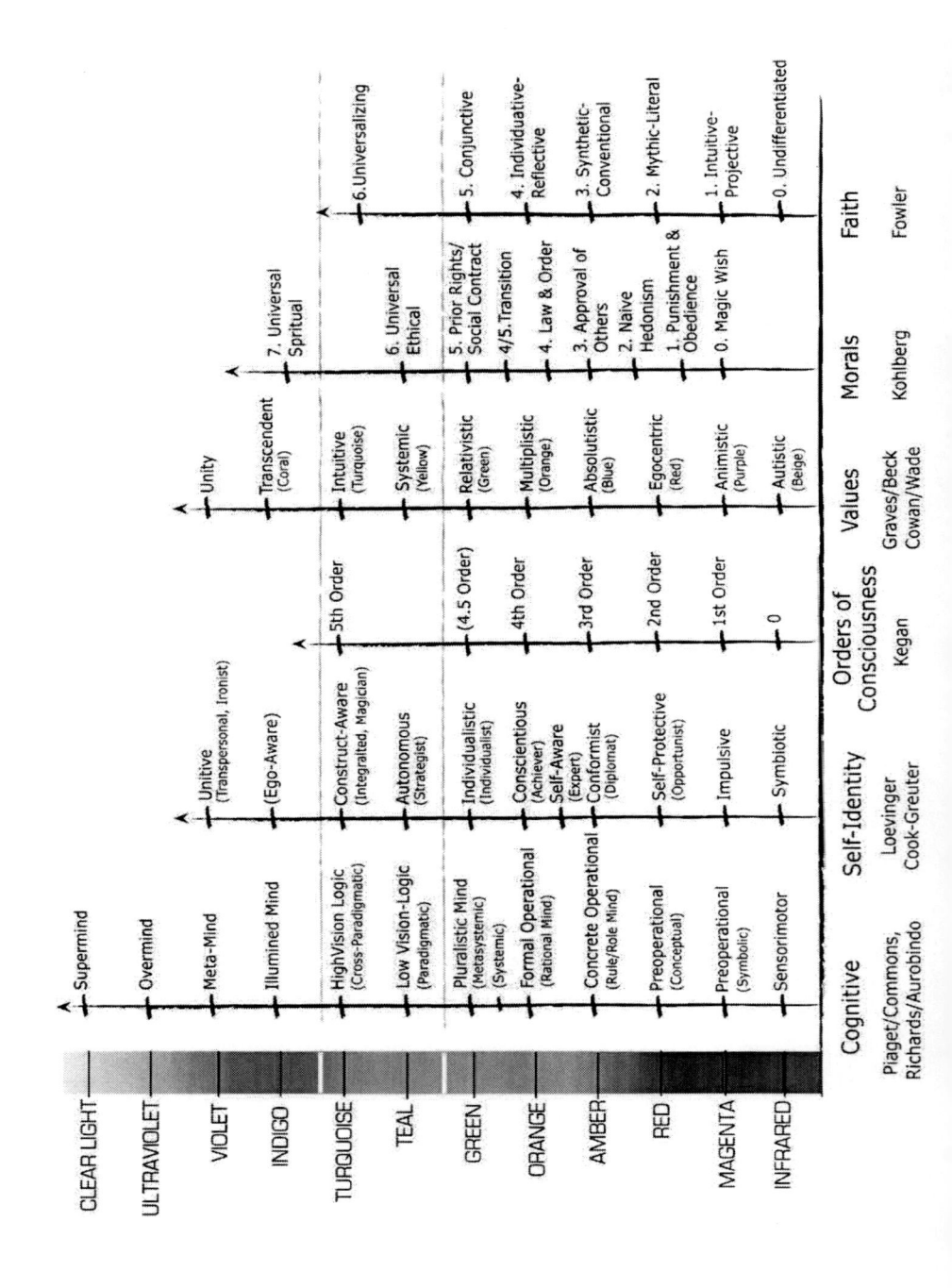

Color	Cognitive (Piaget/Commons, Richards/Aurobindo)	Self-Identity (Loevinger, Cook-Greuter)	Orders of Consciousness (Kegan)	Values (Graves/Beck, Cowan/Wade)	Morals (Kohlberg)	Faith (Fowler)
CLEAR LIGHT	Supermind					
ULTRAVIOLET	Overmind			Unity		
VIOLET	Meta-Mind	Unitive (Transpersonal, Ironist)				
INDIGO	Illumined Mind	(Ego-Aware)	5th Order	Transcendent (Coral)	7. Universal Spiritual	6. Universalizing
TURQUOISE	HighVision Logic (Cross-Paradigmatic)	Construct-Aware (Integrated, Magician)		Intuitive (Turquoise)		
TEAL	Low Vision-Logic (Paradigmatic)	Autonomous (Strategist)		Systemic (Yellow)	6. Universal Ethical	
GREEN	Pluralistic Mind (Metasystemic) (Systemic)	Individualistic (Individualist)	(4.5 Order)	Relativistic (Green)	5. Prior Rights/ Social Contract	5. Conjunctive
ORANGE	Formal Operational (Rational Mind)	Conscientious (Achiever) Self-Aware (Expert)	4th Order	Multiplistic (Orange)	4/5. Transition 4. Law & Order	4. Individuative-Reflective
AMBER	Concrete Operational (Rule/Role Mind)	Conformist (Diplomat)	3rd Order	Absolutistic (Blue)	3. Approval of Others 2. Naive Hedonism	3. Synthetic-Conventional
RED	Preoperational (Conceptual)	Self-Protective (Opportunist)	2nd Order	Egocentric (Red)	1. Punishment & Obedience	2. Mythic-Literal
MAGENTA	Preoperational (Symbolic)	Impulsive	1st Order	Animistic (Purple)	0. Magic Wish	1. Intuitive-Projective
INFRARED	Sensorimotor	Symbiotic	0	Autistic (Beige)		0. Undifferentiated

Chapter 5 - Growing Up: Your Capacity for Developmental Growth

Altitude is an orienting generalization—meaning it's a 50,000-ft. view of development that we can leverage to serve our learning. And this reveals one immediate benefit: As we learn about individual development, instead of having to learn about every level discovered in each line, we can instead start with the much simpler altitude spectrum, expanding in complexity as our knowledge and experience increase. Next, we'll walk through the altitude spectrum, but because altitude is not a line and therefore has no content itself, we will draw content from many of the other lines in order to paint a picture of what each altitude looks like. Figure 3 shows the altitude spectrum along with several of the lines I'll draw from (Previous page).

Using the concept of developmental altitude, we will now explore the development of human consciousness from the earliest, most kosmically ingrained stages called infrared through the most speculative and emergent stage called clear light. To put this into perspective, we will cover stages of development from the earliest australopithecine human ancestors of millions of years ago to the most recent stages reached by possibly only a handful of present-day developmental pioneers. Also, the spectrum from infrared to clear light covers or includes the stages described by every researcher, regardless of their line of focus; most researchers discover stages starting at or beyond infrared, and stopping before indigo. Regardless of when various structures were laid down as kosmic patterns, this exploration is pertinent to us at this time, because each of us start our development at square one—at infrared. And, each of us has the possibility of reaching the highest known stages, helping to then carve those patterns deeper into the Kosmos. This is not a given, only a potentiality, but by increasing your understanding and awareness of levels in general, we could argue that it may increase your potential of expanding your growth even further than it is now.

Finally, one last thing before we start. As we proceed through the spectrum, we'll also track shifts in what are called tiers of development. A tier is basically an arbitrary grouping of levels. Arbitrary not because they are unimportant, but rather because different researchers place tier shifts in different places. The integral map tracks three tier shifts—1st tier, 2nd tier, and 3rd tier—each of which represent what Clare Graves (2005) called a "momentous leap" in consciousness. As we'll see, a tier marks a profound reorganization of consciousness, which clearly distinguishes levels in the new tier from the previous tier.

Infrared

Starting out as our first stage, in tier one, is the infrared altitude. With the evolutionary split between modern Homo sapiens from hominids some 150,000 years ago, the infrared stages emerged as the first in our spectrum of consciousness. Cognition at this early stage is pre-reflexive or pleromatic in the case of human infants who are unable to distinguish between inside and outside or subject and object (Wilber, 1980). Infrared cognition is also described as absolute adualism, meaning it's a stage of oceanic oneness, not of the spiritual variety but a type that is preverbal, pre-spatial, and protoplasmic—which is just a fancy way of saying a sense of oneness prior to differentiation. The next shift, happening again within the infrared altitude, is the initial discernment between self and the objective world. This large step is the first clear differentiation on the path of development, but it is still prepersonal, archaic, concerned with survival needs, and operating fully in the sensorimotor realm—the realm of simple sensory-derived actions and motor functions (Piaget, 1926).

Further development through infrared sees the emergence of the axial and then pranic body as young children sufficiently distinguish their physical body from the environment, and then their proto-emotional body from the physical. Proto-emotions—fear or pleasure—are still prepersonal and based on simple reflex-driven images, which are not complex enough to sustain higher emotion (Wilber, 1980). The self-sense here is described as symbiotic—meaning the self exists in a fusion of symbiosis with proto-emotions and body (Loevinger, 1976). Aside from laying the foundation for structures of later development, infrared, if we successfully navigate it, is training in how to get our basic physiological needs satisfied. Along with that is the development of instinct and a strong survival intuition, which appear in later development as innate biological warnings of danger.

Magenta

Chapter 5 - Growing Up: Your Capacity for Developmental Growth

Emerging some 50,000 years ago, the magenta altitude brought with it the emergence of the impulsive self, driven by an impulse predominance that focuses on anxiety reduction and wish fulfillment. The awareness of punishment and reward are present but psychological causation is not; in its place is a simple form of physical causation (Kohlberg, 1981). Cognitively, magenta sees the completion of sensorimotor and the emergence of pre-operational, symbol-driven thinking that makes simple mental representation of objects, even when they are not present—but this representation is imprecise and it is not mentally reversible—meaning the representation can't be fully operated on in the mind (Piaget, 1926). Also, a child cannot act on these impulses but rather is these impulses and perceptions. Needs have shifted from survival to safety and security. But they are still me-focused needs, which can be satisfied through fantasy and magic (Maslow, 1969). Magenta is characterized by a self who is ritualistically, superstitiously, and stereotypically engaging a world of inanimate objects which have an indwelling of life bestowed upon them (Loevinger, 1976). This magical-animistic thinking is prevalent in faith at this stage, which is powerfully and permanently influenced by examples, moods, stories, and myths of faith held by adults (Fowler, 1981).

Red

The red altitude sees the emergence of more advanced pre-operational thinking that is capable of forming concepts and demonstrating conservation of substance—which is a classic test administered by Piaget (1926) in which he asks children if two equal balls of clay are still equal if one is flattened and the other is lengthened. Conceptual language continues to develop at this stage and allows the self to further transcend the simply present world. Self-sense at red is described as self-protective or opportunist and features a big step towards the self-control of impulses through the anticipation of short-term repercussions of actions (Loevinger, 1976). An individual's focus is still on their immediate security needs, self-protection, and self-gratifying opportunities (Maslow, 1969). Power is used as a tool in social interactions where control is a feasible way to get what one wants, and impulses and perceptions are organized according to a greater stability in needs and habits; this is why the child is sometimes described as his needs, in that those needs regulate his experience (Kegan, 1982). Values are egocentric, focusing on getting attention, being right, and receiving respect and immediate gratification (Beck and Cowan, 1999). Morality is similarly focused; rules are taken literally and followed to avoid punishment. Individualism is concrete and others are allowed the same as self as long as the self's interests aren't threatened (Kohlberg, 1981). Faith features beliefs and symbols held to strict literal interpretation, as a linear narrative orientation replaces the episodic quality of the magenta's imaginative construction and composing of the world (Fowler, 1981).

Amber

The amber altitude emerged with the influx of farming some 10,000 years ago. It has a mythic-membership, traditional, and ethnocentric worldview which still forms a prevalent basis in society in our world. Cognition at amber is characterized by concrete operations or the development of a complete system of mental operations on objects, which exist in a type of "mobile" equilibrium, that allows for fully mental reversibility. Thus, these concrete operations create a logic of classes and relations and feature skills such as classification—in which the child can understand that a Labrador belongs to the class of dogs, which belongs to the class of mammals, which belongs to the class of living beings. Also present is the ability for seriation, which allows for the ordering of objects based on certain properties, such as length (Piaget, 1926). Thinking at amber is described as absolutistic, or black and white, in that it sees only two options, one of which is right. This either/or conception is typically limited to not what is objectively or pragmatically best, but what the group feels is right. Self-sense at amber is conformist and association with the group is paramount (Loevinger, 1976). One chooses to obey rules because they are group-accepted rules rather than for fear of punishment. Values follow suit: it is important to embody assigned roles and strive for a stable, orderly, and predictable world. Also of value is a purpose-driven life that has meaning and direction (Beck and Cowan, 1999). Morality is equally concerned with the group, in that the reason for doing right is a desire to be seen as good in one's own eyes as well as those of others. The social perspective at this altitude is the awareness of individuals in relationship

Chapter 5 - Growing Up: Your Capacity for Developmental Growth

with other individuals. Needs shift to belonging and acceptance, to which self-esteem becomes hinged (Kohlberg, 1981). Faith as well is concerned with conformity. And individuals create a faith consisting of an ideology, or a cluster of values and orientations that individuals are unable to investigate objectively; rather, they are determined by the group (Fowler, 1981). Amber is the pinnacle of ethnocentrism and features the ability to take the perspective of the other or the perspective of the group as poorly differentiated other.

Orange

The orange altitude emerged a few hundred years ago with the European Renaissance. Its modern, rational view grew in prominence through the Age of Enlightenment and came to its fullest expression during the Industrial Revolution. Fueling this age of reason and science was the emergence of formal operational cognition or the ability to operate on thoughts themselves. No longer limited to reflection on concrete objects, cognition moves from representations to abstractions and can now operate on a range of nontangible propositions that may not reflect the concrete world—this is the basis of scientific reasoning through hypothesis (Piaget, 1926). Orange also brings multiplistic thinking or the realization that there are several possible ways of approaching a situation, even though one is still considered most right. Self-sense at orange features two shifts—first to expert and then to achiever. These moves feature an increase in self-awareness, and an appreciation for multiple possibilities in a given situation. Recognition that one does not always live up to idealized social expectations is fueled by an awareness that begins to penetrate the inner world of subjectivity (Loevinger, 1976). This is the beginning of introspection, an objectifiable self-sense, and the capacity to take a third-person perspective (Cook-Greuter, 2004). Needs shift from belonging to self-esteem and values land on pragmatic, utilitarian approaches to life that rely on rational and objective thinking to earn progress, prosperity, and self-reliance (Maslow, 1969).

Morality at orange sees right defined by universal ethical principles. The emergence of formal-operational thinking at orange enables a worldcentric care for universal human rights and the right of each individual for autonomy and the pursuit of happiness. A desire for individual dignity and self-respect are also driving forces behind orange morality (Kohlberg, 1981). A significant number of the founding fathers of the United States harbored orange values. While these moral drives first emerged as a capacity of the orange altitude, this does not imply that culture as a whole, at the time orange first emerged (or even now, for that matter) is able to fully actualize these moral principles. Faith at orange is called individual-reflective insofar as identity and worldview are differentiated from those of others and faith takes on an essence of critical thought, demythologizing symbols into conceptual meanings. At orange we see the emergence of rational deism and secularism (Fowler, 1981).

Green

As the 1950s and '60s began to roll around, the last stage of the 1st tier emerged as a cultural force. With the green altitude, we see the emergence of pluralistic, multicultural, postmodern worldviews. Cognition is starting to move beyond formal operations into the realm of coordinating systems of abstractions in what is called metasystemic cognition. While formal operations acted upon the classes and relations between members of classes, metasystemic operations start at the level of relating systems to systems. The focus of these investigations is placed upon comparing, contrasting, transforming, and synthesizing entire systems rather than components of one system (Commons, Richards, and Armon, 1984). This emergent faculty allows self-sense to focus around a heightened sense of individuality, and an increased ability for emotional resonance. The recognition of individual differences, the ability to tolerate paradox and contradiction, and a greater conceptual complexity, all provide for an understanding of conflict as being both internally and externally caused (Loevinger, 1976). Context plays a major role in the creation of truth and individual perspective, with each being context dependent and open to subjective interpretation. Meaning, each perspective and truth are rendered relative and cannot be judged as better or truer than any other (Cook-Greuter, 1999). This fuels a value set that centers on softness over cold rationality, sensitivity in preference over objectivity, along with a focus on community harmony and equality—which drives the valuing of sensitivity to others, reconciliation, consensus, dialogue, relationship, human development, bonding, and the seeking of a

Chapter 5 - Growing Up: Your Capacity for Developmental Growth

peace with the inner self (Graves, Cowan, and Todorovic, 2005; Beck and Cowan, 1999).

Moral decisions are based on rights, values, or principles that are agreeable to all individuals composing a society based on fair and beneficial practices. All of this leads to the equality movements and multiculturalism—and to the extreme form of relativism which we saw earlier as the context-dependent nature of all truth—including objective facts (Kohlberg, 1981). Faith at the green altitude is called conjunctive and allows the self to integrate what was unrecognized by the previous stage's self-certainty and cognitive and affective adaptation to reality. New features at this level of faith include: the unification of symbolic power with conceptual meaning, an awareness of one's social unconscious, a reworking of one's past, and an opening to one's deeper self (Fowler, 1981).

Teal

The transition into teal marks the move from 1st tier to 2nd tier. Before describing the nature of the teal altitude, let's explore what characterizes the momentous leap to 2nd tier. Perhaps most important is that teal is the first level capable of understanding and honoring all previous levels of development as important and natural. How about a stylized but powerful metaphor? If someone from each altitude is locked into a room for a day, by the end of it, amber comes out thinking red is barbaric and orange is going to hell. Orange sees amber as too institutional and trapped in its myths and green as too mushy and sensitive. Green thinks orange has destroyed everything from the environment to the soul of our unique humanness, and all other levels are seen as misguided but alright. Then we have teal, and no one knows what to think. They don't like teal per se but they can't figure out why exactly. The point here is that teal is the first altitude that doesn't need to aggressively fight for the sole rightness of its worldview. As such, teal is the first altitude to discover ways to get along with, understand, and honor all previous levels.

This shift is the product of a primarily teal cognition and self-sense. Cognition is described as middle vision logic or paradigmatic in that it is capable of coordinating the relations between systems of systems, unifying them into principled frameworks or paradigms. This is an operation on metasystems and allows for the view described above: a view of human development itself (Commons, Richards, and Armon, 1984). Self-sense at teal is called autonomous or strategist and is characterized by the emergent capacity to acknowledge and cope with inner conflicts in needs, duties, and values, all of which are part of a multifaceted and complex world. Teal sees our need for autonomy but also sees autonomy itself as limited because emotional interdependence is inevitable (Loevinger, 1976). The contradictory aspects of self are weaved into an identity that is whole, integrated, and committed to generating a fulfilling life. Additionally, teal allows individuals to: link theory and practice, perceive dynamic systems interactions, recognize and strive for higher principles, understand the social construction of reality, handle paradox and complexity, create positive sum games, and seek feedback from others as a vital source for growth (Cook-Greuter, 1999).

Values embrace the magnificence of existence, flexibility, spontaneity, functionality, the integration of differences into interdependent systems, and complementing natural egalitarianism with natural ranking (Beck and Cowan, 1999). Needs shift to self-actualization and morality is defined in terms of both universal ethical principles and a recognition of the developmental relativity of those universals (Maslow, 1969). Teal is the first wave that is truly able to see the limitations of orange and green morality. It is able to uphold the paradox of relativism and universalism. Teal, in its decision-making process, is able to see deep and surface features of morality, and is able to take into consideration both those variables when engaging in moral action! Currently, Teal is quite rare, embraced by 2 to 5 percent of the North American and European population according to sociological research (see: Miller and Cook-Greuter, 1994).

Turquoise

Even more rare—found stably in less than 1 percent of the population—and even more emergent is the turquoise altitude. Cognition at turquoise is called late vision logic or cross-paradigmatic and features the ability to connect metasystems or paradigms with other metasystems. This is the realm of coordinating principles—which are unified systems of

Chapter 5 - Growing Up: Your Capacity for Developmental Growth

systems of abstraction—to other principles. Confusing, huh?—and exceedingly rare. This type of cognitive ability is behind the integration of fields of knowledge into new transdisciplinary fields of knowledge. Examples would be Darwin's coordination of the paradigms of paleontology, geology, biology, and ecology to form the field of evolution or Einstein's coordination of the paradigm of non-Euclidian geometry with the paradigm of physics to form the field of relativity (Commons, Richards, and Armon, 1984).

Aurobindo, Indian sage and philosopher, offers a more first-person account of turquoise, which he called higher mind. It's a ". . . unitarian sense of being with a powerful multiple dynamisation capable of the formation of a multitude of aspects of knowledge, ways of action, forms and significances of becoming, of all of which there is a spontaneous inherent knowledge" (Aurobindo, 1985, p. 976). Self-sense at turquoise is called construct-aware and is the first stage in Cook-Greuter's extension of Loevinger's work on ego development. The construct-aware stage sees individuals for the first time, exploring the meaningfulness of more and more complex thought structures—with awareness of the automatic nature of human map-making and the absurdities to which unbridled complexity and logical argumentation can lead. Individuals at this stage begin to see their ego as a central point of reference and therefore a limit to growth. They also struggle to balance their unique self-expressions and their concurrent sense of importance, the empirical and intuitive knowledge that there is no fundamental subject/object separation, and the budding awareness of self-identity as temporary; which leads to a decreased ego desire to create a stable self-identity. Turquoise individuals are keenly aware of the interplay between awareness, thought, action, and effects. They seek personal and spiritual transformation and hold a complex matrix of self-identifications, the adequacy of which they increasingly call into question (Cook-Greuter, 1999). Much of this already points to turquoise values, which embrace holistic and intuitive thinking and alignment to a universal order in a conscious fashion (Graves, Cowan, and Todorovic, 2005; Beck and Cowan, 1999). Faith at turquoise is called universalizing and can generate faith compositions in which conceptions of ultimate reality start to include all beings. Individuals at turquoise faith dedicate themselves to the transformation of present reality in the direction of transcendent actuality. Both of these are preludes to the coming of 3rd tier (Fowler, 1981).

Indigo

The transcendent drive of turquoise can unfold into another tier shift—this time from 2nd to 3rd tier. The move to the indigo altitude marks the transition to the level that is arguably the most emergent, but clearly recognizable kosmic groove. Third tier as compared to 2nd is marked by a definitive move to the truly transpersonal domains where the self is to some degree transcended. As such, this is when vertical development starts to take on structural characteristics of spiritual development as described by the contemplative traditions. This is why for several decades it was thought that development through states started in 3rd tier. But, the primary difference is that 3rd tier altitudes are able to take as object all the previous levels of development. This capacity for advanced perspective-taking in the developmental sense characterizes indigo cognition, which Aurobindo calls illumined mind and integral calls the para-mind. This altitude allows for thinking that is no longer of higher thought but is becoming more comprised of spiritual light. With this descent of spiritual light into the reality of illumined mind comes, in the words of Aurobindo:

. . . the arrival of a greater dynamic, a golden drive, a luminous 'enthousiasmos' of inner force and power which replaces the comparatively slow and deliberate process of the Higher Mind [or vision logic] by a swift, sometimes vehement, almost violent impetus of rapid transformation. Illumined mind [para-mind] works not through thought but primarily through vision, which affects a powerful and dynamic integration by illumining thought-mind with inner vision, imbibing the heart with spiritual sight, and the emotions with spiritual light and energy. (Aurobindo, 1985, p. 944)

Kohlberg (1984) postulated a final stage of morality which corresponds with indigo. He called this stage the universal spiritual in that it moves beyond the universal ethical principles and replaces them with an ethical and religious orientation that finds meaning in meta-ethical, metaphysical, and religious epistemologies articulated within theistic, pantheistic, or agnostic cosmic perspectives. From these perspectives,

Chapter 5 - Growing Up: Your Capacity for Developmental Growth

moral principles are seen in a natural law framework that views morality as not a human intervention but rather as principles of justice that are in harmony with broader laws regulating the evolution of human nature that have tetra-emerged in all quadrants. Kohlberg had limited data in this realm, so we'd like to question his inclusion of agnostic perspectives. Can indigo be truly agnostic . . . or truly uncertain of the possibility of divine knowledge? If indigo is agnostic then it does not have the transpersonal drive which defines 3rd tier altitudes. It is not unusual for indigo to have objectified the subtle, dream state, which means that it has a degree of gnosis or knowledge, and unlike orange deism, is less likely to be agnostic about the spiritual essence of the universe!

Violet

At the violet altitude, we get a set of interesting descriptions: Aurobindo's for cognition and Jenny Wade's (1996) for values. According to Aurobindo, the previous two levels derive their completeness through a reference to this level, called the intuitive mind or meta-mind for the integral approach. Again in Aurobindo's words:

Intuition [meta-mind] is a power of consciousness nearer and more intimate to the original knowledge by identity. . . . It is when the consciousness of the subject meets with the consciousness in the object, penetrates it and sees, feels or vibrates with the truth of what it contacts, that the intuition [meta-mind] leaps out like a spark or lightning-flash from the shock of the meeting; or when the consciousness, even without any such meeting, looks into itself and feels directly and intimately the truth or the truths that are there, or so contacts the hidden forces behind appearances. This close perception is more than sight, more than conception: it is the result of a penetrating and revealing touch which carries in it sight and conception as part of itself or as its natural consequence. Intuition [meta-mind] sees the truth of things by a direct inner contact, not like the ordinary mental intelligence by seeking and reaching out for indirect contacts through the senses. (Aurobindo, 1985, p. 983)

We are well aware that Aurobindo's descriptions are often hard to decipher. If you find this to be the case, hold them lightly, and take them instead as beautiful offerings, or vibrant word-paintings of what these higher altitudes feel like to someone who has traversed their vast and ephemeral territories. Values at violet are called transcendent by Wade. The primary motivation for individuals at this level of value is the process of transcending the ego in order to understand the nature of absolute reality, similar to Maslow's self-transcendence needs. Individuals at this stage demonstrate a reverence and appreciation for all life as a manifestation of the Absolute. They seek to overcome attachment to life in all manifest forms via persistent practices that transcend ego, cultivate compassion, and develop abilities to handle paradoxical epistemologies, all of which are not bound by typical conceptions of time, and which cultivate non-ordinary states of consciousness. Notice in Wade's description that this stage is starting to sound spiritual in the more classic contemplative sense. This is partially because Wade, at the time she wrote this, was still adhering to the paradigm of thought that saw the spiritual growth as emerging in the 3rd tier. Since then, the relationship between high structural or vertical development (growing-up) and spiritual development (waking-up), which is best described as a progression through states, has been described in greater depth. In short, meta-mind has more or less permanent access to the subtle state/vantage point, plus access to all previous structures of consciousness up to and including the meta-mind structure.

Ultraviolet

The ultraviolet altitude, from a place of higher cognition, is described by Aurobindo as overmind. In his own words:

> Overmind is the highest of these ranges or layers between the human mind and supermind; it is full of lights and powers; but from the point of view of what is above it (which parenthetically is supermind or the clear light altitude), it is the line of the soul's turning away from the complete and indivisible knowledge and its descent towards Ignorance. For although it draws from the Truth, overmind is the beginning of the separation of aspects of

Chapter 5 - Growing Up: Your Capacity for Developmental Growth

> the Truth, the forces and their working out as if they were independent truths and this is a process that ends, as one descends to ordinary Mind, and lower levels, in a complete division, fragmentation, separation from the indivisible Truth above. The intuitional change of overmind can only be an introduction to this higher spiritual overture. But . . . the Overmind, even when it is selective and not total in its action, is still a power of cosmic consciousness, a principle of global knowledge which carries in it a delegated light from the supramental Gnosis. When the Overmind descends, the predominance of the centralizing ego-sense is entirely subordinated, lost in largeness of being and finally abolished; a wide cosmic perception and feeling of a boundless universal self and movement replaces it. (Aurobindo, 1993, p. 65)

Wilber (2006) refers to this as overmind, the witness, true mind, or true self, and by whatever name, ultraviolet includes all the previous structures up to and including the overmind structure. This differentiates the overmind from big mind or true self, in that the latter are merely states of consciousness, in themselves devoid of structure, whereas overmind possess both the state of true self plus all the evolutionary structures up to and including the ultraviolet witness (or turyia). Big mind can be experienced at any lower structure; overmind, only at ultraviolet. Aurobindo, again, to finish:

> Thought, for the most part, no longer seems to originate individually in the body or the person but manifests from above or comes in upon the cosmic mind-waves: all inner individual sight or intelligence of things is now a revelation of illumination of what is seen or comprehended, but the source of the revelation is not in one's separate self but in the universal knowledge. (Aurobindo, 1985, p. 987)

In regards to ultraviolet self-sense, described by Cook-Greuter (1999) as unitive, we find similar characteristics, expressed here, in her own words:

... a fluid, undulating sense of self that is based on trust of the intrinsic value and process of life. Individuals—enmeshed in the immediate flow of ongoing experience—become non-judgmental witnesses to the being-becoming of a self in moment-to-moment transformation with a constant awareness of behavior, feeling, and perception. At this altitude, the paradox of feeling one's relatedness and one's separateness has resolved and is experienced without tension as a changing perception of a unitive manifestation. Individuals at this altitude relate to a reality that is an undifferentiated phenomenological continuum of unified consciousness where object, word, thought, and theory are seen as human constructs that create boundaries between self and other. Individuals experience themselves ... as part of an ongoing humanity, embedded in the creative ground, fulfilling the destiny of evolution. (Cook-Greuter, 2002, p.34)

Clear Light

Finally, at our last level of individual consciousness we have the clear light altitude, which Aurobindo (1985) and the integral approach refer to as supermind, which descends as the "mind itself super-eminent and lifted above ordinary mentality but not radically changed." (p. 134) By supermind, Aurobindo means a plane of consciousness that is above mind along with the higher mental levels of 3rd tier but which is also radically different from them all. While the other 3rd tier altitudes in the cognitive line—illumined mind, intuitive mind, and overmind—are varying blends of knowledge-ignorance, supermind is the truth-consciousness—again in his words:

... a principle superior to mentality and exists, acts and proceeds in the fundamental truth and unity of things and not like the mind in their appearances and phenomenal divisions. It is a consciousness always free from Ignorance which is the foundation of our present natural or evolutionary existence and from which nature in us is trying to arrive at self-knowledge and world-knowledge and a right consciousness and the right use of our existence in the universe. The Supermind, because it is a Truth-Consciousness, has this knowledge inherent in it and this power of true existence; its course is straight and can go directly to its aim, its field is wide and can even be made illimitable. Whatever may be said of

Chapter 5 - Growing Up: Your Capacity for Developmental Growth

supermind is likely to be not understood or misunderstood. It is only by growing into it that we can know what it is and this also cannot be done until after a long process by which mind, heightening and illuminating, becomes pure Intuition (not the mixed thing that ordinarily goes by that name) and masses itself into overmind; after that, overmind can be lifted into and suffused with supermind till it undergoes a transformation. (Aurobindo, 1985, p. 155)

In describing the ultimate or highest level of development, Wilber (1980) in his stunning book The Atman Project, reminds us that at the clear light altitude, the search for ultimate truth is no longer—for there is only one true self, radical, radiant, all-pervading, perfectly ecstatic in its release, perfectly ordinary in its operation, perfectly obvious in its way. Prior to all that arises, but not other than all that arises, clear light can be realized. It is the permanent realization of nondual suchness, plus all the lower structures. This means the permanent acquisition of nondual turyiatita, or the pure ground of being, plus all previous levels and structure of consciousness that have proceeded supermind. Also, supermind can only be experienced at the high clear light level, whereas suchness or the nondual state can be experienced at any lower level.

Benefits of Altitude

That concludes our in-depth tour through the altitude spectrum, describing the unfolding of consciousness from the most primitive or least complex levels through the highest, most emergent levels. From this point on, you can use the colors to refer to various levels in any line. If you say green, for example, it calls up the general or broad description provided in this section, but if you say green morality, this refers to the equivalent level in the moral line or mid-postconventional morality. As your learning expands, you can venture into learning about each level in specific lines, remembering that as you do the correlations between altitude and other levels are not always 100 percent perfect. Also, worth noting—just because we included descriptions of values, needs, morality, and faith at each altitude, this does not mean that if someone is developed to green in cognition that they are developed to green in other capacities. Remember, altitude is an orienting generalization, which, if we are not careful, can lead us away from the most important characteristic of psychographs—namely, our uneven development! The orienting generalization of altitude is an incredible tool for learning and awareness, and the benefits of this approach are quite far-reaching. When you are just beginning to learn about levels, it is helpful to focus on one spectrum rather than trying to tackle each level in every line. Altitude can also be used as a model of developmental correlation across any line. Take what you know of a line's particular capacity and what you know of the altitude color, combine them and the result is a relatively robust or at least functional understanding of levels in most lines. Finally, this folds into one final set of important benefits, concerning communication about levels in various lines. Because levels in a specific line cannot be used to refer to the levels in other lines, the altitude spectrum helps us keep our communication in check and it makes us more understandable. For example, you can say green moral development, or red cognitive development, or amber ego development, and after learning the degree of complexity these colors represent, you are communicating about postconventional morality, preoperational cognition, and conformist self-development through a simple and common vocabulary—no need to worry if those whom you are speaking to understand the technical language used by each researcher.

Scales of Development

If the altitude colors are the general levels of human emergence, the actual rungs or structures in the developmental ladder, or the waves of unfolding from birth to enlightenment, how do individuals move through this spectrum? Who is it that is doing the movement? What properties govern that movement? How do we understand individual development in a cumulative and holistic way? And, finally, how do we account for the variance seen in individual development? As we round out this lengthy chapter on levels, we will encounter these final topics: the scale of developmental investigation, the forms of development, and the nature of transformation.

To adequately answer these questions, we must first confront the question of scale. At what scale of investigation does this altitude spectrum appear? And at what scale do the properties we've discussed hold more or

Chapter 5 - Growing Up: Your Capacity for Developmental Growth

less true? Developmental research is conducted at three degrees of scale. And each degree reveals a noticeably different picture of development (see: Granott and Parziale, 2002). First, is the scale of micro-development, which models development and learning over minutes and hours? Next, is the scale of meso-development, which models development over hours, weeks, and months? And finally we have the scale of macro-development, which models development over many months and years. So, the simple question naturally arises: Which scale does our current exploration of development concern? That's right, each line and every spectrum we have discussed thus far was discovered through macro-developmental investigation—allowing us to see the unfolding of broad stages over many years. In this chapter, I have confined our investigation to this scale, because it provides you with the broadest, most cohesive picture of development. And, it's the scale at which the principles and properties we've discussed actually hold up. Regardless of which scale we are using, development is still development; it still concerns the increase in complexity of skill, behavior, and consciousness. What shifts at different scales is the subtle behaviors of the three forms of developmental movement: transformation, translation, and regression.

Forms of Development

In addition to three scales of developmental investigation, the integral approach also accounts for three types of developmental movement: transformation, translation, and regression (Wilber, 1995). The following explanation concerns the nature of each form at the macro-developmental scale. Transformation refers to the vertical movement upwards from lower to higher structures. Transformation is what we have spoken about the most in the chapter—it refers, for example, to the movement from amber to orange, or from conventional to postconventional. When we say vertical developmental transformation, we are referring to this type of movement through structures. Horizontal developmental transformation is typically used when referring to development in states.

Translation is also sometimes referred to as a horizontal movement—meaning, rather than moving vertically between stages, we see a shuffling and stabilizing of various surface features within a current stage. Additionally, the acquisition of knowledge could be viewed as a translative function: Just because someone is really smart in, say, theoretical physics doesn't mean, for example, that their self-sense is complexly developed. Someone whose self-sense is orange can acquire subject specific knowledge in the same way someone who's self-sense is teal. As such, an increase in theoretical or cognitive knowledge is more of a translative than transformative function.

Finally, our third movement is called regression, which refers to temporary or permanent movement from a higher level to a lower level. At the macro scale, regression to lower stages is rare, occurring in cases of say organic brain damage, where physiological structures supporting certain higher stage functions are impaired. However at the micro and meso levels, as we are learning new capacities and navigating the emergent dimensions of higher structures, temporary regressions to lower capacities are very common.

The Nature of Transformation

We've seen that the content of each developmental level is different—meaning, for example, that amber is substantively different than green in all lines. But, the nature of developmental transformation between all levels is essentially the same. At each point in development we find this general sequence: (1) The self starts out identified with its current level of development; (2) A higher-order level begins to emerge; (3) The self starts to shift identification from the current level to the new, more complex level; (4) The high order level continues to emerge as the self begins dis-identifying or differentiating from the previous level; (5) The process continues until the self is fully differentiated from the lower level and identified with the higher level; (6) This completes the self's transcendence of the lower level; (7) At this point, the self is able embrace or include the lower level's enduring capacities from the place of the higher level; (8) The self then integrates its functioning at the new level—including and coordinating all enduring capacities from all previous levels (Wilber, 1996).

This process can be stated in many ways, each of which tells us something very important about the pattern or nature of development, evolution, and transcendence: What is whole becomes part. What is

Chapter 5 - Growing Up: Your Capacity for Developmental Growth

identification becomes detachment. What is context becomes content. What is ground becomes figure. What is subject becomes object. What is condition becomes element (see: Wilber, 1980). At each point in development, what is whole at one level becomes part of a whole at the next level. Sensorimotor actions, during the early stages of growth, are the whole of the self-sense. As the preoperational mind emerges and develops, however, the sense of identity shifts to the latter (mind) and the former (body-based actions) become merely one aspect—one part—of the total self. How do we understand the development of this "self" in a cumulative or holistic way? Center of gravity, our next topic, demonstrates exactly how that is achieved.

Center of Gravity

Development is complex; that is one thing we can say for sure. With over two dozen lines, each with its own set of stages, an accurate individual psychograph is tricky to create and even more cumbersome to communicate. Even with developmental altitude serving as a tool for cross line communication, we are left with the problem of referring to an individual's development in a cumulative and holistic, but also concise manner. Having to report on the status of our full psychographs every time we speak about our development just doesn't cut it. Fortunately, a concept called center of gravity fits the bill. Center of gravity is another orienting generalization that allows us to summarize an individual's aggregate level of proximate self-development in spite of its complexity and variable nature. Despite our tendency to do so, an individual shouldn't be pegged as being at a single level. With levels existing as probability waves, even at the macro scale, developmental expression is just not precisely located at a single position.

However, it is interesting to note that when you know someone quite well, you get a strong sense that their development does seem to hover around a certain stage most of the time. Center of gravity is used to describe this place. More precisely, center of gravity refers to a general developmental vicinity of the proximate self in the self-identity line (Wilber, 2006). As such, it is the stage of development around which most other major lines revolve, meaning cognitive development is typically one half to one stage higher—and values and moral are about the same—or within a stage or two at most, below. Remember, this is another orienting generalization, so it won't appear exactly the same way in every person, but it is seems accurate enough in most instances. And it allows us to put a name to the general sense we get about an individual's development. However, please keep in mind that the concept is not yet research validated, and to be most accurate, needs to be confined to development at the macro scale (see: Turiel, 1966). So, if we were to say that your best friend's center of gravity is orange, does this mean every expression they make will come from the orange altitude? Well, not exactly. Our final concept—called developmental range—shows us that your friend's expression will show variance towards higher and lower levels depending on a few variables.

Developmental Range

As we strive to find ways to explain development in a manner that is both accurate and expeditious, it helps tremendously to supplement center of gravity with the concept of developmental range, which has been research validated (see: Fischer and Bidell, 2006), and adds to your potential for accuracy without making the task more difficult. Developmental range describes the span or range of an individual's developmental expression in different contexts.

At the low end of the developmental range is the functional expression. This is a person's typical developmental expression in normal, non-supported, or possibly stressful or non-ideal contexts. In the middle of the range is an optimal expression. This could be considered the relative center of the developmental range, surfacing when the individual is in a typical, non-stressful context where contextual pressures are either normal or tending toward ideal. Then, at the upper end of the range is the scaffolded expression, which surfaces when the context features support, or scaffolding, that makes a more complex expression easier to embody. This support typically takes the form of another person who is aiding us in some way—either through direct assistance or through implicit presence and subtle positive pressure. The result is a push or pull from our optimal expression towards an emergent capacity which we haven't ourselves fully stabilized or integrated into our developing self.

Chapter 5 - Growing Up: Your Capacity for Developmental Growth

Center of gravity and developmental range aim to help you more fully grasp the dynamic and flowing nature of development, while providing you a way to refer to an individual's development in a summative but still accurate manner. With many lines and constantly shifting quadrant contexts, it will cause you trouble if you think that someone is always and solidly at one particular level. But, in lieu of always needing to keep an entire integral psychograph in mind—these concepts allow us to conceive of individual development in a more concise way.

Principles and Properties of Levels

Alright, we're almost complete. We've covered a huge amount of information on a variety of topics from lines to center or gravity. As we bring this in for a landing and prepare to shift to awareness and application of levels, let's conclude by distilling this learning into the key principles and properties of individual development.

Development is the movement toward increasing complexity, where each new level transcends the previous level by adding a novel emergent capacity while simultaneously including capacities from the previous level. Levels go by many names: stages—referring to their unidirectional sequence of unfolding; structures—referring to their dynamic, holistic patterns; and waves—referring to their fluid nature as probability waves rather than rigid developmental rungs. Transformation refers to a vertical movement to higher levels. Translation refers to the process of integrating all contextual and situational dynamics at any given level and regression is the de-evolution to lower levels. The process of transformation renders the subject of one level the object of the subject of the next higher level. Altitude is a useful model for understanding the development of consciousness and complexity across all lines. It is an essential tool for understanding development at the macro scale, which tracks growth over months and years. Center of gravity and developmental range are used to summarize and simplify conceptions about individual's development, while not forgoing the fluid and imprecise nature of developmental expression. Center of gravity is the general level of proximate self-development in the self-identity line and developmental range spans functional, optimal, and scaffolded expressions depending on quadrant factors.

Finally, the majority of this chapter has focused on ontogenetic development, which is the unfolding of the individual through the spectrum we've described. In ontogenetic development, everyone starts at square one or infrared and has the potential to develop to higher waves. The existence of these waves is made possible by phylogenetic development, which, in this case, refers to the development of the human species. In the past, each of the 1st tier altitudes emerged and was laid down as an ever-deepening kosmic groove or pattern through which future individuals began to progress with greater ease (Wilber, 2002). Ontogenetic development is therefore said to recapitulate phylogenetic development. To take this one step further: As each of us continues to deepen the grooves of 2nd and 3rd tier waves, our children's children's children will hopefully have an easier time progressing to the highest of the waves available at this time. Meaning, at some point, 2nd tier will begin to emerge when kids enter high school, whereas currently, most adults haven't developed that far along the spectrum—how about that as a reason to feel a bit more responsible about cultivating your own growth?

As you take your awareness of levels out into the world, you will find that the concept of levels applies to levels themselves. Meaning, you guessed it, there are levels of development in your understanding of levels. From one perspective this isn't too surprising, right? Like everything we learn, our understanding and ability to apply and recognize levels starts out less complex, and can develop into great complexity. Integral researchers are just starting to understand these developmental levels in the apprehension of levels—but it's quite clear that some real developmental action is at play. So, why am I bringing this up? Good question. Levels are powerful—both in their explanatory power and in the power to upset people if used inappropriately, or in a manner that others don't really understand. If you tell people that they have four dimensions to their being, they typically smile and think, "Yeah that sounds about right!" But if you tell them they are green—or, even worse, if they hear that you said it behind their back—it is often quite a different story. In general, people struggle with being labeled and some straight-up rebel against the idea of ranking, seeing it as marginalizing and oppressive. In my experience, many people get quite excited when they first experience the power of levels as a tool—so much so that some take this new hammer out into a world that strangely appears like a bunch of nails. And then they start whacking their way from nail to nail with their new

Chapter 5 - Growing Up: Your Capacity for Developmental Growth

developmentally-informed hammer. Sure, this is a bit hyperbolic, but not really.

The important point here is that whatever the complexity of your understanding—it's critical to keep in mind the true benefit of levels. They help you understand the differences between individual expressions and they aid you in understanding the ways in which we are similar—meaning, we all develop, and we just happen to be at different places along that journey. Levels can also help us communicate better with others and, ultimately, they are a very effective path to cultivating more compassion for other human beings, regardless of how much a particular person has managed to grow up.

References

Armon, C. *Ideals of the Good Life: Evaluative Reasoning in Children and Adults* (doctoral dissertation). Boston: Harvard University Press, 1984.

Aurobindo, S. *The Life Divine*. Twin Lakes, WI: Lotus Press, 1985.

———. *The Integral Yoga: Sri Aurobindo's Teaching and Method of Practice*. Pondicherry: Sri Aurobindo Ashram, 1993.

Beck, D. E., and C. C. Cowan. *Spiral Dynamics: Mastering Values, Leadership and Change*. Cambridge, MA: Blackwell, 1996.

Commons, M. L., F. A. Richards, and C. Armon, eds. *Beyond Formal Operations*. New York: Praeger, 1984.

Cook-Greuter, S. "Postautonomous Ego Development: A Study of Its Nature and Measurement," Dissertation Abstracts International 60, no. 6 (1999).

———. "A Detailed Description of the Development of Nine Action Logics in the Leadership Development Framework: Adapted from Ego Development Theory," 2002, retrieved February 25, 2007, from www.cook-greuter.com.

———. "Making the Case for a Developmental Perspective," *Industrial and Commercial Training* 36, no. 7 (2004): p. 275–281.

Fischer, K. W., and T. R. Bidell. "Dynamic Development of Action, Thought, and Emotion," in W. D. R. M. Lerner, ed., *Handbook of Child Psychology: Theoretical Models of Human Development*. New York: Wiley, 2006, p. 313–399.

Fowler, J. *Stages of Faith: The Psychology of Human Development and the Quest for Meaning*. San Francisco: Harper and Row, 1981.

Gardner, H. *Frames of Mind: The Theory of Multiple Intelligences*. New York: Basic Books, 1983.

Gilligan, C. "In a Different Voice: Women's Conceptions of Self and of Morality," *Harvard Educational Review* 47 (1977): p. 481–517.

———. *In a Different Voice: Psychological Theory and Women's Development*. Cambridge: Harvard University Press, 1982.

Goleman, D. *Working with Emotional Intelligence*. New York: Bantam, 1998.

Granott, N., and J. Parziale, eds. *Microdevelopment: Transition Processes in Development and Learning*. Cambridge, U.K.: Cambridge University Press, 2002.

Graves, C., C. Cowan, and N. Todorovic. *The Never Ending Quest: Clare W. Graves Explores Human Nature*. Santa Barbara, CA: ECLET Publishing, 2005.

Housen, A. *The Eye of the Beholder: Measuring Aesthetic Development*. Harvard Graduate School of Education, 1983.

Kegan, R. *The Evolving Self: Problem and Process in Human Development*. Cambridge, Massachusetts: Harvard University Press, 1982.

Kohlberg, L. *Stage and Sequence: The Cognitive-Developmental Approach to Socialization*. New York: Rand McNally, 1969.

Loevinger, J. *Ego Development*. San Francisco: Jossey Bass, 1987.

Maslow, A. H. "The Farther Reaches of Human Nature," *Journal of Transpersonal Psychology* 1, no. 1-9 (1969).

Chapter 5 - Growing Up: Your Capacity for Developmental Growth

Miller, M. E., and S. R. Cook-Greuter, eds. *Transcendence and Mature Thought in Adulthood: The Further Reaches of Adult Development.* Lanham, MD: Rowman & Littlefield, 1994.

Piaget, J. *The Language and Thought of the Child.* London: Lund Humphries, 1926.

Selman, R. L. *The Growth of Interpersonal Understanding: Developmental and Clinical Analyses.* New York: Academic Press, 1980.

Turiel, E. "An Experimental Test of the Sequentiality of Developmental Stages in the Child's Moral Judgments," *Journal of Personality and Social Psychology* 3(6), 611 (1966).

Wade, J. *Changes of Mind: A Holonomic Theory of the Evolution of Consciousness.* Albany, NY: State University of New York Press, 1996.

Wilber, K. *The Atman Project: A Transpersonal View of Human Development.* Wheaton, IL: Quest Books, 1980.

———. *Sex, Ecology, Spirituality: The Spirit of Evolution.* Boston: Shambhala Publications, 1995.

———. *Eye to Eye: The Quest for the New Paradigm.* Boston: Shambhala Publications, 1996.

———. *Integral Psychology: Consciousness, Spirit, Psychology, Therapy.* Boston: Shambhala Publications, 2000.

———. "Excerpt A: An Integral Age at the Leading Edge," 2002, retrieved July 8, 2009 from http://wilber.shambhala.com/html/books/kosmos/excerptD/excerptA.pdf.

———. *Integral Spirituality: A Startling New Role for Religion in the Modern and Postmodern World.* Boston: Shambhala Publications, 2006.

———. *The Integral Vision: A Very Short Introduction to the Revolutionary Integral Approach to Life, God, the Universe, and Everything.* Boston: Shambhala Publications, 2007.

Chapter 6
Cleaning Up: The Reciprocal Dance of Psyche and Spirit

Michael Brabant, Ph.D.c.

Introduction

We are evolving as individuals and as a world society. As part of this evolutionary process, there is a need to continually shift and refine the perspectives from which integral scholars orient their methods of research and analysis. After all, we have access to a plethora of globally informed knowledge and social practices. In such a complex social landscape, those of us drawing from Wilber's integral model endeavor to see where the partial truths of different disciplinary spaces and cultures fit together in order to weave meaning into the lives we enact internally, interpersonally, and collectively. Many scholars have examined their respective fields with an integral lens to explore the complexity, beauty, and the dynamic interplay of seemingly incommensurate disciplinary fields for the purpose of understanding evolution. Integral thinking has also allowed us to identify the ways these different fields have meaning in light of each other, and how this can set the foundation for an interdisciplinary synthesis of theory and practice. A collaborative and interpenetrating set of practices and insights can open up a space for corroboration with regard to what's next in the process of evolution and how we can robustly participate via intentional methods of cross-pollination.

In this chapter I focus on the relationship between two fields that up to this point have yet to be integrated adequately: psychological healing and spiritual awakening. While plenty of books have been written on the psychology of spirituality,[1,2,3] I suggest there is a need to unpack the relationship between psychological work and modern forms of spiritual development and praxis. While some teachers have a clear delineation between the two, or an unskillful or rudimentary blending, we are *living* the messy and often chaotic process of integrating different parts of ourselves where aspects of our unconscious come forth in the midst of a drive towards superconsciousness. It is assumed that you as the reader are intimately aware of this messiness, for you would not be reading this book about Integral Theory without some desire to integrate who you are in relation to these considerations.

It is important to note that *volumes* can and most likely will be written on the interplay between psychological healing and spiritual awakening from an integral perspective. This chapter is by no means claiming a comprehensive overview. The intention is to scratch the surface by offering some preliminary ideas about how we can integrate what appears to be the most fundamental aspiration we all seek: how to alleviate suffering for ourselves and others and evolve into the clearest vehicles of divine light on this planet, giving our gifts in service of the evolution of the Kosmos. All of our lives revolve around these questions at an integral worldview whether we are healers, researchers, architects, spiritual teachers or working in any profession.

The processes of awakening and development seem fairly linear as they are laid out in the integral model. A person grows up vertically through structure-stages and wakes up horizontally across state-stages. Pretty simple. When you throw in the seemingly uncountable parts of our selves operating under various degrees of awareness (sometimes referred to as subpersonalities), the best argument for awakening and development is that there is a directionality to them rather than any sort of clean linearity. Meaning that we understand we are moving in the direction of greater expansion and complexity, it's just that we don't necessarily know what the road is going to look like moment to moment. Due to the immense scope of this topic and the incredible nuance of each individual's evolutionary process, this paper is going to be laid out in broad categories rather than as a linear progression that can claim any sort of universality.

While this topic is as complex and diverse as a human being's psychological working and karmic unfolding, by leveraging the integral model, we are able to see how richly and skillfully one can contextualize psychological healing within the path of spiritual awakening and vice

Chapter 6 - Cleaning Up: The Reciprocal Dance of Psyche and Spirit

versa. An important framing on this topic to keep in mind is that from an integral perspective we are able to objectify psychology as a field as well as mysticism as a field, in order to see more clearly how the two dance together. This dance, in my opinion, is the most important and foundational dance of all the work that can be enacted in service of the alleviation of suffering of all beings and the evolution of this planet and its inhabitants.

This chapter will suggest a working definition of what an integral awakening looks like, address several topics where awakening and development intertwine, and investigate an emerging paradigm that takes a developmental look at healing as it unfolds towards awakening. May our collective healing and awakening inform the rich dialogue of esoteric spiritual teachings and exoteric psychological approaches to healing, to create a more readily available, skillfully disseminated, and integrally informed approach towards the integration of what Wilber calls our "freedom" and "fullness" as mutually constitutive features of integral enlightenment. I will use the follow phrases coined by DiPerna[4] with regard to an integral approach to spiritual practice: "wake up" (referring to spiritual awakening), "grow up" (referring to vertical development), "clean up" (referring to shadow integration), and "show up" (referring to our full capacity to embody the preceding three aspects of an integral approach to spiritual practice and participate pragmatically in its unfoldment).

Towards a Definition of Integral Awakening

The Wilber-Combs matrix supports us in navigating the complexity of what an integral enlightenment could look like. Not only do we need to develop the complexity of our worldview by growing up through structure-stages, we also need to identify with increasingly subtle vantage points in our subjectivity through horizontal state-stages. An integral enlightenment aims to achieve both the highest worldview that has been developed in human evolution while expanding and stabilizing our awareness fully in nondual realization. However, as Wilber points out there are three "S"s in the Upper Left quadrant that pertain to one's development: states of consciousness, structures of development, and the x-factor of shadow.[5]

Although this paper does not directly have to do with vertical development, we acknowledge the importance of growing up as part of an integral approach to spiritual practice. Noting in the Upper Left quadrant we have both the "S" of shadow work, which we could categorize as a descending spirituality and the "S" of state-training, which we could categorize as an ascending spirituality. Both are crucial for an integral awakening because if we just traversed the path of ascent we could easily fall pray to spiritual bypassing and state-stage pathologies, on the one hand, and if we took just the path of descent, we could take the world of form as the ultimate truth and as a path towards liberation that it simply cannot provide, on the other hand.[6]

The irony of paradox is that it ultimately point towards a greater wholeness, where the partial dualistic truths meld into the nondual one. As we pay attention and practice both the upward path of state-training and the downward path of psychological integration, we move towards embodying integral awakening. It becomes clear that these two paths were never not two and to think of one without the other simply prevents us from fully integrating all of who we are. A typological perspective on the integration of psyche and spirit can also bear fruit in the process of unfolding.

Typologically Informed Awakening and Objectification

Saniel Bonder, founder of the path of Waking Down in Mutuality, speaks about the need to acknowledge a hypermasculine approach towards spiritual growth[7] and its partiality as well as limitations. We can understand and watch out for a predominantly masculine drive onward and upward and not as much of a feminine embrace of what is here and now. As mentioned earlier, despite the lack of linearity towards an integral approach to waking up and cleaning up, there is a strong directionality. While a hypermasculine approach to growth can support the evolutionary momentum, it can also lead to psychological pathologies that taint spiritual realization.

There are two forms of pathology that Wilber speaks of in regard to developmental findings: one being structure-stage pathology and the other state-stage pathology.[8] At each fulcrum between levels of vertical development, certain pathologies can arise leading to a bleeding of former

Chapter 6 - Cleaning Up: The Reciprocal Dance of Psyche and Spirit

worldviews that one has transcended and not totally included. These pathologies can then come through in an unconscious ways. In many cases these are identified as subpersonalities, which become shadow material that jeopardize the integrity of each developmental level, thereby reducing the solidarity of all aspects of one's self identity at a given worldview. The idea of Boomeritis,[9] where aspects of red or tribal level of development are regressively operative within a green or pluralistic level of development is a common example of this. This problem points towards the need to integrate such split-off or dissociated aspects of self, so we can actually act from an integral consciousness (if this is where we are stabilized). Via psychological integration, we can act without these trigger points unhealthily and unconsciously blending previous transcended and not fully included aspects of previous developmental levels.

Wilber also talks about state-stage pathologies. Using a more recent approach towards state-stage development to help contextualize this understanding, the use of vantage points vis-à-vis Daniel P. Brown, refers to one's stabilized identity at a given state-stage from gross to nondual.[10] When one is coming from a vantage point of nondual awareness, it is not simply a state that one has access to (i.e., Wilber's framing of access to gross, subtle, and causal through waking, dreaming, and deep sleep in the Upper Right quadrant); rather it is one's permanent (or semipermanent, as we shall soon see) vantage point of reality. For instance, if someone is stabilized in a nondual vantage point, they view reality not from their personality, but from nondual awareness itself. If a spiritual teacher has not integrated aspects of their personality structure, for example with their relationship to power due to unintegrated feelings of powerlessness when they were younger, when their teachings become broader reaching and money and/or accolades come about, they can be triggered into losing their vantage point of nondual awareness, move into their personality and abuse their power. Since this aspect of personality was coming from shadow, they probably would not recognize that they temporarily dropped from their nondual vantage point and often explain away such acts with a spiritualized rationale.

As we take into account these state-stage pathologies, we can see that they are imperative to address in order to establish complete integrity of each state-stage that acts as a foundation for the next. What is dangerous is that the appearance of a solid nondual vantage point can actually be plagued by these psychological cracks of pathology that arise in usually ugly and destructive ways. By filling these cracks, there is a strengthening of one's realization and capacity to maintain one's established vantage point more easily and consistently. This approach is a more feminine understanding of embracing and drawing up all of those integrated aspects of self rather than simply driving forward towards deepening vantage points in a nondiscerning, hypermasculine fashion.

Another usage of typology to inform both cleaning up and waking up is through the use of personality typology. The Enneagram is the most popular model of typology in integral thought, so I will use this system as an example. It is important to note that personality typologies are best utilized in light of the integral model; they can be helpful in aiding individuals in objectifying their personality, as well as destructive if viewed as the truth of their personality that can solve complex problems such as psychopathology.[11] With that being said, typologies can be very helpful in supporting the process of disidentifying with the content of consciousness as well as the personality structure which contains and filters such content.

Identifying blind spots that one with an underdeveloped Enneatype enacts on a regular basis can be objectified and over time integrated in awareness so one no longer sabotages their relationship to self, other, and the world. When I use the Enneagram with clients, they are often shocked at how "pegged" they feel by the Enneatype they identify with most. It is a similar reaction that someone has when they first come to the realization that the thoughts they think are not necessarily universal truths they must believe. At first, understanding this unconscious patterning within the personality is very helpful and simultaneously there is an implicit understanding that their personality as a whole is a total construction. The personality is simply an adaptive tool we created in order to "survive whatever difficulties we encountered at that time, [and] we unwittingly mastered a limited repertoire of strategies, self-images, and behaviors that allowed us to cope with and survive in our early environment."[12] From the perspective of the Enneagram authors, Riso and Hudson, these strategies that were coping mechanisms covered up our divine essence and enabled us to receive love from our family of origin in the way that they were able to give it to us.[13]

Understanding the personality as simply a useful disguise over our divine essence can support a meta-disidentification from the personality as a whole. When one is working towards objectifying their subjective experience through inquiry with the Enneagram, it is simultaneously with

Chapter 6 - Cleaning Up: The Reciprocal Dance of Psyche and Spirit

the awareness that the whole personality is ultimately a facade. I've found this actually loosens one's identification with the personality at its core. In a sense, this understanding greases the gears of disidentification with the personality, which predisposes them to realize more easily that the personality is not as solid a part of their ultimate identity when they reach the causal vantage point where the personality is realized as ultimately illusory.[14] In this way, one works at bringing awareness to their shadow, all the while not taking it so seriously. This bidirectional process seems to enable a smoother, faster, and more integrated healing process leading towards stabilized spiritual development. As the shadow is more thoroughly integrated it creates the firm foundation for the flowering of awakening to flow more easily without state-stage pathologies pulling it down to shallower vantage points. From a greater sense of integration and perspective on reality, we have a responsibility to act from these perspectives as much as possible in our daily lives.

Self/Other Accountability

We are individual agents of consciousness working towards waking up for ourselves and for the collective we are inextricably linked to. Just being interested in a book like this implies that the developmental perspective that you orient from carries a lot of responsibility with it. We are now aware that evolution is moving through us, as us, by what has been called the "evolutionary impulse." From the coiner of this term, Andrew Cohen:

> God is dependent on *us*. Indeed, the evolution of consciousness, which is the evolution of the interior of the cosmos, is entirely dependent upon the conscious evolution of human beings at the leading edge. There is no other way for God, that primordial energy and intelligence, to evolve in and through matter.[15]

God depends on us?! This can be a daunting task to take seriously in the throes of our everyday human predicament when our life does not stop to allow us the space to make time to heal, to engage in practice, and to evolve. From this perspective we must become accountable to this impulse that is awake within us. There is no way we could possibly find lasting contentment without stepping forward into this responsibility, for it is not something that can go away by burying our heads in the sand and acting like this is not the case.

This leads us to a tenant of Cohen's Evolutionary Enlightenment that is particularly pertinent in this argument that states: Face everything and avoid nothing.[16] This tenant nicely exemplifies the accountability that we have for ourselves that is interdependently linked to the other and the All. We are called to face everything inside of us that is not the boundless unconditional love that is the fabric of our reality. As Rumi put it, "We must not seek love, we must seek and find all the barriers we have built against it." It is the prayer to live as unconditional love that can trigger a more rapid opportunity for us to face all the barriers that are within us to authentically embody the unconditional radiance of Spirit. Since most of these barriers are psychological in nature, the psychological work *is* a deep spiritual practice as it is rooted in the intention is to become the embodiment of Spirit.

Cohen also speaks poignantly to the intertwining nature of psychological and spiritual work:

> If your life-context is merely personal, your psychological, emotional, and cultural wounds can seem overwhelming. But where you see them as a very small part of a very big picture, you'll be able to handle them and keep them in perspective. You will accept that your karma is your responsibility, not anybody else's.[17]

Our practice, our healing, and our awakening matter so deeply to all of consciousness. If we are true integral practitioners, we must become accountable to the Kosmos through the deep psychological and spiritual work that is before us on this path.

Motivational philosopher Jim Rohn stated, "you can't hire someone else to do your push-ups for you." You cannot hire someone to meditate for you, to face your fears for you, to cry your tears for you, and to evolve for you. This accountability spans both psychological work and spiritual practice and is the essence of showing up. All of what was talked about before and will be talked about shortly is a moot point unless we recognize the responsibility that we have and thus become accountable to living our life as an expression of answering the call of that responsibility.

Chapter 6 - Cleaning Up: The Reciprocal Dance of Psyche and Spirit

Furthermore, it would do us well to realize that we are not just being accountable to ourselves in this task of showing up. We are also facing what needs to be faced and doing what needs to be done on behalf of the entire evolving Kosmos that transcends and includes our individual bodymind.

This leads us into the question, What is our highest priority, and is our life structured to reflect this priority? Paul Tillich boils down the motivation for spiritual development to the question, "What is of ultimate concern?" As integral evolutionaries we know that spirituality was left out after modernity came on the scene, being replaced by morality and partnered with art and science.[18] Spirituality is not just the mythic version of dogmatism enacted in a widespread manner in premodern times; it is the living and breathing prayer that underlies our intention to evolve. It rests as *the* underlying motivation for our incarnation on this planet that we can now consciously operate from. Are you accountable to that priority? Does your daily life align structurally with a trajectory leading to the fulfillment of that priority? The more we align ourselves with what is of ultimate concern, the more barriers to being a clear manifestation of Spirit will emerge, and oftentimes that will mean dealing with the psychological conditioning keeping us in separation and samsara.

Another way our spiritual practice informs our healing is through our ability to bring full awareness to our psychological wounding. Clinical psychologist and spiritual author John Welwood states that our basic disease is that we consistently struggle against, judge, and condemn certain aspects of our experience that cause us suffering of some kind. It is this process that keeps us inwardly divided and separate from the totality of our being.[19] If we are pushing away part of our experience (which is actually part of our own wholeness and by default the nondual reality we live in) consciously or unconsciously, we simply cannot transcend, include, and integrate it into our being. To allow all the contractions in our being to arise to the surface enables us to see them, embrace them, and therefore include them into our awareness. For many people, these repressed traumatic experiences (by trauma I am referring to a broad spectrum of experience leading to the creation of shadow material) are simply too overwhelming to be seen directly, at least at first.

Our spiritual practice enables us to create more spaciousness in our subjective experience of awareness. If you have been practicing meditation for any period of time you will know that things that used to really bother you, simply no longer elicit the same degree of aversion that they once did. This falls in line with what Wilber talks about in meditative development; he says as we develop, suffering of our own and the world hurts more but bothers us less.[20] We simultaneously become more sensitive to the world as an extension of our own nondual identity and yet have the spaciousness in our awareness to embrace others with increasing empathy and care. This capacity serves us well in our psychological growth work; for the degree to which we transcend the world of form is the degree to which we increase our capacity to descend deeper into the world of form (the world of form in this case meaning psychological wounding and unconsciousness, where we can more readily embrace all of who we are and both discern more clearly and face more fully all that is unconscious within us).

A final note on accountability has to do with preliminary practices prior to beginning meditative practice. With the availability of esoteric practices and the commodification of spirituality, the preciousness of these teachings can be diluted or even distorted to some degree. In great eastern contemplative traditions, preparatory practices were taken up for five to ten years by students to help the mind and body become fit for meditative development prior to even beginning formal meditation practice.[21] This would be a preposterous notion to many in a Western culture of "give it to me now," where the individual has become the source of authority on all matters of *ultimate* concern. Daniel P. Brown suggests that in the West, psychotherapy can act as a surrogate preliminary practice to help the mind become more fertile ground for meditative development to take root. However, he does suggest that psychotherapy alone does not adequately help practitioners cultivate the broad range of skills and understanding that traditional preliminary practices in the contemplative traditions produce.[22]

As integral practitioner-scholars, we know the value of practice. An integrally-informed engagement with the mind, body, spirit, and shadow as outlined in an Integral Life Practice[23] would be a good start to supplement the psychotherapeutic facet of preparatory practices. Of course as integralists, we focus on integrating many things together, and so our meditative practice will be engaged simultaneously with other facets of our life practice, thus serving as preparatory practices for contemplative development. Therefore we must remain accountable to ourselves and the Kosmos to prepare our body-minds for genuine spiritual development and

Chapter 6 - Cleaning Up: The Reciprocal Dance of Psyche and Spirit

remain accountable to engaging in "preparatory" practices all the way up through nondual realization. As discussed earlier, state-stage pathologies can be insidious, especially for those with access to deeper spiritual vantage points. Thus it is imperative that we continue to clean up as we continue to wake up. As integrally-informed musician Stuart Davis's lyrics state, "the higher that we climb, the more the ladder sways." By remaining accountable to the nuance of our shadows as we develop spiritually, we are more likely to stabilize our realization and use it in service of supporting the awakening all beings. What we don't want is to hide our unconsciousness from ourselves, only to see it emerge in harmful and not-so conscious ways later.

Intellectual Use of Realization

With all the access to spiritual writings and teachers, we are able to see how unenlightened we are compared to many masters that have come before us. We can actually leverage other's realization intellectually to support the flowering of our own. An important starting point on this topic is a quote from meditation teacher Daniel P. Brown, "successful spiritual development entails finding a balance between intellectual understanding of each stage of meditation and actual meditative experience. Placing too much emphasis on either alone significantly decreases the likelihood of genuine progress."[24] This is an important both/and distinction to be made when implementing the insights that will be suggested below. While actual meditative realization as well as intellectual understanding are two sides of the coin of integrated spiritual development, I believe we can support our spiritual realization and psychological healing by using the intellectual insights gleaned from other people's realizations as stepping stones towards embodying our own.

One such realization is that of emptiness. In a basic sense, emptiness means that nothing has an essence or nature of its own. We label things that we have experienced based on the sum of their parts; these labels help us explain and categorize things as complex as our personality or as seemingly simple as a pencil. The pencil for example, has no pencil-ness. Rather, it is simply wood, lead, some metal, rubber, and paint that we label from our cultural understanding as "pencil." There is no innate value of the pencil other than the meaning that we place upon it based upon our conditioning and cultural agreements. Similarly, the personality is simply a product of our conditioning, the emotions running through our system, the life experience we have, the way we look, the way others have treated us, etc. However, all of these pieces have no essence or meaning other than what we, most often unconsciously, give to them. The pencil and our personality have relative meaning and that meaning is useful as it helps us function in our everyday reality. However, there is no ultimate meaning to any content within awareness because it is all awareness. Brown speaks to this in reference to the objects that the normal distracted mind views: "The common element in this list of objects is that they all imply epistemological realism, in which the ordinary mind is said to act in an artificial way to produce the illusion of seemingly real, self-existent entities apart from the mind."[25] Mind in this context is used to mean awareness itself. The quotation implies that everything that we label as object is ultimately subject. We are both a subject that is arising in time and space with a personality that sometimes uses things called pencils to write words on things called paper, and we are not a subject and are irreducibly connected to everything.

It is through the deepening of our vantage point that we begin to realize emptiness of relative reality. As we stabilize a subtle vantage point, we see the ultimate emptiness of thoughts but are still confined within an understanding that our personality is real.[26] There is more nuance to this but for sake of simplicity, understand that at the nondual vantage point in the gross waking state, the subject/object duality collapses and the experience of the ultimate emptiness of thoughts, personality, time, and space are realized. This has occurred for thousands of years in contemplative traditions when practitioners reach the higher stages of spiritual realization.

While intellectually knowing that everything is ultimately empty will not shift you into a nondual awareness, I suggest that this understanding can help you see the relative nature of the content that arises in your awareness and makes it easier to work with. If we can understand, for instance, that our thoughts and emotions are ultimately devoid of meaning other than what we place on them, we can begin to more easily see how we are perpetuating the false notion that what we experience through these mediums is ultimately true. It can turn into a sort of game within your awareness to recognize for instance the idea that, yes, you are experiencing subjective suffering when you believe the self-talk

Chapter 6 - Cleaning Up: The Reciprocal Dance of Psyche and Spirit

that you are worthless, incompetent, and hopeless. That dire story understandably elicits suffering! However, when you can recognize, even on a surface level, that in some unconscious way you are perpetuating that story by believing your thoughts at face value, then you have an opportunity to relax when those thoughts arise and open to the fact that they may not be as true as you once thought. As we loosen our grip on our thoughts and other concepts of reality, that which is not true has an opportunity to release and create space to live from a place closer to the Truth of who you really are. The key is to take responsibility for the suffering we have perpetuated without getting lost in any blaming of ourselves or others.

By recognizing the emptiness of our emotions, we can see that, although at times subjectively uncomfortable or painful, we can stop the struggle against these conditioned parts of ourselves and get curious about them as they arise. From my experience, as this happens, emotions become more like energy that moves through the body-mind to be released. German spiritual teacher Thomas Hübl refers to shadow material within the body-mind as energy that has not been able to fulfill its natural cycle. Innate in unconscious material is a drive to become conscious. This process actualizes to the extent that we allow this natural evolutionary cycle to take place. By recognizing this process, and by understanding the fact that we are actually fueling the cycle remaining incomplete, we can more easily relax our unconscious struggle and allow whatever needs to happen to complete that cycle. This can take the form of crying, being vulnerable in front of another person, expressing rage, or a myriad of other responses. As the energy of our incomplete emotional cycles are allowed, we no longer need to allocate psychological energy in keeping them unconscious and can leverage that freed up energy to consciously direct it towards further transformation and service in the world.

A final note is on the notion of embracing all of reality as part of the nondual nature of the universe. It's so easy to intellectualize this wisdom, but much harder to apply this wisdom to oneself and the repressed, shut down, pushed away aspects of our personality that impede our actual realization of this truth. One of the main mechanisms perpetuating our separation is pushing away parts of ourselves. It's easier to see the nondual nature in the beauty of a flower or in someone else's random act of kindness, than in every facet of our own being. What about in the part of you that guards yourself from opening your heart because of a relational trauma that gave you good reason to contract the heart, so no one could ever break it again? This and all other aspects of yourself that you are not so proud of are equally part of the nondual One.

As we "choose" to operate from a fraction of who we are and not the totality of it, we are perpetuating the self-contraction. John Welwood calls it "creating an identity based on contraction."[27] The compensations that keep unconscious material out of our awareness, turn into stories that then morph into self-fulfilling prophecies that further solidify our stories that keep us separate! Welwood speaks of at least three main components to psychological stress: one being the pain of overwhelming feelings, the second being the contraction of the body-mind to avoid feeling that pain, and the third is the energy it takes to continually defend, justify, and prop up this partial version of ourselves.[28] I would add a fourth: the incongruence with what our true nature is and what our contracted identity tries to maintain. One anecdote I see for this insidious problem is awareness. Spiritual practice of course can be a powerful vehicle for cultivating awareness, along with psychological inquiry with a therapist, coach, trusted friend, and working with a typology such as the Enneagram. Another anecdote that is supported by awareness is to maintain a vigilance to see when we are pushing uncomfortable emotions away from ourselves or shutting down to another person who triggers part of our contraction. If we can recognize that every time we push something away we are delaying our healing and our awakening, there will be a much different motivation to begin to open to the pain that needs to be felt and experienced; and thereby cultivate a foundation for our awareness that is embracing and inclusive rather than negating and exclusive. It takes time to develop skill and lucidity around these subtle choice points, yet is well worth the effort.

Bringing the Mountain to the Marketplace and Bodhisattvas in Psychotherapy

It was once appropriate for some spiritual people to live a monastic life, isolated from the intensity of Western culture and focused solely on awakening. While this can be enticing to some, in this time of global crisis and rebirth, we are called into action—to wake up, to grow

Chapter 6 - Cleaning Up: The Reciprocal Dance of Psyche and Spirit

up, to clean up, and with all that we have gained through this perpetual process, to show up to how life wants to use us. It is imperative that we take our realization and sense of integration and enact our unique gifts into the world and heal individuals, the collective, and the planet. Mariana Caplan speaks to this beautifully:

> This is not a time for monks on mountaintops. It is a time to pursue our spiritual work with depth, focus, and efficiency and bring whatever morsels of wisdom we discover to all of our structures and systems—families, schools, politics, and policy—in order to transform these structures and infuse life force and integrity back into a suffering Earth and cultures that are increasingly void of spirit. Insight and awakening must be actualized externally.[29]

Spiritual teacher Lee Lozowick coined the term "enlightened duality" referring to "the realization of nonduality as expressed in and through the body and the full expression of all of life, experiencing and enjoying it as it is, without identification."[30] This sort of embracing inclusivity, mixed with deep emotional presence and a degree of nonattachment, is how we can engender fearlessness and heartfulness through all of our actions. There are big challenges ahead of us and at the leading edge of consciousness, we are the ones we have been waiting for to steward this evolutionary shift. We are at a time in human history where consciousness is able see and embrace the partial truths of all worldviews that have come before. This is not a matter of right and wrong, it is a call to make our realization actionable and to embody skillful means with all beings we encounter on this path.

A theoretical distinction bringing more clarity to this idea is DiPerna's use of trans-duality. He speaks about the notion of nondual reductionism, in which practitioners can view nonduality as ultimately real and therefore duality as less valid. This is simply another form of bypass because in fact nonduality transcends and includes duality, so he uses the more precise term "trans-duality."[31] This small and important distinction helps one stay grounded and cognizant to the pitfalls of having a nondual experience and perhaps seeing the fruitlessness of doing deeper psychological work because everything is experienced as Spirit itself totally connecting the seer with the seen. If we can place this nondual reductionism on our radars, then when we begin to engage in such a broad-stroke move, we can understand that there is most likely still work to be done in our psyche that will only deepen our nondual vantage point and strengthen the degree in which it is stabilized.

It is from this nondual vantage point, or nondual glimpse, or even just an outpouring from our heart to serve people, that we may come across the Bodhisattva vow. The Bodhisattva is a Buddhist term for an individual devoting their whole existence to awakening to full Buddhahood to alleviate suffering of all beings and support *them* in awakening to full Buddhahood. These beings are said to remain reincarnating over and over again until every sentient being is enlightened.[32] Of course within an integral frame, enlightenment is a loaded term that is misused and misinterpreted. So to clarify things from an integral perspective, the Bodhisattva vow is to awaken to a nondual vantage point and tirelessly engage in service, full of compassion, for all beings still stuck in a vantage point where suffering remains.

A pitfall of taking this vow formally or informally would be to focus so much on serving others that we actually use that service as a way to escape looking deep into our own hearts and diligently practicing to wake up and clean up as fully as we can. Hence the second half of the title of this section, "Bodhisattvas in Psychotherapy." It is essential that we remain humble in our service for all beings, recognizing that this is no small task, but one that necessitates a deep commitment to our own waking-up process. As we have explored in this chapter, the cleaning-up process is inextricably linked to waking up and therefore through our humility and integral approach to awakening, we must remain open to continuing to clean our vehicles so the clear light of awareness can shine brighter and with more integrity, moment by moment.

Of course there comes a time on the path when the desire to clean up no longer comes from a place of lack or a need to fix. The motivation simply arises to further clarify our being to be a vehicle for the clear light of awareness-love. From an integral evolutionary approach to the path to waking up and growing up, the frothy edge continues to expand in each moment. Therefore, we can never attain the fullest possible development both vertically and horizontally because it is perpetually expanding. All we can do is aspire to awaken and to integrate our unconsciousness throughout the course of our life in order to stay true to the Bodhisattva that we are. Like it or not, as we are on this integral

Chapter 6 - Cleaning Up: The Reciprocal Dance of Psyche and Spirit

trajectory, our development gets to a point where we *feel* the suffering of all beings, we identify as all beings, and there is nothing else to do but alleviate suffering in the way we best can. As Wilber points out, the greater our development, the greater evolutionary ground there becomes for pathology to arise.[33] It is therefore essential to remain open to our blind spots and the ways in which unconscious personality tendencies distort our realization and development. This does not need to look like Bodhisattva psychotherapy necessarily. Having a sense of humility, vigilance, and community that can both challenge and support you, will go a long way in ensuring that your development is as clean and clear as possible while you continue on your path of healing, awakening, and serving the world.

An Emergent Paradigm

We are embedded in systems of healthcare, paradigms of psychological healing, and other contexts that recognize various degrees of awareness and crucial components of well-being. So much of the traditional paradigm towards healing compartmentalizes our mind, body, spirit, and psyche and treats illness or symptoms as parts; it does not necessarily recognize how these parts interact and affect each other. While integral applications in medicine and psychotherapy are increasing, the paradigm that they are operating from is the same as it's been, but now includes levels of development and multiple perspectives on health and dis-ease. While this evolution of an existing paradigm is welcomed and needed, there are other healing paradigms that can more readily be optimized to serve the evolution of consciousness.

One emergent paradigm that recognizes more aspects of being related to health, and that is becoming more integrally informed within the last few years, is called Reorganizational Healing (ROH). While we are evolving our approach to the synthesis and interdependence of psychological healing and spiritual awakening, it is helpful to understand and apply a paradigm towards healing that recognizes this necessary organic union (which is also more explicitly emerging).

We can say that a Western medical model or allopathic medicine can be labeled as Restorative Therapeutics (RET). Of course within this paradigm, mind-body medicine and other "updates" are becoming more prevalent, *and* more or less operating within this restorative therapeutic model. Even many alternative therapies operate from this model. We can define the aim of RET to "fix" the parts of oneself that are "broken" in order to restore an individual back to a previous level of functioning within a "normal" range of functioning based upon results of lab tests and other measures.[34] This approach to working with dis-ease focuses upon a "cure" rather than "healing." Curing focuses on eliminating symptoms that arise from dis-ease in order to bring people back to a previous level of functioning where they were not experiencing their current symptom. Donny Epstein, the creator of ROH states that "curing as an attempt to control our experience generally interferes with our ability to move into the unsolicited experiences we need to restructure our lives."[35] Restorative therapeutics are essential to the profession of healing when acute circumstances arise. However, a western allopathic approach to treating dis-ease, oftentimes a reductionistic approach, can leave out the individual's perception of their dis-ease, cultural beliefs and relationships with key figures, and social connections and broader frameworks in which an individual lives. It can also mark a devolution of the individual to a previous level of functioning rather than supporting the evolution of the entire human being.[36] As Epstein stated, we need to restructure our lives when our current way of relating to life is being met with feedback from our body-minds telling us we need to evolve our approach.

The paradigm of ROH "facilitates a dynamic responsive awareness to enable optimization of structural, perceptual, behavioral and energetic elements in a coherent sequenced fashion"[37] and "is rooted in dynamical systems, transformation, awakening, personal discovery, somatic awareness, and subtle energy systems as well as the relationships between the self and other in society and culture"[38]. This paradigm for healing recognizes that dis-ease of any kind is providing the individual with information about what needs to be seen, restructured, and evolved in order to meet the demands of the evolutionary impulse that is manifesting itself through that individual. Epstein views dis-ease and suffering as "agents of healing when viewed as perfect creations of disconnected, misdirected, or blocked consciousness."[39] It is not about getting rid of these blockages by regressing. It is about taking the information that the blockages provide and finding novel and resilient ways to evolve into an orientation to them that serves the evolution of the individual as a whole.

Chapter 6 - Cleaning Up: The Reciprocal Dance of Psyche and Spirit

As part of the framework, Epstein has created what he calls the 12 Stages of Healing that act as a spectrum of development through the ways one orients towards whatever is ailing them over time. The initial stages look very personal, such as the first stage having to do with feeling the sense of suffering that one is going through and accepting both that nothing is working at this time and one is currently helpless to do anything, in that moment.[40] The latter stages begin to look much more transpersonal, such as stage 11 in which one recognizes the responsibility they have for what they feel, begins to engage in life without attachment, and starts to love and serve others while communicating with oneself and others through one's wounds instead of from them.[41] Much like stabilizing in a nondual vantage point, the personality does not go away, it is simply seen as translucent, and awakened awareness is able to shine through it. Similar to stage pathologies discussed above, "If stages are missed or bypassed, your chances of "slipping" on the healing path are greater because you will not yet be flexible enough to deal with the new information inherent in each stage."[42] This deeply connects to the importance of being thorough in including the wisdom of the stages we transcend in order to form a stable foundation for a stabilized sense of wholeness and awakened awareness. While the details of ROH will not be introduced in this chapter, it is important to understand that there is an emergent framework that holds the intention of this chapter to skillfully and intentionally see the ways in which psychological healing and spiritual awakening are deeply reciprocal.

Conclusion

We have explored some initial understanding of how our psychological healing path and spiritual awakening path are not two and how we can actually leverage each of these aspects of our practice to support the other. Never were these processes separate, and this chapter and those like it strive to clarify what happens in the dance between nirvana and samsara in our own body-mind-hearts. As we stay grounded in an integral approach towards awakening, utilizing the complexity of the intellectual frameworks, the potency of transformational tools, and the guidance of the wisdom of both contemplative traditions of spiritual development and western psychological healing, we can more thoroughly, efficiently, and skillfully navigate the messy perfection of the path of healing and awakening. May each of our lives be a shining example of humility, radiance, and integrity, in order to create a solid foundation for our hearts, so we can radiate unconditional love and shine the clear light of Spirit in service of the alleviation of suffering of all beings, including *you* and the evolution of the Kosmos as a whole.

Notes

1. Gay Watson et al., eds, *The Psychology of Awakening: Buddhism, Science, and Our Day-to-Day Lives* (York Beach, Maine: Samuel Weiser, Inc., 2000).

2. John Welwood, *Toward a Psychology of Awakening: Buddhism, Psychotherapy, and the Path of Personal and Spiritual Transformation* (Boston, MA: Shambhala Publications, Inc., 2000).

3. Larry Culliford, *The Psychology of Spirituality: An Introduction* (Philadelphia, PA: Jessica Kingsley Publishers, 2011).

4. Dustin DiPerna, *In Streams of Wisdom: An Integral Approach to Spiritual Development*. In press.

5. Ken Wilber, *Integral Spirituality* (Boston, MA: Integral Books, 2006), p. 140.

6. Ken Wilber, *Sex, Ecology, Spirituality* (Boston, MA: Shambhala Publications, 2000), p. 330–331.

7. Saniel Bonder, *Waking Down: Beyond Hypermasculine Dharmas* (San Anselmo, CA: Mt. Tam Awakenings, Inc., 1998).

8. Ken Wilber, *Integral Spirituality* (Boston, MA: Integral Books, 2006).

9. Ibid., p. 104.

10. Dustin DiPerna, *In Streams of Wisdom: An Integral Approach to Spiritual Development*. In press.

11. R. Elliott Ingersoll and David M. Zeitler, *Integral Psychotherapy: Inside Out/ Outside In* (Albany, NY: State University of New York Press, 2010).

12. Russ Hudson and Don Riso, *The Wisdom of the Enneagram: The Complete Guide to Psychological and Spiritual Growth for the Nine Personality Types* (New York, NY: Bantam Books, 1999), p. 28.

13. Russ Hudson and Don Riso, *The Wisdom of the Enneagram: The Complete Guide to Psychological and Spiritual Growth for the Nine Personality Types* (New York, NY: Bantam Books, 1999).

14. Dustin DiPerna, *In Streams of Wisdom: An Integral Approach to Spiritual Development*. In press.

15. Andrew Cohen, *Evolutionary Enlightenment: A New Path to Spiritual Awakening* (New York, NY: SelectBooks, Inc., 2011), p. 48.

16. Ibid., p. 135.

17. Ibid., p. 132.

18. Ken Wilber, *Integral Spirituality* (Boston, MA: Integral Books, 2006).

19. John Welwood, *Toward a Psychology of Awakening: Buddhism, Psychotherapy, and the Path of Personal and Spiritual Transformation* (Boston, MA: Shambhala Publications, Inc., 2000).

20. Ken Wilber, lecture, 2005.

21. Daniel Brown, *Pointing Out the Great Way: The Stages of Meditation in the Mahamudra Tradition* (Somerville, MA: Wisdom Publications, Inc., 2006).

22. Ibid.

23. Ken Wilber et al., *Integral Life Practice: A 21st-Century Blueprint for Physical Health, Emotional Balance, Mental Clarity, and Spiritual Awakening* (Boston, MA: Integral Books, 2008).

24. Daniel Brown, *Pointing Out the Great Way: The Stages of Meditation in the Mahamudra Tradition* (Somerville, MA: Wisdom Publications, Inc., 2006), p. 3.

25. Ibid., p. 293.

26. Dustin DiPerna, *In Streams of Wisdom: An Integral Approach to Spiritual Development*. In press.

27. John Welwood, *Toward a Psychology of Awakening: Buddhism, Psychotherapy, and the Path of Personal and Spiritual Transformation* (Boston, MA: Shambhala Publications, Inc., 2000), p. 138.

28. John Welwood, *Toward a Psychology of Awakening: Buddhism, Psychotherapy, and the Path of Personal and Spiritual Transformation* (Boston, MA: Shambhala Publications, Inc., 2000).

29. Mariana Caplan, *Eyes Wide Open: Cultivating Discernment on the Spiritual Path* (Boulder, CO: Sounds True, 2009), p. 25.

30. Ibid., p. 235.

Chapter 6 - Cleaning Up: The Reciprocal Dance of Psyche and Spirit

31. Dustin DiPerna, *In Streams of Wisdom: An Integral Approach to Spiritual Development*. In press.

32. Pema Chödrön, *No Time to Lose: A Timely Guide to the Way of the Bodhisattva* (Boston, MA: Shambhala Publications, Inc., 2005).

33. Ken Wilber, *Integral Spirituality* (Boston, MA: Integral Books, 2006).

34. Simon Senzon, Donald Epstein, and Dan Lemberger, "Reorganizational Healing as an Integrally Informed Framework for Integral Medicine," *Journal of Integral Theory and Practice* 6, no. 4 (2011): pp. 113–130.

35. Donald Epstein, *The 12 Stages of Healing: A Network Approach to Wholeness* (San Rafael, CA: Amber-Allen Publishing and New World Library, 1994), p. 3.

36. Simon Senzon, Donald Epstein, and Dan Lemberger, "Reorganizational Healing as an Integrally Informed Framework for Integral Medicine," *Journal of Integral Theory and Practice* 6, no. 4 (2011): pp. 113–130.

37. Simon Senzon, Donald Epstein, and Dan Lemberger, "Reorganizational Healing: A paradigm for the Advancement of Wellness, Behavior Change, Holistic Practice, and Healing," *The Journal of Alternative and Complimentary Medicine* 15, no. 5 (2009): 475–487, p. 476.

38. Simon Senzon, Donald Epstein, and Dan Lemberger, "Reorganizational Healing as an Integrally Informed Framework for Integral Medicine," *Journal of Integral Theory and Practice* 6, no.4 (2011): pp. 113–130.

39. Donald Epstein, *The 12 Stages of Healing: A Network Approach to Wholeness* (San Rafael, CA: Amber-Allen Publishing and New World Library, 1994), p. xv.

40. Donald Epstein, *The 12 Stages of Healing: A Network Approach to Wholeness* (San Rafael, CA: Amber-Allen Publishing and New World Library, 1994).

41. Ibid.

42. Ibid., p. xvi.

Chapter 7
Showing Up: The Power and Potential of "We"

Andrew Venezia

Over the last few decades—a single heartbeat in the history of human culture—in quiet corners here and there, we have begun to see and participate in a beautiful and emergent experiment in conscious and intentional practices of relationship and shared awareness. These practices, and the spaces of conscious relating that they open, have taken on the name "We Space." In recent years, We Spaces have expanded from being something touched on by pockets of isolated groups to become a buzzword in integral-evolutionary circles. My intention for this paper is to present a simple and clear overview of We Space phenomena, while also delineating and describing its relevance to current issues of theory, practice, and consciousness in contemporary culture. I hope to help capture some of what has happened in the last few decades and to facilitate the further emergence of this way-of-being-together.

The context of this book is an apposite place for such a discussion for two main reasons. Firstly, the emergence of We Space is radically novel on our planet as far as we know. Since we are very much still midwifes, or even envisioning something yet at the stage of conception, an almost journalistic style is much more appropriate than an academic one. What follows is therefore both description and narrative. I am attempting to describe where we have been and where we might be going as an entry into understanding what exactly is unfolding right now. While I do not have the space here to weave in my own embodied narrative in relationship to We Space and its practices, the third-person description stems from my own experience and understanding of these spaces, having been a student and participant in many different forms of We Space in the last several years. At the end of this chapter you will find an appendix that offers further avenues and practice for those interested.

The additional reason why this book is such an appropriate venue for this discussion is that this subject implicates and is in turn implicated in some of the major issues that Integral Theory, practice, and application is currently addressing, many of which are represented in this book: psychological development and maturity, Shadow work and psychological healing, consciousness practices, community building and collective individualism, embodied action, sustainability, and evolutionary philosophy, just to name a few that I will briefly discuss in this chapter.

The format of this chapter will allow each topic to serve as a foundation for what follows, while also clarifying and expanding on what has come before. I will first introduce the concept of We Space and give a very brief overview to get us situated in the topic at hand. I will then weave this thread through the different topics just mentioned, including theoretical highlights and contexts as well as short practical examples of We Space practices.

What is "We Space"?

While the phrase "We Space" has not been around for very long, in integral and evolutionary circles it has already come to indicate a rather broad swath of distinctly different "intersubjective" practices. As the term "intersubjective" itself can be confusing or disorienting, for this chapter I will be using it to point at that dimension of reality that is interior to our collective experience. As an individual, I have my own subjective experience that is not available to any other subject; you can not see through my eyes, nor feel through my hand. Intersubjectivity, by contrast, is the inner dimension of shared meaning, culture, and relationship—the space within which you and I experience our relationship, and that is created as the field of our interactions. Intersubjectivity thus understood is an intrinsic element, according to Integral Theory, of all life.

To uncover the unique territory described by "We Space" in this chapter, we need to make one further distinction. While I share an intersubjective space with my dog, for example, my dog and I do not share

Chapter 7 - Showing Up: The Power and Potential of "We"

a We Space in the sense used in this chapter. A fundamental element of We Space is the self-reflexivity of intersubjective awareness, where the subjects know that they are relating. This self-reflexivity begins in the abstract and personal realms, and can potentially develop into spaces where each participant experiences one shared awareness, aware of itself through each participant. Similarly, then, We Space as I am using it does not refer to the intersubjective interaction that might be present between a mother and her baby, for example, or even the majority of interactions between adults. While I do not wish to denigrate the importance of such prior and foundational intersubjective spaces, for the purposes of this chapter I will be using We Space to indicate an intentional and self-reflexive intersubjective awareness.

As mentioned, there is a whole range of We Space practices being experimented with today falling under this definition. At one end of the spectrum we have practices that are designed to bring about deep connection and intimacy between people, to begin to transcend the barriers of the modern hermetic sense of self. At the other end of the spectrum are groups of people tapping into a radically emergent and awake sense of shared consciousness. Between these two places lie a great number of practices designed to elicit and stabilize self-reflexive intersubjective awareness. For this chapter, We Space indicates all of these. As this, essentially, is an emergent and newly developing way of relating, my account is not meant to be exhaustive, or even accurately descriptive, but suggestive and evocative. For the rest of this chapter I will be weaving a thread around the potentials that seem to be emerging from these spaces of engagement as I have experienced and understand them. A fuller and more practical sense of what We Space is and represents should come out of this weaving.

Psychological Development

In Integral Theory and the models that it draws its understanding of development from, psychological development is theorized in one sense as represented by the ability to take increasingly complex perspectives. The simplest and clearest example is Swiss psychologist Jean Piaget's famous experiment with schoolchildren, where he colored a ball two colors by hemisphere, so that with the ball placed properly, the children could see only one color at a time. In preparation for the experiment, the children were allowed to examine the ball so they could see that it had two colors (let us say red and blue). At an early stage of development, when the ball was placed between the child and the experimenter and the experimenter asked the child what color they saw, the child responded accurately ("red!"). When asked what color the experimenter saw, however, the children would name the same color ("red!"). Only after several years were the children able to take the perspective of the experimenter as different from their own and name the color the experimenter was in fact looking at ("blue!").

It is a basic tenet of Integral Theory that our development is described by a progression through levels of meaning-making marked by the ability to take increasingly complex perspectives of reality, and that these levels create the basic structure underlying the individual's worldview. For the purpose of simplicity, in this chapter we will be looking at three progressively more complex developmental levels, which I will be referring to by the name of their corresponding worldviews as shorthand: the modern, the postmodern, and the integral. Any person evincing a developmentally earlier structure of consciousness will not have created an ego capable of self-reflexive awareness, and so will also not be able to reflect upon intersubjectivity. Any developmentally later levels of consciousness, on the other hand, are too conjectural and rare to be of practical interest here. I should also note that people are complex beings, and that the levels of consciousness, as I will be using them in a shorthand way here, are grossly simplified and are purely used for illustration. Theorists in any field I mention would likely beat me over the head for the stack of omissions I am quite consciously making in this chapter for the sake of a few general points, and of course I will be using the term "Integral Theory" as if there were a single theory, another shortcut for the sake of introduction. People are never just at one place on any developmental scale. We each display several levels of consciousness in one day—and it is my understanding that people can be making meaning from several different levels at once, due to the nature of the way in which we construct and define what levels are. There is, nevertheless, an overall and generally irreversible directionality to psychological development.

With this caveat in mind, We Space practices represent one potentially potent way to create the kinds of supportive and challenging environments that appear to nurture psychological development in all of

Chapter 7 - Showing Up: The Power and Potential of "We"

its complexity. Why might that be? Let us back up a step, quickly. Integral Theory works with a model of reality that is perspectival and enactive, where perspectives are the foundational building block of reality, and which bring (enact) "what is" about. While also concerned with ontology, or the philosophy of what is real, while discussing psychological development and levels of consciousness the focus is more on epistemology, or the philosophy of how we know what we know.

Integral Theory does not assume a singular underlying metaphysical reality. What this practically means for our discussion is that different developmental levels of consciousness are not simply looking at the same world through different lenses—they are looking at different worlds. As this in itself is an extremely abstruse topic and only tangentially important for this introduction, let us simply continue with the understanding that as one develops psychologically, what one takes to be real develops as well.

The modern self generally thinks and believes in a world and self that are each solid and separate as being "real." The modern sense of self has the strongest boundaries of any of the self-senses—in itself healthy and crucial for further development. In addition, there is the underlying assumption of a single metaphysical reality—a single and representable truth that can be discovered through inquiry: logical, philosophical, and scientific.

For the postmodern self, what one takes to be real becomes somewhat more illusive. Questions of context and situation enter the picture for the first time, and it becomes apparent that several people can have different perspectives on what seems to be the same "event," and that all perspectives might be valid. If there is a single marker of postmodern consciousness as a developmental stage of meaning-making, it might be the emphasis on the inclusion of voices that had been marginalized by the modern self, whether interior "parts" of the self, or from "other" cultures not considered mainstream. The self begins to recognize different loci of control within the self, while one's unique history and culture become seen as foundational and formational to one's identity. A middle class Indian-American person represents a unique blend of influences on identity and worldview; it will be different for someone who grew up in a favela in Brazil.

With an integral sense of self, while we affirm the formational nature of one's developmental contexts in creating a historical sense of self, several nuances open that change one's sense of identity and reality, eventually opening up into a sense of self-as-awareness, within which one's story, or the self of personal identifications, is arising moment to moment. These nuances include the "Shadow," or the observation that what I am as a psychological being includes motivations that I may be less than conscious of, and may even deny or repress. This further develops into the realization that all of what I consciously identify myself with carries a compensatory negation. If I prefer peace, for example, I am also predisposed to be uncomfortable with energy and excitement, and I am likely negating the more energetic side of life in my pursuit of peace—something which, paradoxically, can make my life and the world a much less peaceful place. The integral self-sense also becomes much more tolerant of paradox and uncertainty. This allows for a much more fluid sense of what is real, and what I am within and as this reality. The contexts of my life, rather than making my interiors inaccessible to others, can be shared to reveal an underlying humanity. Rather than the sliding scale of infinite contexts making meaning arbitrary, as can be the case with postmodern consciousness, meaning can be generated through the prioritization of contexts based on relevance and complexity, and through the affirmation of the subjectivity of meaning. This can eventually open up into a radically imminent sense of self and reality, where reality is revealed by the experience of consciousness arising within and as awareness.

The ways that We Space can create a developmental container are of course dependent upon the injunctions of the practice space, and the developmental level of the participants. They all rely to some extent, however, on the holding space of relationship: an environment of curiosity, exploration, and safety, though these words will be understood differently in different contexts—what is safe in one context to one person may not be in and to another. I'll be using as an example a simple exercise called a sentence stem completion. One example of a sentence stem completion exercise would be with two individuals sitting across from each other, each repeating a single sentence stem. The first individual might start with "being with you, I feel . . ." and then complete the sentence. The two would then take turns saying "hearing that, I feel . . ." until the time for the exercise was over. For the modern self-sense, the exercise can open up the indescribable reality of another person's being, and that that person might well have an entirely different viewpoint than he, as this

Chapter 7 - Showing Up: The Power and Potential of "We"

exercise can also illuminate assumptions that we make about others and their reactions that turn out to be unfounded. One might expect the phrase "Hearing that, I feel angry," to elicit a different response than "Hearing that, I am entirely unconvinced of your anger," which might in turn elicit a surprised laugh. Equally revelatory to the modern self-sense can be discovering the territory opened up by sharing in the moment, that one's own self can prove equally surprising.

Another helpful exercise for this self-sense is "Open-Hearted Listening," the injunction being that one person with a grievance approaches the second person, asking if they would be willing to listen in an open-hearted manner to the first. Accepting the request, the second person is enjoined to listen, and to repeat what the first is saying, without responding or interjecting their own opinions or interpretations of the material being discussed. As the participant is enjoined to listen without defense to another's position, and then repeat to ensure that they have understood the other, this challenges the modern self-sense's claim to their viewpoint as being correct, and opens them up to different interpretations of a single event, and to how their being affects and is in turn affected by "others."

The sentence stem and similar exercises can help someone move from a postmodern self to an integral self-sense as well. While any activity that calls attention to the present moment is generally thought to be an aid in development, the injunction to pay attention to the present moment *as* one is constructing a sense of self can be particularly trenchant. Take for example an exercise to share your life story. If you are given five minutes, you will have one version of your story. If you are then given twenty seconds to share your life story, you are likely to come up with a very different story. The essentials might be the same, but the format will create a very different overall picture than a five-minute format will. For the modern self, this exercise can call attention to the fluidity of one's identity, that in different contexts, the self appears differently. For the postmodern self, calling to attention that one is in-the-moment creating and presenting a story, that one is essentially "making it up on the spot," and that one can take advantage of the limits of the context as a creative opportunity can similarly be revelatory. From this space one can begin to notice that "I" is actually *not* located in any of the stories being communicated. I am the observer of that story—in no way separate from it, but also not to be found or limited within it. Here we are approaching a late-integral sense of self, where one's identity is beginning to open up into awareness itself, and to detach identification from the contents of awareness. We Space practices present a unique way to both support an individual in community, while simultaneously challenging their notions of what is real, bringing about the development of more and more complex perspectives of reality. We Space as a container for Shadow work presents a further spur to development, which we will turn to next.

The Shadow

Up until this point, I have been working with an implicit definition of what our self-senses are. I will now make this definition explicit as a way of transitioning into a discussion of the Shadow. As mentioned, developmental levels represent different ways of answering the question "What is real?" and further, of answering the question "who am I?" Within these rather general and foundational ways of meaning-making, we discern individual and idiosyncratic varieties of making meaning. Starting again with the modern self-sense, which is the culmination of the ego, we note that every ego is composed of an accumulation of positive identifications. Those positive identifications arise within a space of negation, which constitute the Shadow. Take, for example, the question: is the glass half full, or half empty? This is not merely an arbitrary question. While the question is usually about whether one is a pessimist or an optimist, and personalities are far more complicated than one simple dualism, this nonetheless illustrates an extremely important principle. The question itself presupposes that there is an answer. There is not (or the answer is "Holy Mole! There's water in that glass!"). Our self-senses are an activity of constantly posing dualistic questions, assuming an answer, and taking that answer to be real. In saying that the glass is half full, the optimist asserts this as reflective of reality as it is, saying simultaneously and surreptitiously that it is not half empty. One who claims that it is half empty is doing the reverse. The point is that this is an *activity*, a filtering of what is (the glass has water in it) which we take to be the way that things are, period.

This becomes more trenchant when we move from a glass of water to real life. Say, for example, that my predisposition is towards being

Chapter 7 - Showing Up: The Power and Potential of "We"

a bright and sunny person. Life is inherently positive, and I am always looking for the best in every situation, and for the next exciting thing to do. This is a caricature, of course, but again serves to highlight a point. My ability to be sunny is one thing on a day-to-day basis. When crisis strikes, however, if I am unable to face that there is a serious issue to be dealt with, I may be causing more trouble by ignoring it. My attachment to an identity formed out of the positive association with "sunny-ness" and the negative association with "gloomy-ness" is a complex out of which both my ego, or sense of self, and Shadow emerge. The glass, though, is neither "really" half full, nor is it half empty.

This is not simply tangential to the topic at hand. Not only is psychological development beyond the modern and postmodern senses of self a process of re-owning previously negated Shadow material just as much as it is the development of "positive" traits, but Shadow material is also largely available to be activated and opened in a group context. To be sure, as our personalities and senses of self develop embedded within an intersubjective, relational field, much of the work of psychological healing *must* be done in relationship. In working with a group, I am likely to find someone who embodies those very traits about myself, or humanity at large, that I most dislike. Someone will be gloomy, or will appear to be angry, or uncaring, or ingratiating. Whether they are this quality or not is largely beside the point, which is to investigate your own activity of seeing the glass as full or empty. In consciously engaging in a context where this tendency of human psychology is made explicit, and where each individual has the intention to work with their Shadow, We Space work can be powerful. Indeed, while Shadow work can be done in many other ways, when face to face with someone and truly feeling Shadow material triggered, it is hard to intellectualize the work. There is a simple test, after all. If I still feel like "he's a jerk" and that's that, in a supportive community context, I will inevitably be called to do more work.

Shadow work, as mentioned, elides nicely with developmental work: they are the left and right hand of growth. As we move from a postmodern sense of self, where personality traits have an underlying and external reality, to an integral sense of self, we begin to become self-reflexively aware of the ways in which we habitually pay attention, what we emphasize and ignore. This happens first mostly in reflection, after-the-fact. As we become more used to inhabiting self-reflexive awareness as the present moment, we begin to catch our projections and constructions as we are making them, something which heralds the shift from an egocentric self-sense, including the modern, postmodern, and early stages of the integral self-sense, to a truly transpersonal self-sense, where even the boundary between "I" and "not I" which is fundamental to the rest of the identified self-sense begins to become transparent.

There are two ways to approach Shadow work in an explicit We Space context. First, as mentioned, in any community there are likely to be members who will trigger some aspect of yourself that you either reject or deny. Secondly, there are exercises that explicitly call forth Shadow aspects to be worked with. Even the simple sentence completion exercises can be helpful, if framed correctly. One powerful sentence stem for this is: "you seem . . . are you?" Practices such as this focus and clarify one's ability to observe their own inner state and to notice when one is sensing personal material, and when one is sensing the other. If I see anger in everyone while no one else experiences anger, it is likely mine. There are additionally a number of practices that ask the individual to bring a Shadow element forth and embody it. Parading around a room of support crowing like a rock star may for many people be both an extremely challenging and an extremely rewarding activity.

Practices of Consciousness

I have remarked that most We Space practices rely on a careful attention to the present moment. The sentence stems mentioned above, for example, require an actual process of checking in with what is present in one's self. Further We Space practices place this attention on different aspects of awareness, but all require this attunement to self, other, and to the present moment. As such, they are in themselves not only relational practices, but meditative practices as well.

The present moment itself changes throughout meditative practices. What seems at first to be no more than a taste of presence becomes a steady stream. Thoughts and images, sounds and sights appear and pass away. Eventually, the present moment opens up as the space of awareness itself, something timeless and spaceless. One begins to rest in the recognition that nothing happens outside the present moment. Time and space become seen as constructions. Rather than "reaching" a place where the present moment expands, one realizes in a direct and

Chapter 7 - Showing Up: The Power and Potential of "We"

experiential way that linear time and three-dimensional space that have seemed to be simply givens in life are byproducts of a way of paying attention, and are developmental. Eventually, awareness transcends all dualities, even that between awareness and its contents, what is self and other. Objects and differentiations arise as awareness disclosing awareness to itself—something called nondual awareness.

This is the fulcrum of the chapter. I have remarked earlier that one's sense of self consists of ways of paying attention. Linear time and three-dimensional space are similarly ways of paying attention. Both arise from a very particular way of paying attention that can be called "mental," or "egoic." Linear time, three-dimensional space, and the abstract virtual self, here also called the ego, are intricately tied together. The modern and postmodern self-senses are encapsulated within this mental way of being. What I am calling in this paper the integral stage is helpfully thought of as two stages. The first is a transitional stage, where one begins to become aware of their ego-Shadow complex mostly in a reflexive, third-person, and abstract way, where I can understand *that* I have a Shadow, and I can analyze this Shadow with the help of time, but am usually not aware of when I am enacting Shadow material *in the present*. This is another way of saying that moment to moment, I am identified with my ego structure, and that my self-sense is not transparent to me. I do not see my self-sense as an activity or an enactment, but as my own solid self. In the later stages of integral awareness, I start to see my projections as they are happening, and begin to see my habitual ways of paying attention.

Engaging in advanced We Space practices, such as Enlightened Communication, or Theory U, the central injunctions are around being aware of the space between the participants, and engaging from a place beyond one's ego. Rather than speaking from the egoic self-sense, participants are enjoined to speak from an emergent and shared consciousness. In terms that Theory U uses, participants are encouraged to speak/listen not only from an open mind, a practice which challenges the modern self-sense to see the possible third-person truths of another's position; and not only from an open heart, a practice which further asks us to listen from within another person's perspective and to encounter them as a second-person; but to listen and speak from a place of open will, something which challenges our mental-egoic selves to be as present and surrendered to the moment as we can be, which can be as powerful as a personal meditation practice. This shift to an engagement with the group from a space of self-reflexive awareness I believe to be the most profound and meaningful element of the We Space practices that are emerging now in a large way, and holds potential ramifications for how we organize ourselves as a human society. Properly, We Space originally indicated these spaces of engagement, and even more advanced spaces of engagement from awakened, nondual awareness, a usage that I agree with. The term, however, has broadened to mean intersubjective awareness of any type, including the practices that lead up to this greater We Space, and so I have accepted this usage. Practices that aim at healing one's psychology and/or shifting the self-sense to a postmodern or integral level of interpersonal engagement are preliminary to practices which engage the group mind in a field of radical emergence, but they are also essential for two other reasons. A strong personal We Space provides a sustainable foundation for a strong awakened We Space, and in any case most of humanity is not on the cusp of an awakened We Space engagement. We may have a revolution by just engaging each other as humans in personal We Spaces.

I have briefly mentioned that the mental self is built on a fundamentally dualistic activity. Where there is water, and a glass, the mental self sees the glass as either half full or half empty. Also as noted, this activity constitutes what one experiences and believes to be real. What is striking is that *everyone undertakes this activity in a slightly different manner— everyone's ego is built on very different underlying senses of what is real*. Not only do we have a different underlying and personal sense of what is real, but when we engage with each other, we are fundamentally banging our assumed realities off of one another. Advanced We Space practices help teach us to surrender our self-sense in the experience of the co-creative moment, as we stop claiming that the glass is half full or empty, and begin looking at the water.

Theory U, and practices like "The I of the We" explore this kind of space. In "The I of the We," participants sit in a circle, and sense into or imagine the energetic threads between them, building and strengthening the group field. A question is asked to populate the center of the circle, and the group intends to sit and receive thoughts as images or words that might help address the question. When speaking to the group, participants are instructed to pay attention to where they are sharing from. Are they sharing for selfish reasons, from "me" to "me?" Are they sharing from their personal sense, but in service of the group, as an

Chapter 7 - Showing Up: The Power and Potential of "We"

offering, from "me" to "we?" Are they sharing through their personal sense but, sourced in an awareness beyond their personality, through "me" to "we?" Or are they sharing and speaking as the field of emergent consciousness, downloading future potentials into the present, from the "We" to the "we?"

I have been speaking of the self that is sourced from awareness as a permanent psychological developmental achievement that I've been attributing to late-integral consciousness, but there is a second way to think about it: as a temporary state. Just as with meditation, where one can carry a certain day-to-day self-sense, while having access to profound altered states on their pillow, so can one live life in the modern self-sense, but learn to surrender to an open self-reflexive intersubjective awareness in an appropriate context. In a postpersonal space, and further into an awakened nondual space, even the boundary between what I am and what I am not, perhaps the most fundamental of the constructions that we take as being real, is seen through, as the group experiences itself as one awakened awareness looking at itself through the different practitioners. We may well find that these awakened group practices are able to introduce individuals to the nondual state of consciousness in a more reliable manner and with a greater support structure than traditional meditation.

Collective Individualism

Though both traditional meditation and We Space practice appear to be effective in the process of self-awareness that leads to mature psychological development, with We Space having an edge in terms of embodied Shadow work, and while both open us up to presence in the moment, meditation itself does not engage the critical dimension of reality that is relationship. Bringing two awake human beings together does not necessarily bring about an awakened We Space, just as bringing a match and gasoline in the same room does not make fire—the match must be lit, and must be applied to the gas. The potentials illuminated by advanced We Space practice point to the importance of both of these facets of life: our human societies will only meet the needs of today if our unique individuality (our becoming most and fully ourselves), is woven together in a way that does not compromise our ability to join together in collective action, and if our ways of being together do not compromise our unique individuality.

One integral theorist, Don Beck, has coined the term "collective individualism" for such a culture. Where previous themes of human culture have been organized around the split or tension between the individual and the collective, either emphasizing conformity and sacrifice of the individual self in service of the whole, or emphasizing the inviolability of individual agency. A culture of collective individualism is a culture that blossoms out of the embodied knowledge that the dividing line between self and other is another way of asking whether the glass is half full *or* empty. It is, of course, both.

In a group where every member is in some way able to cognize this both/and perspective, that is, where the activity of cognizing self/other has become transparent to consciousness, the boundaries between what psychological material is "mine" and what is the "other's" begins to break down. Projections can become connections, and roles become fluid. If, for example, anger is present in a We Space circle, where that anger is "coming from," one group member or another, becomes less important. That there is anger, and that this anger is a universal human experience, becomes more so. In the sharing of our most intensely personal material, and the recognition that others share the same pattern, we can embrace our patterning as something universally human—our most personal material is also profoundly universal. Here another interesting thing happens: in entering consciously into these experiences and acting them out, in being given permission in a container of acceptance to fully express and experience the whole range of humanity, we begin to transmute these energies into their positive correlates. Anger can become clarity and even compassion as its energy becomes transparent, no longer repressed or indulged. When I and others are not resisting what is arising as a threat to our implicit constructions of what is real, when shame around the experience of our emotional selves is dropped, and when the patterns we are seeing are played out not only for our own individual healing, but for the healing of our humanity, we can create profound healing spaces for individual and group woundedness.

The role-playing that becomes common in this kind of group can be approached purposefully and explicitly as an exercise by almost any group held by those with sufficient ego maturity and lead to profundity. For example, one individual in a group of three might take on the role of

Chapter 7 - Showing Up: The Power and Potential of "We"

being God. She sits in this viewpoint for a minute, feeling into what it would be like to look on the second participant as God, with all the love that God has for God's children. The second participant is asked to receive this love, and can then speak to God whatever she feels or wants to say or ask, while the third person acts as an observer—an important role which helps to keep the energy of a dyad from concretizing, and which points to the synergistic power of observers. This is not simply role-playing —while one way to think of this exercise is that we are "playing" God, the more profound orientation is that what we call God is everywhere, and by consciously holding the energy of being and speaking to God we are calling our attention to this presence, and able to bring it down into a profound space of relationality.

Of course, if we were waiting for all of the population to mature to the point where they could hold these paradoxes and act on them to bring about a collective individualist culture, we'd be waiting a long time. There are, then, two interesting aspects of culture that potentially come online in the later stages of integral consciousness. The first is what we have largely been discussing: smaller peer groups of people able to source their enactments of consciousness from a space beyond identification with the ego, whether as a permanent psychological development or a temporary context-dependent state. This can have such a profound effect on individual's development and presence in the world that we would see an effect on the rest of the culture if this was the only thing that happened. It is not. In integral consciousness, when one does not exclusively identify with their attachments and constructions of reality, one is no longer allergic to the constructions of others. Everyone's perspective is true, partially. Just as in the above discussion where a personal arising of anger becomes something not to resist, or necessarily express, but something to be welcomed with curiosity and engagement, so other people's unique constructions of reality become unthreatening. Rather than fight another individual or group's way of being in the world, in the way of, say, the culture wars, a person enacting integral consciousness can identify with the energy being expressed by anyone, while affirming that which is positive, and calling it forward. While I do not believe we have seen this much on a large scale, the potential exists for a small group of individuals expressing integral consciousness to nurture a community in a holding space where the gifts of each are called forth into their full potential in service of the greater community.

Embodied Action and Sustainability

As practicing in a We Space allows one to confront, embrace, and make transparent in the moment the ways one has been cognizing reality into a series of dualities, including the duality between the mind and the body, it presents a powerful methodology for coming into embodied action. By "embodied action" I mean action that is in alignment with one's sense of morality and purpose and sourced from a body-heart-mind that is expressing a singularity of intent, rather than a split body/mind that is, at least as this stage of consciousness is most commonly enacted currently in the west, at odds with itself.

We Space has the potential to harbor psychological development and lead to a more embodied human being as almost a byproduct of the work. As discussed just above, it also creates the medium through which the individual can embody the collective and act on its behalf. In a larger scope, when I am aware of the self and the world as being half full and half empty perspectives, then the world *is* an aspect of my self, and my community *is* an aspect of my self—my actions becoming co-extensive with this embodiment.

For the larger issues of sustainability within the current climate of global crisis, We Space represents more than just a means to a more embodied individual, however. In the space of radical emergence opened up in Theory U practices, for example, at least two important things happen, each mirrors of the other. Firstly, where my individual will is surrendered to the experiential process of the group, not to gain acceptance (which is not an act of surrender), but to allow the current of emergence to flow unimpeded into manifestation as an act of service, my own personal agenda is less likely to get in the way of discovering profound solutions to whatever problems are being addressed. The group can address whatever is present as a whole—imagine a team of horses running in different directions, as opposed to one in which each horse is headed in the same direction, the energy of each expressed for a single purpose. Secondly, the knowledge each individual has can be drawn upon where needed. Rather than filtering action through a single locus of control that may or may not be qualified to address each aspect of the question at hand, and who may or may not be able to understand what

Chapter 7 - Showing Up: The Power and Potential of "We"

each contributor brings to the table, action and direction is determined by the space in between the participants. The group itself has a life of its own, not entirely reducible to its individuals, but neither dominating them. In later stages of We Space, the group is attuned to a transcendent awakeness. *For the level of complexity of the organizational and cultural difficulties now facing the human species, nothing short of an awakened We Space will do. We need to act decisively and singularly in the service not of a projected future, but of the radically emergent possibility of the present moment.*

Evolutionary Spirituality

While I have not to this point mentioned the word explicitly, all of this points towards an emerging sense of spirituality very closely aligned with the integral worldview, called evolutionary spirituality. The main tenant of evolutionary spirituality is that consciousness evolves in the direction of greater complexity, simultaneously emerging as greater and greater expressions of differentiation and cohesion. We, in our practice, can engage with and step into this terrific energy of evolution, called eros, while embracing all of manifestation, an energy called agape. As the universe is always evolving, there is no final state to attain that can be called enlightenment as we have traditionally thought of it. We may still attain nondual consciousness, or "classical enlightenment," as a permanent trait, but this consciousness must be brought out to engage with the world: it is no longer sufficient to meditate in a cave or a monastery for one's life. We become all of us householders, called to a life of meaning and purpose, and inherent in this engagement is that we must learn to collectively engage surrendered freely to the service of the highest good. Similarly, as our humanity is evolving as one consciousness, we must embrace and support those around us. Just as a chain is only as strong as its weakest link, so does our future development as a species and planet depend on all of us. As we become identified as consciousness itself, involved in this process of evolution, we also become aware of the future *not* as a projection of the present moment based in past experience, but as an open field of potentiality which is present and rooted in this moment and affected through our conscious engagement with it.

Conclusion and Acknowledgements

I have run quickly through the idea of a We Space and some of its implications in a cursory and roughshod way. If this interests you I suggest that you contact some of the groups mentioned in the appendix. I have also been focused on giving a thin overview of several different aspects of We Space in current practice, and where we might be headed in the next few decades. I have unfortunately only given some basic examples of actual We Space practices, and have not touched upon the full depth of any of these practices, let alone covered the full breadth of practices available. Again, I encourage those interested to explore some of the groups mentioned below.

Though I have mentioned several times the singularity of consciousness, and how We Space practices can enlist a number of perspectives in the furtherance of a single group consciousness, we are also at a time of great experimentation with these technologies, and the flowering of perspectives upon the flowering of practices being developed now can only be a benefit. It is my hope that this chapter may contribute to the blossoming of We Space in whatever small way, helping to bring us into a world where culture is the invocation of the gifts of all, where every person is needed and called to contribute to their fullest abilities exactly the gift they most desire to give. May it be so.

My deep thanks to Dustin DiPerna, Christina Vickory, and Bill McCart for their work with the We Practice Community; to Terry Patten, Dustin DiPerna, Miriam and Stephan Martineau, Mike Wombacher, Thomas Hübl, Olen Gunnlaugson, Geoff Fitch, Patricia Albere, and Jeff Carreira, who have helped clarify my understanding of the phenomenon of We Space; and to all of the amazing human beings that I have been exploring this space with over the last several years, including and especially my beloved Karen. My humble thanks as well for Dustin's invitation to write this chapter. May it contribute to the birth of a radiant and flourishing human being.

Chapter 7 - Showing Up: The Power and Potential of "We"

Appendix: We Space Practice

Enlightened Communication: Andrew Cohen's group EnlightenNext has been working with We Space for a very long time. I have been told but cannot confirm that Cohen coined the phrase "We Space." www.enlightennext.org/about

We Practice Community: A practice group that explores We Space experimentally and from many different directions. http://wepractice.org

Theory U: Otto Scharmer, the father of Theory U, is also the founder of the Presencing Institute, through which we support the work of Theory U in the world, in the service of the emergence of a more humane social system. www.presencing.com

Thomas Hübl: I am oddly unable to say anything about Thomas. He is a marvel. www.thomashuebl.com/en.html

Authentic World: Authentic world works with a form of practice called Circling that I find to be unparalleled for its ability to make the personal realm transparent. www.authenticworld.org

Evolutionary Collective: Jeff Carreira and Patricia Albere bring a synergistic and vivacious energy to the cutting-edge exploration of conscious community. www.evolutionarycollective.com

Next Step Integral: Stephan and Miriam Martineau have been engaged in this collective experiment for over twenty years, and their Community Seminars are profound experiences of the emergence of a collective individualist holding space. http://nextstepintegral.org

I can obviously not cover the breadth of We Space practices happening at this time. I encourage exploration—the rabbit hole goes deep!

Chapter 8
The Biggest Taboo

H.B. Augustine

If someone you know, love, and trust told you that (s)he remembered a past life, and that the experience of remembering it was just as distinct as the experience of remembering one's dream from a previous night, how would you interpret what this person is telling you? Would you be inclined to regard the individual as crazy or delusional, despite being someone you know, love, and trust? Would you believe what (s)he says is true? Would you choose to suspend your intellectual judgment, due to the magnitude and implications underlying this theory presenting itself to you as being real? While it is easy to see only one possibility or another, "the person is telling either the truth or (s)he is not," this simplistic binary is more complex and chaotic than meets the naked mind.

Every binary consists of two extremes or opposites, which necessitates a relationship or shared space between them. This relationship brings blurredness and uncertainty to the seemingly perfect, clear-cut solution that the particular binary superficially evidences. The binary that results from a trusted person telling you that (s)he remembered a past life, superficially evidences the "(s)he is telling either the truth or is not" scenario. Yet, when analyzed with greater intellectual awareness and proficiency, one realizes that the solution addressing this predicament is not and cannot be reduced to a belief in either "pure truth" or "pure falsity." Granted, and as is true for all binaries, some cases involve exclusively one extreme/absolute or the other, to a significantly greater extent than other cases. For example, if this person who you know, love, and trust walks into the room and informs you that it just began raining outside, then—most likely—you would have no problem believing him or her.

While slightly different, this example nonetheless connects with the previous case in that a person you know/love/trust is informing you of what (s)he believes was an authentic experience. In one case, the experience was remembering a past life; in the other case it was seeing rain outside. The gray area of this binary of human experience ranges from concrete physical perception to what so-called mystics call the "depths of consciousness"—the "transpersonal" experiences constituted by perceptions of more than just (ordinary and physical) sensation, emotion, and thought.

How do we interpret or make sense of a seemingly intelligent, sensible, honest human being who claims ability to have an out-of-body experience at will, for instance? The experience and general claim that this individual communicates definitely falls *significantly* outside any sort of societal norm. Yet, what does such abnormality mean?

Some norms are seemingly more valuable than others. For instance, the norm "Murder is wrong," at least *seems* a lot better than the norm "Homosexuality is wrong." Our duty as scholars and citizens, I believe, is to understand the significance of all norms, both individually, in and of themselves, and collectively, in relation to one another. The norm for which I feel most passionate reveals itself in the abnormality of transpersonal or "mystical" experience. This area interests me because it has applied to my own life for the past four years, both logically/textually and phenomenologically. Transpersonal/mystical experience, what I shall hence signify as "trans-mysticality," is both fascinating and significant because if it is true—meaning that it is true in both a metaphysical and epistemological sense—then the way traditional, modern, and postmodern ideologies alike interpret the human condition needs to change.

I question these ideologies, along with the cultures responsible for or associated with them, because virtually the only current explanation for trans-mystical experience is that the individual who claims to experience it is psychologically impaired or disillusioned (e.g., schizophrenic). Trans-mysticality is so negatively and fearfully abnormal culturally that it limits peoples' ability to reason whether the "abnormality" is in fact so negative and fearful, or is instead both positive and truthful. I see with first-person, second-person, and third-person experiential accounts that there must be some truth, some value, and some significance at least, due to the vast

Chapter 8 - The Biggest Taboo

evidence that implies some authenticity about trans-mysticality. Generally, my objective with this work is to make a case for trans-mysticality apropos of its negative-normative discrimination and disregard on a massive social scale. Namely, my goal here is to inspire the reader to see that 1) trans-mysticality's taboo is excessive and for the most part unuttered (especially within the intellectual community), 2) there is a vast, integrative, and comprehensive amount of legitimate evidence that gives reason to see beyond this taboo, and 3) there is immense value to opening one's mind toward the possibility that one's most influential worldview inadequately accommodates trans-mysticality's oft-neglected truth-value.

The structure of this work shall go as follows. First, I will elaborate on the relationship between ethical normativity and epistemic normativity. After establishing what this relationship is, I will holistically cover and analyze the second category in accordance with the history of philosophy and critical thought in general. I will demonstrate that epistemic normativity includes four primary variables while spanning four general contexts or paradigms. These variables are rationalism, empiricism, reductionism, and holism, and these contexts/paradigms, or eras, are ancient, medieval, modern, and postmodern. With this information reviewed and considered, I will then elaborate upon the theoretical framework that most resonates with my understanding and, therefore, shall reach toward achieving success with my research, rationalization, and writing. Broadly speaking, this framework is called (among other names) integral, integrative, holistic, triangular, three-dimensional, and/or spectrum-oriented.

Having established my understanding of theoretical frameworks in general, along with my framework of choice in particular, I will use it to holistically review the most relevant information encompassing both ends of the spectrum, so to speak. In addition to covering the whole spectrum of belief in trans-mysticality, I shall cover another spectrum: the spectrum of testament to trans-mysticality, ranging from "pure subjectivity" (first-person) to "pure objectivity" (third-person). Having reviewed all information adhering to such a theoretical framework, I will analyze each of three main perspectives toward trans-mysticality and will identify as many positives and negatives related to each one as is feasible.

After exhausting this analysis, I will consider the relationship between these three ideologies and their positives and negatives, and will end my work by pointing toward the most contradictory and problematic view, along with the most coherent and valuable one. I will finally conclude by leaving the reader with some thoughts on the greater significance of this research. Our exploration shall now consider the relationship between ethical normativity and epistemic normativity, ultimately in relation to the greater subject that is trans-mysticality and its excessive abnormality today.

Theoretical Framework for Upcoming Exploration

The difference between these two categories of normativity seemingly aligns with the difference between connotation and denotation, the difference between "goodness" and "truth," the difference between ethical philosophy and epistemic philosophy. Ethical philosophy deals with the value of human decisions, while epistemic philosophy deals with the *truth*-value of human inference(s). It would seem that both categories affect one another, more or less interdependently. A person's ethical worldview can influence his or her epistemic worldview, and vice versa. A fundamentalist Christian's belief in the ethical wrongness of, say, homosexuality can influence his or her believing the category to be untrue or unnatural. Conversely, an atheist's belief in the epistemic wrongness of God's existence or inherent goodness to reality can influence his or her belief that systematically torturing people for fun is no different, ultimately, from attempting to save the world.

In light of this distinction and its significance, I accept in principle, or as a given, that *truth is inherently valuable*. If truth is inherently valuable, then a relationship between "truth" and "value" or "goodness" is made proportionately indispensable or interdependent. The pursuit of greater truth in any circumstance is *better* than not pursuing greater truth. In the case of trans-mysticality, considering and finding this phenomenon's epistemic normativity sheds a theoretically equal amount of light upon our understanding of its ethical normativity. Therefore, I will seek to maximize comprehension on the epistemic normativity of trans-mysticality, given the context and limits of this undertaking. It is necessarily impossible to maximize such comprehension without first maximizing comprehension on the subject of epistemic normativity itself. In philosophical terms, this subject includes the branches of metaphysics,

Chapter 8 - The Biggest Taboo

epistemology, and logic, beginning with the earliest ancient thinkers and continuing up to the past century.

Although the possibility of an answer to this question has inspired thousands of years of disagreement, the entire conversation is now available for virtually anyone to see via digital means. The digital sphere encircling global society brings not just seemingly chaotic/excessive plurality, but also—with the acknowledgement of such plurality—a way to understand the entire whole as a coherent and simple system rather than some fragmented and complex soup. I suggest there is a way to understand the problem of epistemic normativity by recognizing the categories underlying the entire multi-millennial conversation itself. Some find this last claim enormous and absurd, but someone born into the age of information/knowledge/plurality can find this perspective a great privilege and plain fact. Having access to the entire conversation allows for coherence and comprehension. Relative to my perspective, such an understanding of epistemic normativity, due to accessing and seeing its entire historical conversation, denotes four primary variables or categories. As I see it, the relationship between all of these categories, again, is one of coherence rather than fragmentation.

First, there is the binary between rationalism and empiricism, which roughly aligns with the binary between mind and body, between "science" and "not-science." Rationalism deals with epistemic normativity by placing significantly greater emphasis upon ideas as such, on pure reason, rather than upon physical observation, while empiricism deals with epistemic normativity by doing the exact opposite. Second, there is the binary between reductionism and holism. Reductionism operates analytically or deductively, breaking any theory or inference into its complete, semantic, hierarchical structure, while holism operates not-analytically. Holism operates synthetically and "abductively," emphasizing not individual isolation but preexisting relationships. In the case of epistemic normativity, the connection between these two binaries reflects the connections between mind/interior and body/exterior, and between individuals/parts and collectives/groups. Naturally (and unfortunately), philosophers living prior to our pluralistic global context did not have the luxury of seeing this whole conversation and its ultimate coherence.

Looking at the conversation, I see Plato, Augustine, and Descartes epitomizing the rationalist position and Aristotle, Aquinas, and Locke epitomizing the empiricist position. I also see Russell epitomizing the reductionist position and Quine epitomizing the holist position. Plato, Augustine, and Descartes together value reason over experience. Rationalism, in general, is significantly more sympathetic toward the possibility of trans-mysticality's epistemic normativity. It does not matter how absurd or outlandish my friend's claim sounds relative to the not-so-absurd and not-so-outlandish experiences that I myself have had to this point. Instead, what matters most is how much *reason* I possess to believe in what (s)he has claimed based on my preexisting relationship with this person. If my respect and trust for the individual could not be greater, then reason tells me that I ought to believe in what (s)he has communicated. However, Aristotle, Aquinas, and Locke would disagree, insisting that if I myself have never experienced what my friend has claimed, then its epistemic normativity relative to my understanding remains neutral or meaningless. Moreover, empiricism would contend that if the experience is not grounded physically, then it bears no significance. (The latter point makes things difficult for the trans-mystical claim of experiencing an "energy body" that is literally "not-physical.")

Consider now the more particular difference between reductionism and holism. Russell believes in the power of analysis and deduction so much that his perspective sees the world as a structure of categories to which we humans have rational access. Quine believes that such inherence, such structure, such categorization is contradictory, because everything, and our recognition of everything, depends upon everything else, and because the mental maps to which we humans access to interpret the world are not representations of how the world *actually is* but are simply *webs of belief* manifested from the process of social conditioning alone. In the historical conversation about epistemic normativity, we see holist-rationalists, such as Quine, reductionist-rationalists, such as Plato, holist-empiricists, such as Foucault, and reductionist-empiricists, such as Russell. Furthermore, in this conversation, we see the evolution from an ancient, to a medieval, to a modern, to a postmodern context.

It would seem that the first and second contexts overemphasized rationalism and reductionism, the third overemphasized empiricism and reductionism, and the fourth overemphasized (and overemphasizes) empiricism and holism. What began as thinking about ideas alone by oneself has transformed into a perspective concerning epistemic normativity that enacts many different groups; each attempt to make sense

Chapter 8 - The Biggest Taboo

of the environment by means of physical observation rather than "metaphysical speculation." Today's postmodern context would certainly have issue with the rationalistic-reductionistic tendency of the present discussion in its proposing this ultimate coherence underlying history's conversation about epistemic normativity. Indeed, the above variables or categories are nowhere to be found in physical observation; moreover, their mention seemingly assumes that categories *as such* can be real in and of themselves rather than in relation to everything else. This postmodern objection is partially legitimate. While there may be the binary or category of "rationalism versus empiricism," there certainly cannot be any absolute divide or cut-off point between these two ends or theoretical extremes.

Any binary implies a gray area or blurred space. Any binary implies a spectrum. Ken Wilber, the scholar whose work has most influenced the theoretical framework to which this discussion has led, recognizes such a spectrum in his view on epistemic normativity and our method for maximizing it. Although Wilber uses the term "broad empiricism" to denote his methodology, this paradigm does not pertain any more to "empiricism" alone than it pertains to "rationalism" alone. He acknowledges the difference and relationship between first-, second-, and third-person epistemic claims. An example of first-person knowledge is the purely subjective experience of seeing rain outside. An example of second-person knowledge is the intersubjective experience of being informed of rain outside by someone who just had that purely subjective experience. An example of third-person knowledge is the objective experience of assessing data that is not first-person and not second-person, and realizing something about the significance or meaning of this data (for example, being informed via television that there is a 99 percent chance of rain tomorrow).[1]

First-person knowledge is purely subjective. It corresponds to the rationalism end of the spectrum, because rationalism is all about the "mind alone." In sharp contrast, third-person knowledge simply cannot be attained by the mind or individual alone. This form of knowledge requires sufficient quality and quantity of second-person and/or first-person sources. It corresponds to the empiricism end of the spectrum, because empiricism—defined more generally than just "physical experience"—is all about convention and "common sense." Second-person knowledge corresponds to neither end of the spectrum because it is the necessary liaison between these two. It would seem as though two fundamental predicates of legitimate second-person knowledge are respect and trust—that is, respect and trust for the person who makes the original/first-person claim. Not only does Wilber's model account for the rationalism-empiricism binary, but it also accounts for that between reductionism and holism. Both first- and third- person knowledge concern the individual—the former concerns the individual person, while the latter concerns the individual idea that is claimed to be objectively true. Second-person knowledge is social or relational. It depends upon others and one's relationship with them. Furthermore, it is knowledge based upon respect and trust, rather than private perception or public testament.

I see that the most comprehensive way to understand epistemic normativity and its application to the topic of trans-mysticality is this spectrum-oriented methodology outlined by Wilber, which coherently transcends and includes the more particular and constitutive perspectives already discussed. The most comprehensive view that one can gain concerning the epistemic normativity of trans-mysticality is the view that considers information, data, or evidence *in alignment with this spectrum*. Such material must come from first-, second-, and third-person accounts simultaneously, and from accounts that do not share the same holistic, spectrum-oriented methodology or epistemic view concerning trans-mysticality. Thus, beginning with first-person information, I shall now provide evidence that gives me reason to see the epistemic normativity of trans-mysticality.

First-Person Evidence Affirming Trans-mysticality

The first experience that I alone have had (disregarding others claiming to experience anything similar) is called ego death. This experience, occurring multiple times throughout the past four years, has allowed me to realize that my ultimate identity is not physical, not emotional, not mental, and not individual. If this claim about human identity does not constitute "trans-mysticality" for the reader, then I apologize; however, I believe that many people would regard me as crazy or insane to believe this. The first time that I experienced ego death was while having a lucid dream, which is a dream in which one realizes that one is dreaming. Acknowledging the dream for what it was, I realized that literally everything constitutive of this experience was "not real," meaning

Chapter 8 - The Biggest Taboo

"not physical" or "not waking-state phenomena." I realized that literally any aspect of the experience that I could perceive or identify *was not real*.

The dream-sensations were not real, the dream-emotions were not real, the dream-thoughts were not real. My dream-body, the experience of myself as an individual, was not real. Yet despite the fact that all my experience was unreal, "I" still existed—but absolutely nothing perceivable constituted this "I." I existed as the source of perception, but not as the objects or phenomena I perceived. I was simply *pure being*. Subsequently, I realized that if I am pure being, most fundamentally, then my ultimate identity could not be conceptually or linguistically reduced to any limitation or thing. Several other experiences while meditating invoked the same authentic realization concerning identity. While sitting in stillness/emptiness, I realized that *I still am*, despite not thinking anything. I realized that I am not a mind or thinking thing, because I still exist even when that "mind" and the thoughts constituting it disappear for uncertain stretches of "time."

Another trans-mystical experience/realization that I have had personally is seeing auras of light, ranging different colors, engulfing people's bodies. I do not know if these auras are the invention of my mind or if my mind is recognizing an inherent category of reality. However, this perception is very real for me, aside from its epistemic normativity beyond the scope of first-person inference, exclusively. For several years now, I have also been able to focus my perception on certain areas of my body and, in doing so, "activate" a noticeable amount of energy or "subtle sensation" concentrated and limited to that specific location. For instance, if I sufficiently concentrate on the space between my eyeballs, then, suddenly, I feel a slight tingling or prickling in that top-middle region. The perception gains intensity as I further realize/experience a certain rotation or spinning of that energy activated. I have tried to see whether I can create the same experience on any bodily location rather than the areas to which my phenomenological success has been limited. However, this attempt has proven to be unsuccessful, showing me that there must be something quite special or significant about the particular locations allowing me to activate such energy.

The amount of second-person information about trans-mysticality to which I have access is significantly greater than the amount of first-person information.

Second-Person Evidence Affirming Trans-mysticality

The following individuals have each been important parts of my life for the past two and a half years. I could not have more respect for any of them given all their credentials of which I am aware. The amount of trust that I have for four of them is equivalent to the amount of trust I have for my closest family members and friends, while the amount of trust that I have for the other three is equivalent to the amount of trust I have for my closest professors and instructors. In this section, I shall describe my specific relationship to each one and then I shall list all of his credentials along with all of the trans-mystical claims that he has given me reason to believe constitute epistemic normativity.

Two years ago, I met Michael Richardson. Richardson played Division I college basketball at Wright State University before transferring to Georgetown College. While studying ethics at Oxford University, he realized that the path he was on did not align with his authentic self. This realization moved Richardson to shift away from a focus on medicine and to earn a degree in English and to become an ESL teacher and student of Zen Buddhism in Japan. After graduating, he went to live by himself on his family's farm in Kentucky for five consecutive years, without contact from anyone else, only meditating and writing. During the fourth year, Richardson claims to have experienced *kensho*, which is a Zen term that denotes sudden awakening to nirvana or nothingness. This realization prompted him to burn all twelve hundred typewritten pages that he had accumulated to that point while living by himself on the farm—symbolizing for Richardson that, after this authentic awakening experience, every single word in the English dictionary literally had a profoundly different meaning for him. He then went on to write a poetry anthology titled *Suicide Dictionary*, which was published by O-Books later that year.[2] As of now, he stewards C-Cam (short for Creativity Camera) and the Renaissance Project.[3] My relationship with Richardson led me to connect with his good friend and entrepreneurial partner, Doc Barham.

Barham works as a "transformation expert." Since March 2010, he has been my mentor, life coach, and dear friend. Barham has been featured in the *Los Angeles Times, Fast Company, Psychology Today,* the History Channel *(Ancient Aliens), Business Insider,* the *Huffington Post,* as well as PBS. His client backgrounds include Zappos.com, Playboy, NASA, NFL,

Chapter 8 - The Biggest Taboo

Oprah.com, PGA, CMA, the Oprah Winfrey Network, NBA, World Series Poker, NASCAR, and the NCAA. Specifically, Barham's individual clients include NBA All-Star Elton Brand, along with ex-president of digital media for Oprah.com and the Oprah Winfrey Network, Robert Tercek. The latter figure remarks that:

> Doc has been my personal professional career coach for several years, and he has helped me achieve great results. I give him my highest recommendation. In 2005, I worked with Tony Robbins, and after that I did a project which involved more than 200 professional coaches, so I had the opportunity to meet several excellent coaches. In my experience, Doc Barham is the best coach I've ever worked with.[4]

Barham has also experienced remote viewing, kensho, and subtle-realm masters. Furthermore, he claims to experience any chakra (supposed energy vortexes connecting one's physical, emotional, and mental bodies) at will. He also claims to have communicated with extraterrestrial beings while dreaming, a week before experiencing several UFOs hover several hundred feet over his vehicle for several minutes while near Area 51. One of Barham's mentors and friends is a *chi gong* master named Master Jo.

I have not yet met Master Jo digitally or physically, but have heard about him from Barham and saw a video demonstrating his abilities featured on *Ripley's Believe It or Not*. Jo has known kung fu since age seven and chi gong since age sixteen. In the video demonstration, he raises a towel to near-boiling temperature without even touching it. The ability is shown using infrared camera technology. It is affirmed by Dr. Michael Upsher, a well-known MD who has experienced Jo's energetic healing treatment and who claims to know that it is real.[5] Another acquaintance of Barham, his meditation teacher whom I have not yet met but respect and trust, is Dr. Shinzen Young.

Young, a longtime Zen master, authored *The Science of Enlightenment* series.[6] Young's own teacher is over one hundred years old, making him the oldest living Zen master on this planet. Aside from Young's experiences of spiritual enlightenment, perhaps even more astonishing is his claim of profound visionary experiences for several consecutive years while studying under a "Taoist wizard" in his mid-twenties.[7] These experiences were such that he saw blatant and coherent subtle/psychic phenomena merged in his everyday physical settings (e.g. perceiving nonphysical visions of beings from greater dimensions while sitting awake at his home)—which, if interpreted by conventional psychology/ psychiatry, would constitute schizophrenia. Yet, like all of these second-person sources of trans-mystical knowledge, Young seems not only extraordinarily gifted intellectually, but also equally wholesome both emotionally and morally.

With Barham, I also met Mick Quinn (digitally) in July 2010. We have remained in regular contact since that time. Quinn used to be a serial Wall Street entrepreneur. After experiencing kensho more than ten years ago, though, he realized that maximizing his personal development in all areas of growth mattered much more than merely making money. Quinn coauthored *The Uncommon Path of Awakening Authentic Joy*, which reached number one in its Amazon category of Consciousness and Thought. He regularly appears on the radio with Jack Canfield, author of *Chicken Soup for the Soul* and star of *The Secret*, along with Dr. Deepak Chopra, who *Time* magazine named among the top one hundred most influential people of the twentieth century (as the "poet-prophet of alternative medicine"). Quinn now works in a Guatemalan slum with his wife teaching Integral Theory to students and helping increase food, power, and stability.[8] During a Facebook discussion that involved numerous participants concerning the reality of chi gong—namely, a video that displayed one master's supposed ability to ignite newspaper without touching it physically—Quinn claimed that his old master, now dead, was not only spiritually advanced but also energetically powerful such that he could (telekinetically) knock down objects from across the room. The last person with whom Barham connected me, beginning in the spring of 2011, is his own mentor, Dr. Pete Peterson—who started working for the government before age thirteen as an inventor and engineer.

According to Peterson, not only has the government been suppressing information about trans-mystical/paranormal phenomena since the early twentieth century, but he himself has invented technology of fantastic proportion, which has been suppressed by government powers, but which—for instance—reverses gravity, or allows any message to be communicated anywhere in the universe instantaneously.[9] Barham and Peterson together claim that he has three PhDs and decades' worth of independent research spent with dozens of Nobel Prize winners. Aside from his credentials, among Peterson's other trans-mystical claims are that he used to throw "spoon-bending parties" during the 1970s, and, perhaps even more unbelievably, that he is permanently awake—meaning that he *always* lucid dreams and that his experience of time relative to the dreaming state is equivalent to hours and even days relative to the waking state. According to his description, Peterson lives not just one life, but many lives/roles simultaneously, continually experienced during his perpetuated state of lucidity while dreaming. For instance, one of these dream worlds that he experiences/visits each night features several family members who have been dead relative to the waking state—yet, according to Peterson, he visits these alternate realities each night, lucid the entire time, experiencing a reality that is as meaningful and complex as the reality that one experiences while awake. He also claims to know individuals whose energetic power is such that they can literally fly—meaning they can levitate their own bodies at will.

Now that I have provided second-person evidence suggestive of trans-mysticality's epistemic normativity, I will review the most prominent and cited third-person sources that do likewise, followed by sources that attempt to debunk or disclaim it. The order of this review will be chronological for practical reasons.

Third-Person Evidence Affirming and Negating Trans-mysticality

Ninian Smart argues in "Interpretation and Mystical Experience" that distinguishing between the experience and the interpretation of mystical experience is imperative for scholars to do.[10] While the experience of "oneness with God" may be an authentic experience of something, Smart contends that interpretation still plays a powerful and often overlooked role in relation to the subject's labeling this experience, whatever it is, with religious language. "Phenomenologically, mysticism is everywhere the same... [but the] truth of interpretations depends in large measure on factors extrinsic to the mystical experience itself" (87). Put differently, Smart sees no reason to believe that trans-mysticality, as experience, is not real. He is not denying the reality of trans-mystical claims. However, Smart is certainly remaining skeptical about what these experiences *mean*, as opposed to that they are real.

Psychiatrist Ian Stevenson argues for the reality of past lives in *Twenty Cases Suggestive of Reincarnation*. This work features twenty separate instances that, from a scientific standpoint, individually and collectively make a case for the trans-mystical experience of remembering one's past life(s). In the words of Stevenson:

> The case usually starts when a small child of two to four years of age begins talking to his parents or siblings of a life he led in another time and place. The child usually feels a considerable pull back toward the events of the life and he frequently importunes his parents to let him return to the community where he claims that he formerly lived. If the child makes enough particular statements about the previous life, the parents (usually reluctantly) begin inquiries about their accuracy. Often, indeed usually, such attempts at verification do not occur until several years after the child has begun to speak of the previous life. If some verification results, members of the two families visit each other and ask the child whether he recognizes places, objects, and people of his supposed previous existence.[11]

Each case follows this method of scientific reasoning to demonstrate that such data could not be reflective of mere chance or pure coincidence, but rather indicative that the children featured are not insane or delusional but quite the opposite—though (perhaps) not yet rationally or intellectually mature.

Frances Beer argues in *Women and Mystical Experience in the Middle Ages* that this phenomenon was largely ignored and suppressed during its time due to the excess of patriarchy and its equating such trans-mystical claims with witchcraft, sorcery, and heresy.[12] Beer speculates whether this bias against trans-mysticality, by associating it with feminine treachery and sinful disobedience, was culturally inherited by the Enlightenment-age thinkers to follow—which would explain the sharp distinction that such revolutionaries made between "reason," "truth," and "science" on the one hand, and "magic," "witchcraft," and "occultism" on the other. The text outlines writings of numerous women from this particular context who clearly demonstrated a certain disregard for submitting to the (ironically) anti-trans-mystical, Church-dominated status quo. Speaking on this "courageous independence," Beer asks whether it was "because [these

Chapter 8 - The Biggest Taboo

women] were unusually strong-minded . . . or [whether] the confidence [spoke] out [because of] their spiritual experiences." He adds:

> . . . Some special strength must have been required to enable them to receive and articulate such powerful, and potentially shattering, visionary experiences. . . . However reluctant some modern readers may be to accept the validity of these revelations, there can be no question as to . . . their utter confidence in what they have been shown. (8–9)

David Young argues in *Being Changed by Cross-Cultural Encounters: The Anthropology of Extraordinary Experience* that anthropology, as a discursive whole, still receives a subtle but considerable influence from imperialism.[13] The Tibetan villager may no longer be labeled as "other," but the Tibetan shaman, the Sufi saint, the Taoist sage still fall under this category of "otherness" for the majority of anthropologists. He states:

> When the anthropologist has an extraordinary experience [that] challenges his/her conception of reality, the experience can be suppressed and the "threat" minimized. Or the experience can be accepted as valid and one's schemata reorganized to accommodate the new reality. In either case, the investigator may choose not to relate these experiences to others because of fear of ostracism. . . . because of [this fear], an entire segment of cross-cultural experience common to many investigators, is not available for discussion and scientific investigation. (8)

Fear of ostracism within the intellectual collective is a powerful, repressive force. The origin of this fear is rationalist bias:

> As a child of Western culture, anthropology is the heir to an intellectual tradition that, until recently, has not taken extraordinary experiences seriously. The case of dreams and visions can be used to illustrate this point. As a result of the eighteenth-century Enlightenment, intellectuals dismissed visionary experiences as the source of a belief in spirits and ghosts. Experiences of such phenomena were described as hallucinations . . . (8)

Young proposes an "experiential" rather than "rational" approach —which shifts the researcher's focus from abstract rationalization that treats the trans-mystical claimant as "object" to experiential conscientiousness that instead regards this person *as a subject*. Charles Laughlin honors this paradigmatic adjustment in his chapter "Psychic Energy & Transpersonal Experience: A biogenetic structural account of the Tibetan Dumo Yoga Practice." Laughlin takes such an adjustment even further, though, insisting that while some scholars indeed utilize the experiential rather than rational approach in order to acknowledge the subject for "what it is," very few academics take the measures to "incubate alternative states themselves" (101). Why? Because "most westerners, including most scientists, are very poor phenomenologists" (104). Laughlin walks his talk, supposedly, by himself engaging in the experimental/ subjective element of his research. In recounting one such experience, Laughlin writes:

> One of the earliest and most profound experiences I had of psychic energy was during a weekend "loving kindness" retreat in 1979. Part of the work was to imagine a rose in the heart region . . . numerous visual images spontaneously arose during this retreat . . . At one point while in steady state of absorption and blissful peace, the image of a beautiful blond female figure dressed in a red schift appeared walking away from me in my left visual field. (109)

It seems only fitting that a discipline as relatively progressive and contextualized as anthropology recognizes the subtle flaws and limitations imposed upon it. If fear of ostracism still plays a role in *this* community's integrity, then I can only imagine how much more of an influence such fear has upon traditional scientific disciplines, such as physics, biology, and chemistry.

Mark Kasprow argues in "A Review of Transpersonal Theory and Its Application to the Practice of Psychotherapy" that trans-mystical experiences can be significantly beneficial for individuals with a "healthy ego development" in helping cultivate "the highest human qualities, including altruism, creativity, and intuitive wisdom," but also that they can be somewhat the opposite for individuals with an unhealthy ego

Chapter 8 - The Biggest Taboo

development—instead leading to psychosis. This relationship between trans-mysticality and "craziness" is important to consider. What is the main difference between someone who is holistically healthier subsequent to trans-mystical exploration and someone whose psyche is instead greatly fragmented or conflicted? After all, hear the words of a famous spiritual master named Nisargadatta Maharaj:

> Look, my thumb touches my forefinger. Both touch and are touched . . . I find that somehow, by shifting the focus of attention, I become the very thing I look at and experience the kind of consciousness it has; I become the inner witness of the thing. I call this capacity of entering other focal points of consciousness "love." Love says: "I am everything." Wisdom says: "I am nothing." Between the two my life flows. Since at any point of time and space I can be both the subject and object of experience, I express it by saying that I am both, and neither, and beyond both.

As Kasprow remarks in light of Maharaj's statement, it is extremely easy for someone to interpret the quote as reflective of severe schizophrenia—an unhealthy delusion regarding self and reality. He cites Wilber in order to make sense of this apparent predicament between trans-mystical authenticity and schizophrenic psychosis:

> Wilber uses his model of prepersonal, personal, and transpersonal stages to explain the apparent similarities between regressive psychotic states and experiences of mystical, transcendent union. Many poets, philosophers, and clinicians have pointed out the apparent similarities between the utterings of madmen and those of sages. In both psychosis and "enlightenment," individuals appear to have altered ego boundaries and to think and act in irrational ways.
>
> *However*—
>
> . . . in the case of a psychotic regression, this is a pre-rational, pre-egoic state, and in the case of healthy mystical experience, it is a trans-rational state built upon and extended beyond a

normal, healthy ego. Wilber names this confusion between the two conditions the "pre/trans fallacy," and Freud's criticisms of religion as a regressive defense may be partly understood in terms of this error.

The significance of Kasprow's work, here, is this relationship between psychotic regression, which arises due to unhealthy ego development, and healthy mystical experience, which is not below the threshold of rationality but rather beyond it. The experience of trans-rationality can still be researched and understood rationally—but the experience in itself cannot.[14]

As mentioned briefly, rationalist bias, or "scientistic bias," gets in the way of researching trans-mysticality in addition to Wilber's pre/trans fallacy. James McClenon argues that:

> Paranormal and anomalous experiences, seemingly a subcategory of mystical perception, are often ignored by academics due to scientistic bias. . . . More than half of American national samples report such episodes. The most common forms of experience include apparitions, precognitive dreams, waking extrasensory perceptions, out-of-body experience, sleep paralysis, and contacts with the dead.[15]

Yet I am not sure which bias/fallacy is more irrationally discriminative against giving trans-mysticality the third-person/academic voice that it deserves. To generalize, it would seem that the "average person," if you will, is more inclined to categorize the trans-mystical claimant as "crazy," "schizophrenic," or "unhealthy," while the average scientist is more inclined to categorize that individual as "irrational," "unintelligent," or "biased." This review will now shift from acknowledging and considering third-person sources that are "pro-trans-mysticality" to ones that are "pro-commonsense" or, as implied, "anti-trans-mysticality."

James Randi is perhaps the quintessence of this opposing worldview. He first made an international name for himself as an escape artist and magician. Today, Randi devotes his time and effort to debunking trans-mystical claims with his James Randi Educational Foundation, which serves as "an educational resource on the paranormal, pseudoscientific,

Chapter 8 - The Biggest Taboo

and the supernatural"—which, according to my definitions of trans-mysticality and epistemic normativity, and considering the track record of JREF,[16] translates to "an educational resource devoted to disprove any epistemic normativity related to trans-mysticality." While the image of this organization appears to take a neutral, objective, unbiased, and open-minded stance in assessing the truth-value of trans-mystical claims, this does not seem to be true, for several reasons.

The foundation's most well-known offer, perhaps, is one million dollars for any individual who demonstrates to its team, in a systematically controlled scientific manner and setting, that his or her supposed trans-mystical ability is real. For the past fifteen years, hundreds of claimants have attempted to demonstrate their ability in accordance with such a structure—but no one has convinced Randi and his board of anything paranormal, pseudoscientific, and/or supernatural. This fact seems rather strange considering the amount of evidence suggestive of trans-mysticality's epistemic normativity but, when considered more thoroughly, actually makes simple psychological sense. Randi and his foundation are not and cannot be as truly neutral, objective, unbiased, and open-minded as it would like the public to believe. The reason why this statement holds true is even simpler: Randi, and the worldview that he represents, does not want to be proven wrong. Ironically, science, which in theory should be totally objective, is in many ways far more enslaved by its own ego than is the individual who claims egoic transcendence.

Psychoanalysis on the language of JREF's articles webpage painfully indicates an immense amount of negative emotion, namely ridicule, projected in response to the claimants who have recently been "debunked," as evidenced in the titles to these articles. "Journalist Promotes Nonsense," "Down-Under Developments," "Dump This Series," "Apologies," . . . "Dumb Is As Dumb Does," "Geller Reviews," "Australia Takes a Backward Step," "Those Stupid Patches," "Hot Item," "How to Swindle the Suckers," "Another Healer Blooms," "Sentenced," "That Bogus Patent," . . . "Magic Rebuffed," "The Bates Debate," "Sylvia In the Suds," "Buy Now," "Enough Damn Lightbulbs," "More Patent Office Nonsense," . . . Science—*true* science—has no business messing with ego, emotion, and ridicule—or so it would seem relative to what science is in theory. Yet far too often, what may be true in theory does not translate as being true in practice. This unscientific contradictory language may in fact be most illustrated in Randy Moore's article "Debunking the

Paranormal: We Should Teach Critical Thinking as a Necessity for Living, Not Just As a Tool for Science."

I believe that the language and logic underlying Moore's work here is indeed quite reflective and accurate of the general viewpoint crusading against this possibility that not all trans-mystical experiences are crazy or stupid. The article begins by noting "our" gradual decline of scientific literacy throughout the decades. "Pseudoscience" has gained more and more prominence, brainwashing more and more people to be simply delusional. For instance, "The popularity of astrology and similar pseudoscientific shams attests to the unwillingness to think critically" (4).[17] As Moore sees it, astrology is not real science because it has much more to do with the categories of business and fantasy than with those of truth and reality. Just look at all the pop astrologers who make their living by adding color and excitement to their customers' lives. For Moore, the fact that something like astrology is so commercialized means that it has more to do with emotion than with reason. For Moore, such con-artistry leaves otherwise innocent agents of reason tragically vulnerable to being ripped off.

He continues by sarcastically explaining that if someone wants to know the sex of his or her unborn child, and if this person believes in trans-mysticality, then (s)he might as well ask a so-called fortune teller about it rather than have the doctor check its DNA structure—since, clearly, if trans-mysticality is at all real, then it should have the same practical utility as conventional science. This belief assumes that "science," whatever that should mean, is not only the best means for acquiring knowledge and understanding, but is also the only means, really. Why? Because "There are no sacred truths, no forbidden questions and no testable issues too sensitive to be questioned. Unlike religion and the paranormal, science values criticism and thrives on debate" (4). Indeed, "science" has absolutely no dogmas, no biases, no fallacies, no neuroses, and no psychoses of its own, no "forbidden question" that its adherents are too afraid to ask. Even though fear of ostracism is certainly at play (and currently winning the game), there is no "testable issue too sensitive to be questioned," despite that "science" is worried frantically in the back of its collective mind that, in parallel, its most dominant worldview relative to more recently emergent ones is being outdated and replaced, just as the Church's most dominant worldview succumbed to the Renaissance, Reformation, Scientific Revolution, Enlightenment, etc.

Chapter 8 - The Biggest Taboo

Moore rhetorically asks, "What's the evidence for talking with dead people or predicting the future? None, of course. Moreover, psychics and ESP violate the commonsense knowledge that all communication requires our normal sense" (7). Yet alas, this statement is based upon two dogmas or assumptions: 1) that there in fact is no evidence for talking with dead people or predicting the future, and 2) that all communication really requires only our normal sense. Moore responds by proclaiming that, "If you're going to accept spirits and ghosts as real, you might as well accept headlines such as 'Elvis's Ghost Is Caught in Mom's Vacuum Cleaner'" (7). Yet alas, again, the statement makes a category judgment before that statement is even thought through or written. This category judgment, using my terms, is that trans-mysticality is fantasy and science is reality. Moving along, "Paranormal hokum is a multi-billion-dollar business [taking advantage of] people's inability or refusal to think critically. . . . Nevertheless, the paranormal will probably remain a big business because it provides a convenient blue sky and rainbow" (9). The latter part of this claim further reinforces the aforementioned category judgment—that "a convenient blue sky and rainbow," or whatever myth this phrase signifies, is not nor cannot be real in the same way that pure, infinite energy, infinite simplicity, transforming into differentiated, infinite phenomena, infinite complexity, can itself be "real."

But if the obedient scientist were to rethink his own deprived mythology such to reinterpret it as something as wondrous and fantastical as the myth/idol/joke that Moore means by "convenient blue sky and rainbow," then perhaps he would come to realize that, from one perspective, even the big bang theory is proof of "magic"—proof that while science is supposed to map reality, reality is *not necessarily* "not-fantasy." This category judgment is so simple—yet so subtle and determining, simultaneously. If fantasy *can* equal reality, then the psychological or emotional resistance against opening one's mind to the first-, second-, and third-person evidence indicative of trans-mysticality's epistemic normativity significantly lessens. Moore adds " . . . we can't force students to submit their beliefs to tests of scientific reasoning and logic. Many people's beliefs are much stronger than their willingness to think, their desire to learn or their ability to reason" (9). Psychoanalytically, this statement could easily and (again) all too ironically apply to Moore himself and the worldview that his article so captures. His belief that trans-mysticality is fantasy and science is reality may indeed be much

177

stronger than his "willingness to think," his "desire to learn," or his "ability to reason." But there is hope for the crusade against trans-mysticality—for " . . . we can teach students the value of basing their decisions on logic and evidence rather than on blind faith, hocus-pocus, mythology, religious dogma and fantasy" (9). Again, as evidenced in this last remark by Moore, trans-mysticality is fantasy and science is reality and, even more psychologically entrenched, fantasy cannot be reality. Nietzschean pacification has indeed lulled the soul's once ecstatic love affair with goodness, truth, and beauty.

While I could cite more examples of discourse that make a case against trans-mysticality, I do not think that this is needed. I have provided ample first-person, second-person, and third-person evidence pointing to the reality and value of trans-mystical experience—which is essential, in this case, because the stance that I have taken throughout this research faces the burden of proof far more (on the surface) than does its opposition. Still, to illustrate the logic and psychology of this latter stance, the fewer sources that I have incorporated nonetheless compensate for such quantitative deficiency, by their exemplifying this particular worldview, and from my in-depth conversation with and psychoanalysis of them. The remainder of this project shall engage in a dialogue between three most relevant worldviews in hope of assessing their respective "pros" and "cons" in relation to the subject of trans-mysticality, and then using this assessment as conclusive testament to the present essay. The reader now has a much more comprehensive outlook on the research topic as a whole. It is time to determine how this individual should interpret such a topic.

Contributions and Shortcomings of Three Main Perspectives on Trans-mysticality

Francis Fukuyama implements a strategy in *The End of History and the Last Man* that I seek to utilize for this final section. He acknowledges three most relevant, or encompassing, ideologies that have been in conflict with one another especially throughout this past century. These ideologies are traditionalism, liberalism, and postmodernism. The method is particularly effective because it not only acknowledges the "biggest players in the game," so to speak, but it also compares and contrasts them. I shall

Chapter 8 - The Biggest Taboo

do likewise for the remainder of this paper. These three perspectives are to be called anti-trans-mysticality, neutral-trans-mysticality, and pro-trans-mysticality. Moore epitomizes the first view, for reasons already stated, while Wilber epitomizes the third view, for reasons already stated. For reasons now to be stated, Foucault epitomizes the second view.

The process/system-oriented holism in Foucault's epistemic style moves him away from considering matters of *positive* goodness and truth. Foucault abstains from making any *deliberate normative assertion* both epistemically and ethically. Instead, he—and the perspective that he represents—chooses to analyze preexisting norms and their relationship with the historical structures and processes that led to their construction and perpetuation. Foucault's ideology epitomizes the neutral-trans-mysticality view because it could care less about the epistemic/ethical normativity of trans-mystical experience; it cares only about analyzing and understanding *how* this subject has become so abnormal and taboo—for the most part. Someone like Foucault chooses to suspend judgment concerning what Moore and Wilber instead choose to judge. Moore prejudges that trans-mystical claimants are all full of shit, put crudely. Wilber judges that some trans-mystical claimants are actually full of truth. Foucault would judge that trans-mysticality is definitely far more abnormal and repressed than the gross majority of academia gives credit—but without the intellectual strength and courage that Wilber has. Please know that while I already see more comprehension and value in Wilber's position, it would be improper and irresponsible of me to dismiss the other two ideologies just as immediately, without any regard for their respective contributions along with their respective shortcomings.

Starting with anti-trans-mysticality, it is plain to see that this viewpoint is valuable because of its skepticism and reliability. Skepticism, arguably, is equally as important for any intellectual dilemma as imagination or realism. Skepticism serves a natural/inherent and useful function—that is, skepticism in appropriate moderation. Anti-trans-mysticality's skepticism makes its method most substantial and reliable, which reinforces public respect and trust for conventional science, and convention in general. However, the skeletons of this perspective's pros have grown excessively in direct accord with its very flaws and contradictions. These shortcomings, put simply, are absolutism and extreme bias. I cannot help but think that many scientists and people in general who fit this ideological category share roughly the same mindset/

worldview as an absolutistic, extremely biased priest alive during medieval times, except their religion or mythology has shifted from absolute overemphasis of the Above, of Platonic idealism, to absolute overemphasis of the Below, of Nietzschean materialism.

Neutral-trans-mysticality's positive features, or contributions, include flexibility and concreteness. This perspective shares the same empiricist/overemphasis of the first perspective, but its holism (rather than reductionism) allows it to be significantly more fluent or flexible than anti-trans-mysticality because, understood plainly, systems/contexts—relative to this "human condition," at least—are changing far more rapidly than are the universe's more inherent tendencies. Foucault's worldview demonstrates both such flexibility and concreteness. However, neutral-trans-mysticality commits the same absolutism as anti-trans-mysticality does, except not from regarding only the Below and not the Above, but from absolutely overemphasizing the Many over the One—intersubjectivity over both subjectivity and objectivity.

If intersubjectivity is all that matters, if there is only context and our being conditioned by it, and if there is no such thing as "truth" or "goodness" in some inherently normative sense, then trans-mysticality becomes meaningless despite all the evidence that implies its meaningfulness. However, if subjectivity, intersubjectivity, and objectivity ("I," "We," and "It(s)") are valued just as much as intersubjectivity alone, then the postmodern ideology that Foucault represents, in alignment with this second possible way of interpreting trans-mysticality, ceases to be postmodern and, in light of this topic, it ceases to be neutral. So the second major shortcoming of neutral-trans-mysticality is not extreme bias (or anywhere near the same degree as with anti-trans-mysticality), but instead, for lack of a better word, apathy. Yet—the time in which we now live does not call for apathy—it calls for curiosity, spontaneity, courage, action, wholeness, wisdom, love.

Concluding Remarks on the "Cash Value" of This Research

Perhaps my understanding of psychology does not apply here, but I am convinced, based on first-person account, that simply realizing the greater possibility that trans-mysticality is real can transform that individual for the better, enhancing or incepting qualities such as

Chapter 8 - The Biggest Taboo

spontaneity, courage, action, wholeness, wisdom, and love. I am also convinced, based on second-person evidence, that experiencing and living the reality of trans-mysticality oneself brings *exponentially more* goodness and truth than merely realizing its greater possibility. We live in a context that is dominated by anti-trans-mysticality and neutral-trans-mysticality. Either "fantasy" is unreal, or we can never know for ourselves and should not even bother trying. Yet, as pro-trans-mysticality, Wilber, a rapidly growing community of others, and myself agree, the previous statement/inference/belief should be, and is in fact, "either 'fantasy' is real, or we have nothing to lose and the opposite to gain from attempting to know ourselves."

Granted, we must of course honor all unique contributions that the other two perspectives bring. There is value in a moderate degree of skepticism; there is value to concrete demonstration; there is value to scientific convention; and there is value to flexibility or fluency due to acknowledging the importance of systems, relationships, and collectivity in general. But there is also value to seeing the coherence and connection between two seemingly indifferent or contradictory worldviews (in addition to seeing the two in the first place), so as to synthesize one that both transcends and includes them in apposite moderation and optimal wholeness. Perhaps an entirely new worldview or evolution in collective consciousness is, and has been, emerging. Perhaps the emergence of this new, comprehensive, holistic, and integrative way of thinking and living shall positively transform today's global society/culture *exponentially more* than the emergence of modernity/liberalism positively transformed the unhealthy, outdated, and/or exhausted society/culture of *its* time.

Make no mistake; my intention with this work, as a whole, is not to convince the reader that trans-mysticality definitely has epistemic normativity. Rather, it is to show the anti-trans-mysticalist and neutral-trans-mysticalist hold subtle flaws in their worldviews in relation to the greater completeness and unity of the pro-trans-mysticalist's worldview, as epitomized by Wilber and defined by holisticity. My goal with this paper is to inspire its reader to see that 1) trans-mysticality's taboo is excessive and for the most part unuttered (especially within the intellectual community), 2) there is a vast, integrative, and comprehensive amount of legitimate evidence that gives reason to see beyond this taboo, and 3) there is immense value to opening one's mind more and expanding one's conscientiousness toward the possibility that one's (most influential) worldview is really inadequate to maximize this opportunity that we scholars, and agents of positive global change, have before us.

This opportunity as I see it is quite literally—and likely—a Second Renaissance, a Second Reformation, a Second Enlightenment, a Second American Revolution, a Second Industrial Revolution, etc., but relative to this pluralistic, global, exponential context that marks planet Earth at this time. This opportunity, *these opportunities,* are such that we individuals can co-create a world in which the human potential is maximized and all life on Earth is allowed to thrive and flourish in fantastical equilibrium and abundance. Perhaps now is finally the time when humankind can wake up from its cocoon and emerge soaring as a magnificent butterfly. In light of such speculations and such emotional and hyperbolic language, know with certainty that I myself hold with maximum conviction that addressing and fixing trans-mysticality's taboo is ineffably worthwhile, especially for anyone intelligent and privileged enough to have just processed all of this information.

Notes

1. Ken Wilber, *A Brief History of Everything* (Boston: Shambhala Publications, 1996).

2. Paul Lonely, *Suicide Dictionary: The History of Rainbow Abbey* (Ropley, UK: O-Books, 2007).

3. Michael Richardson-Borne's Facebook page, created Nov. 2007, accessed Dec. 1, 2011, facebook.com/michaelrich.

4. DocBarham.net, 5 July 2011, retrieved Dec. 2, 2011, docbarham.net.

5. "A Qigong [chi gong] Master Emits Heat From Hand at Over 200 Degrees," *Ripley's Believe It or Not!* YouTube, 6 Oct. 2009, accessed Dec. 2, 2011, www.youtube.com/watch?feature=player_embedded&v=qWCn8PkHeuk.

6. "Meditation in Action," July 5, 2006, web Nov. 29, 2011, www.shinzen.org.

7. Doc Barham, Michael Richardson, and H.B. Augustine, Ask Integral Experts: Asking the Questions, Living the Answers," 1 July 2010, accessed Dec. 5, 2011, http://xtraordinaryoutcomes.com/interviews.

8. Mick Quinn, author of *The Uncommon Path*, accessed Dec. 1, 2011, www.mickquinn.com.

9. "Project Camelot Interviews Dr. Pete Peterson: Part 1 of 3," Project Camelot, *YouTube*, created Sept. 2, 2009, accessed Dec. 3, 2011, www.youtube.com/watch?v=ooSRh7V68uk.

10. Ninian Smart, "Interpretation and Mystical Experience," *Religious Studies* 1.1 (1965): pp. 75–87, accessed at jstor.org on Dec. 1, 2011.

11. Ian Stevenson, *Twenty Cases Suggestive of Reincarnation* (Charlottesville: University Press of Virginia, 1974).

12. Frances Beer, *Women and Mystical Experience in the Middle Ages*. (Woodbridge, Suffolk, UK: Boydell Press, 1992).

13. David E. Young and Jean Goulet, *Being Changed: The Anthropology of Extraordinary Experience* (Peterborough, Ont., Canada: Broadview Press, 1994).

14. Mark Kasprow and Bruce Scotton, "A Review of Transpersonal Theory and Its Application to the Practice of Psychotherapy," *Journal of Psychotherapy Practice and Research* 8.12 (1999).

15. James McClenon, content pages of the encyclopedia of religion and social science, Hartford Institute for Religious Research, July 14, 2006, accessed Dec. 5, 2011, http://hirr.hartsem.edu/ency/mysticism.htm.

16. The James Randi Educational Foundation, Oct. 2000, accessed Dec. 4, 2011, www.randi.org.

17. Randy Moore, "Debunking the Paranormal: We Should Teach Critical Thinking as a Necessity for Living, Not Just as a Tool for Science," *University of California Press* 1 (Jan. 1992): pp. 4–9, accessed at jstor.org on Dec. 4, 2011.

Chapter 9
The Gateway into the Future: Mysticism for Our Times

By Thomas Hübl

Mysticism is the love of God. Mysticism is the love of the One. Mysticism is what fills our heart most deeply and expresses the longing for profound unity, the deep connection with God within.

Mysticism motivates the poets, and it inspires great scientists and seekers who sense that there is a call in their soul to do all that they do in order to recognize this unity within themselves. The beauty of mysticism lies in this love.

A modern mysticism always carries the timeless wisdom within it and it acknowledges that outer life continues to develop. We need answers to contemporary questions. God—the sacred space or the mystic depth dimension—needs a place in our society. If we give this priority a place in our life then everything else follows from it. We have our economics, our sciences, our politics and our education—they all follow and are aligned with this single priority.

Now, at the beginning of the third millennium, we are facing complex questions about life. There are global financial crises, global warming and environmental pollution, famine, ethical questions in science, and much more. All of this concerns us as a collective humanity. What would a culture of awareness look like, a society with answers to these burning questions of our time, and how do we get there? What does a modern path of mysticism beyond a traditional God image look like, and which path can we take to unite the power of the ancient traditions with the evolution of life now? We would need to abandon our ego-oriented view of the world to open ourselves up to a much larger perspective.

For instance, let's imagine that interpersonal friction among human beings is reduced and that we all feel much clearer, more sensitive and connected. We all see everything in everyone else and we allow the flow of much more information in and between us. We become aware of where the "field" of the Earth and its evolutionary intelligence needs more energetic support, and where and how our own evolutionary potential needs to be developed.

Let's imagine too that we are developing a truly global awareness rather than holding an intellectual idea about it. We would feel that a continent like Africa is not separated from the rest of us but is tangibly a part of us all. We would organize collective events for collective shadow work to address the burning issues at hand. We would sense precisely where energy is blocked and where there is a free flow. The entire field of the Earth would be transformed and—as part of this—we would be making way for a new dimension in our human experience.

How could these ideas become reality? When does a vision become real? We want to take a closer look at the possibilities of a shared approach in many people at the same time, so as to increase the focus of awareness and to open up a gateway into the future that even now is taking place in the present.

The Future—Now

Again and again we hear people talking about the future and they generally mean what will happen tomorrow. But the future is the potential into which we can develop. Tomorrow may simply be a repetition of today if it amounts to no more than the continuation of habit. Only if tomorrow is a creative new tomorrow will we be living evolution. Then we will not hope for a better tomorrow but instead will be so present in the now that we develop beyond ourselves and see and experience the bigger picture of humanity.

This is how a new world is created. If we realize our potential we also create a new basis for living from which we can see and interpret reality. This is a new achievement in human awareness.

Chapter 9 - The Gateway into the Future: Mysticism for Our Times

As human beings we are currently experiencing an increase in the collective focal point of consciousness. With a high level of synchronisation and through the practice of the present we can immerse ourselves in a new collective experience. A new "We" will arise from this (see glossary for these terms). A "We" that is not just a collection of individual "me"s but rather a whole new perspective on humanity. We no longer see just people but also the inner worlds in which they experience themselves.

A Transparent World: Transparent Communication

The quality of our habitual communication expands in quantum leaps when we learn to perceive the inner spaces of experience of the people we are with. Transparency means that we are attuned with people and situations—that we learn to see them from an inner perspective, "from inside." It means that we can potentially see everything in everyone else, that we can understand people in their depth, and that we no longer take at face value the whole theatre of life acted out on the stage of life every day. Instead, we begin to allow for the mystical aspects to life in our everyday experience.

What we are calling Transparent Communication requires authentic expression and a particular kind of listening. It requires all the impulses that arise in us in this moment. The more strength and directness that are expressed unfiltered, and are at the same time connected in us, the more authentic we are. All energy or power in us that cannot live moves in front of our perception as a filter. The unlived potential forms the prison in which we find ourselves every day. If we manage to allow the free expression that is connected to the whole then no energy is suppressed in us. We feel freer and at the same time more creative. Our potential can realize itself and the feeling of life-flow arises.

Transparency like this happens when our body-minds (the sum of physical sensations, emotions, and thoughts) become more translucent, when we learn a form of communication that is empathic and at the same time takes place within a transpersonal space. This happens when we perceive much more information than is normally available to us. It provides a new basis for interaction and realization and is the foundation of a new "We."

Thousands of Years of Knowledge in Every Single Moment

Mysticism is the radical path of awakening through all times and in the ordinary everyday "marketplace of life." That is why we call it timeless wisdom: it is independent of the face of time. However, it expresses itself through this face. It is not limited to a specific form but constantly invents itself anew with the evolution of life and consciousness.

Thousands of years of knowledge can be found in the great wisdom traditions. We see there an inner core of principles and we find the "science of awakening" there too. We see an outer casing of culture that forms around this. In all great world religions, like Judaism, Buddhism, Christianity, or Taoism, there is an inner practice of this timeless wisdom. When we understand this more deeply we see that there are similar principles everywhere, that life consists of *being and becoming*, that it contains a deep consciousness aspect that is always present. The principle of the development of souls and the enlightenment of our soul can be found in every single tradition.

To recognize the depth dimension of reality is the great endeavor of all times. But only those who place alignment to God, to the One, in the very center of their lives can achieve this. Only when our whole life is based upon this can we lead an awake life that contributes to an awake culture.

The practice of a mystic is a practice of mindfulness, presence, compassion, love, and clarity. We begin to practice these aspects in every daily life situation: when we walk on the street, when we are in relationship or when we work, when we sit down and when we take time for this holy space in order to listen to the deeper aspect of ourselves.

Mystics deepen this inner science in such a way that they learn to understand reality more deeply by looking within. A by-product of this are "skills" such as the ability to see people more deeply, to anticipate situations, to act in a way that originates in wisdom and spontaneity as opposed to conditioned, learned behavior patterns. All of this means more intuition, more insight, and more freedom.

Mysticism appears "mysterious" (Greek: *mystikós*) because we enter worlds that we usually do not perceive. The mystic dimension is just the dimension in which "we happen" without knowing that we happen in

Chapter 9 - The Gateway into the Future: Mysticism for Our Times

it. That is why it is mysterious and draws forward skills that often appear wonderful or miraculous to us.

Mysticism is only peripherally connected to faith. When we speak of mysticism we speak of entrusting ourselves to a practice and engaging in an experiment of consciousness. And this experiment will bring us experiences. Whoever knows a deeper state does not need to believe in anything. Mysticism is beyond "I believe in God" or "I do not believe in God." We devote ourselves to a practice that aligns us in such a way that we see the effects of this in our reality and that these effects cannot be denied. Thus there is a point in time when we simply know deep within. Not only rationally but in our hearts, we know the presence of God.

Sharing the Presence: The Sangha

> *"Where two or more gather in my name, I am there in your midst."*
> —Matthew 18:20, New Testament

Only when we make awakening the focus of our lives and our culture will we shape a way of life that is sustainable on all levels. For this we need some creative cultural tools.

To place awakening at the center of our lives is radical. There are many part-time mystics but relatively few people who really reach deep down. Let us ask ourselves whether awakening really is at the center of our lives and how this is reflected in our daily life. We will see that we have the opportunity to take a new step forward in collective consciousness, that we can form islands of awareness in our cultures where spiritual practice occupies a central place. This ultimately leads to a more holistic understanding of our human dynamics.

Practicing with others forms the ideal framework to live authenticity and transparency. A supportive atmosphere of togetherness provides the container to speak and share the truth of each moment with each other, to practice transparency, and to dive deeper into a profound understanding of the principles at work. By focusing in common alignment on the source, the essence, God, the group energy field helps us to go deeper, allowing for the development of more compassion and awareness. Members in a sangha support each other in awakening the authentic part within themselves and in trusting their intuition and perceptions.

Most people need a regular practice of meditation or praying, and of course a practice of mindfulness in everyday life, in order to achieve a deeper inner alignment to God or the Light within us. If we strengthen this on a daily basis then this part is more and more present in our reality. For some people this happens very spontaneously, radically, and profoundly. For other people it is a steady process of growth throughout several years.

When Evolution Creates Stress

As with every development, two forces are at work within us: the evolutionary impulse and the force of habit. In the mystical tradition we call these two free energy and the structure of life. To live in an aware way means that we orient ourselves towards the inner light—the evolutionary impulse—in such a way that it becomes stronger than the habits of our personality; stronger than the automatic aspects of everyday life which we have grown so fond of.

If we live our lives according to an evolutionary impulse then we grow through the pressure that is created in our bodies, our feelings, our thoughts, and ultimately in our life circumstances. New potential strives to unfold constantly. The call of evolution resonates within us. If we hold ourselves back through habit we will not heed this call and pressure will build up—evolutionary pressure. Either we learn to channel this creatively and follow the call of our souls, or we get caught up in the dramatic aspects of our various crises. A crisis is a sign that this evolutionary pressure is not being attended to; it has now taken form as "crisis."

There comes a point in spiritual development at which our inner affinity becomes stronger than the noise of the outside world. This means that we are motivated more from the future and no longer live in ways primarily characterized and influenced by millennia of human history. The future—the potential into which we are developing—becomes an inner and overriding driving force. We no longer act reactively but are more strongly connected to God, the one presence, the light. In this way we develop before pressure or tension arises in our bodies or our lives.

Chapter 9 - The Gateway into the Future: Mysticism for Our Times

Inner wisdom is not always pleasant for people. The process of awakening may not be an easy one because wherever we see our ego confronted there can also be pain.

Some people devote themselves to their spiritual practice to such an extent that they authentically contact deeper and more profound levels of consciousness within themselves and this leads to an expansion of their lives. We can experience ourselves and also our collective processes from a much wider perspective and have more freedom, space, scope for action, and thus also more wisdom at our disposal. This is a great challenge since awakening always has something to do with the transcendence of reality, and thus our habits.

Stumbling over Stones in the Flow of Life: Habits

True mystics of all times were and are very radical people since mysticism challenges human habits continually so that we stay in the flow of evolution. Habits are opposed to the evolutionary flow; we form them, identify with them, and would love to anchor them in this way. But life *is* permanent movement. Life constantly provides pressure in order to develop us further. If we do not do this then tension, symptoms, and also illnesses occur. If we evolve further then expansion happens and we are "in the flow." The mystical texts all describe wisdom as the flow of life. This means that we can become conscious in ever-deeper levels of our self and develop our potential.

A Spiritual Teacher

Most people need a teacher because their passion for the Divine—for awakening—blazes repeatedly and dies down repeatedly too. This alone cannot transcend old habits. Teachers keep reminding students of their burning passion until it no longer dies down on its own. They become companions on the path that is being created through them. We call this nonlinear learning. We don't learn by exploring the path we already know. Instead we take the path that only reveals itself through each step as we take it. This is devotion to God.

Surrender to a teacher is trust based on love and therefore can take us to spaces beyond that which we know. A spiritual teacher is someone who can reveal this doorway because the light and higher intelligence flow through them so strongly.

A competent teacher can perceive the student's level of consciousness and is able to discern the right moment and intervention necessary to help him or her achieve breakthrough. Without this help students tend to get stuck in their developmental dynamics, where aspects of reality are experienced as relative to each other, and forget the context within which this development is taking place: namely within an awakened consciousness.

Truly competent spiritual teachers have consciously integrated different stages of growth within their own development. A teacher must be at home on all levels and be aware of their own strengths and weaknesses if they are to be a mirror for their students. A spiritual teacher is basically nothing more than a conscious authentic reflection of various aspects of the student's life.

Spiritual Competence

Whenever we come into higher dimensions of consciousness we recognize a reality that is larger than the one we had previously experienced. We grasp a larger context. Only when we have entered higher subtle or causal states ourselves are we able to share this with others. Not before. If we talk about mysticism then we are talking about committing ourselves to a practice and conducting an experiment in consciousness. And this experiment will result in experiences. However, we need to break through into the Absolute in order to take a look at the Relative from the level of the Absolute.

Being awakened does not mean being perfect in every way, but awakened people are capable of recognizing the perfection of the Whole. They know that there is nothing that is not connected to everything else. But this does not mean that those who know this are themselves perfect; we need to drop this notion.

Just recognizing the unformed primordial ground alone does not automatically provide a ticket to the integration of all of the worldly levels. It is an insight that raises a highly realized individual out of the relativity

Chapter 9 - The Gateway into the Future: Mysticism for Our Times

of life as the only epistemology, yet it does not make that person a universal genius. Neither is it realistic to believe the paradisiacal aspiration that someday a human can reach a state of ultimate tranquility, relaxation, and beauty. Of course inner peace arises in those who awaken. This is a peace in that which is. A "yes" to that which is. However, this does not mean there is no longer pain.

If humans give God—the essence or timeless wisdom—the space he, she, or it deserves then this is space beyond thought and comprehension. A spiritual teacher knows and has experienced this. This means that an intervention from the teacher that comes from this place of authentic connection cannot be compared to that which most people know or are familiar with.

A teacher is someone who can navigate freely through reality and make important contributions using this higher connection. They can enter into empty territories and into nonknowing without hanging on to the conditioning. And yet they know that the goal is not Emptiness alone.

The Absolute and the Relative

Deep immersion in the unformed Ground of being is indeed beneficial for spiritual practice for a while, but separating Emptiness from the worldly loudness of Form itself creates duality. What we are seeking is a nondual insight. In other words: Emptiness includes Form and Form includes Emptiness. We are Form and Emptiness as not-two or nondual. Once we realize this then we know that having profound experiences alone is not enough. Neither is just being adept at the technical issues of development enough. We need both.

The ultimate step of Awakening is that the insight of the Absolute returns to the world of the Relative. This deeply anchors life in reality via the body-mind (our physical sensations, emotions, and thoughts). One is totally immersed in this world but has the transcendental knowledge at the same time of not being of this world. That is transmission. Light transforms material into higher and higher planes. It is like a lamp burning within life itself, and not just a finger pointing towards the Absolute.

Awakening has something to do with people waking up from the view of reality that they know into a new way of being aware of the world. They cannot determine this in advance through their previous understanding of the world. This is an important point in spiritual practice. If spiritual practitioners acknowledge this they will also be able to see and accept the competence of not-knowing in a spiritual teacher. In our world that is characterized by rationality, we demand more and more knowledge and predictability, but this has both a positive and a shadow side.

We often exclude nonlinear, multidimensional development. We could compare this to trying to avoid the holes in the cheese. We want to get rid of the not-knowing element because it doesn't look very economical or efficient. However, this affirmation of the unknown is an important thing since the conditioning of "wanting to know" is so very strong. In spiritual practice it is "the holes" that interest us most because they are the entry to superconscious intelligence in a system that consciously recognizes itself as a Self.

The Collective Consciousness

As we know from experience, there are times in which we feel free and open and other times in which the waves of life crash over us and clarity seems to be washed away. But in this there is a level of our self that we can experience constantly as the sum of all moments. This is the level of awareness that we have adopted for ourselves. The collective consciousness also lives through such a level.

The sum of all experiences defines what sort of society we live. In this way, for instance, society is actually determined by the state in which I walk down the street. This might sound very far-fetched, but it does make sense in terms of the human collective. The development of my consciousness has an influence on the entire world and vice versa! Thus we see the paramount influence of the evolution of consciousness on the culture in which we live.

We need a contemporary spiritual practice that supports us in how we develop on a physical, emotional, mental, collective, and spiritual level, so we can develop a mysticism of the third millennium that is an expression of timeless wisdom and that is—at the same time—capable of facing our current issues and crises.

Chapter 9 - The Gateway into the Future: Mysticism for Our Times

A Creative Step Forward

A synchronisation of many fields of consciousness and an orientation towards the awakening of humanity can have a huge healing effect upon mass consciousness and thus also on the growth of every individual.

We can organize large events, for example, to specifically address current and common themes. Through the increase in synchronization between and within ourselves, we open up to the possibility of enabling energy to flow from the supraconsciousness into daily life. In this way we can all contribute to expanding the blueprint of experiential reality and to opening up to new human possibilities. This allows us to identify new ways of acting, thinking, and feeling which may alter the course of our lives and of all lives.

We are not even close to starting to realize the potential of human consciousness and our common creative force. We merely hear rumors, packaging these as forms of self-idolatry. And yet if we just take one creative step forward we discover a balance in which both creativity and transcendence find their right place.

Thus a contemporary mysticism is a mysticism that no longer holds to traditional God images but instead opens the space for a rational, scientific evolutionary step. It is a mysticism that reaches rational and scientifically educated people in a way that they do not experience as regression but as progress. A mysticism that has answers to burning questions raised by the technological explosion in our lives, by the globalization of world society, and so on.

When this mysticism touches the areas of economy, politics, education, medicine, and science, then these areas become subject to a constant "update," because the development and evolution of humankind originates in this mystic core. This is where inspiration and innovation originate; this is the evolutionary impulse in action. It is with this that we want to consciously connect.

"Digital" Awakening

The digital postmodern era has brought forth new possibilities of interaction and of language. The everyday "marketplace of our lives" in the age of instant communication has changed drastically. In part we live through the Internet.

We can speak of a "digital" awakening when we integrate a highly developed communication technology into the awakening process of the world. If we take the last developmental stage of humanity—the dawning of a global awareness—then we can see in this an opportunity for advancement, like a new musical instrument that we want to learn to play.

Can we use the mass media as an energy source for a new possibility of reality? Can we set up virtual universities on the Internet in order to fulfill our hunger for awakening? Can we organize large-scale digital events that deliver this awakening directly into our homes? The Internet can take so many forms. We can use it as a commercial medium and lose ourselves in virtual worlds, or we can transform it into global consciousness.

In summary, there are several practices to help us answer the questions being asked of us collectively:

- the practice of meditation or praying, in order to achieve a deeper inner alignment to God or the Light within us.
- the practice of transparency, in order to transform interpersonal friction and unawareness into clarity and synchronization.
- the practice of attentiveness and alertness, to ground us in "the now" and to look beyond the apparent boundaries to the development of humanity.
- the inner affiliation to the evolutionary impulse, in order to recognize our future potential in the here and now and to allow us to become alive.

In all of this we must realize that a great many different human perspectives coexist and that all of these have their relative truths. But they cannot claim to be generally valid for everyone.

Following on from this, we need culture-shaping tools that pave the way to a culture of awareness. Through practice we can work to achieve a new "We" as a collective consciousness—or we must get there through crisis. If we develop freely because we realize the future in the now then we will succeed in the transition to a new tomorrow without the

Chapter 9 - The Gateway into the Future: Mysticism for Our Times

need for and the pressure of crises. This is a tomorrow that has a profound effect in the now.

This signals the new dawning of a trans-rational mysticism that speaks the language of our time and at the same time cultivates a timeless wisdom. The eons of all times are reflected in the face of eternal mysticism, and yet they are also expressed as a perennial underlying movement in the course of our current events. This is the beauty and the miracle that we can evoke in every moment. We want to create spaces in which this mysticism of the third millennium is again cultivated, resulting in a civilization that provides a sustainable life for all—on all levels.

Glossary

Focal point of consciousness: The level of consciousness where we hold consciousness on a consistent basis. It is the sum of all contracted and expanded moments. In those moments in which we fall into reactive patterns of behavior our focal point of consciousness drops to that of identification with the personality, and is thus no longer free to remain present in the moment. Our past conditioning has a strong influence on the now. In moments of connectedness we perceive the world with a high level of consciousness, which raises the focal point.

Synchronization: A tuning-in and a deeper awareness of other spaces of experience leads to a synchronization in fields of consciousness. This creates a more coherent vibrational state, allowing more potential to unfold with less friction. This is the basis of intimacy and of collective intelligence.

A new "We": A new "We" is the synchronization of many people in a field of presence and attentiveness. A transpersonal perspective places personal experience within a larger focus of consciousness. This creates space for (more) collective intelligence that can be expressed through us.

Digital: The term digital refers to a humanity that experiences much less interpersonal friction and separation, and through this achieves a "digital we." In this way we realize a much higher level of intelligence as a collective and are able to answer a number of global questions. A "me/us" relationship is analogue, so to speak, whilst a new "We" is digital.

Part 3: Action

Chapter 10
Embodiment

Rob McNamara

What Is Integral Embodiment?

"Integral," from one perspective, means to integrate. The heart of integral is invested in including, embracing, and encompassing as much of the territory of your life as possible. Can you synthesize and envelop the full territory of life? This is the unspoken aim or the implicit movement and gesture of the integral impulse living within you.

So when we talk about integral embodiment we are most simply talking about *how you can embrace and inhabit the fullness of your embodiment*. It is here in this simple act, to embody, that you will find the key to that which your heart most yearns for yet simultaneously fears the most. First, let us look into what it means to embody and then why embodiment is a deeply important consideration for you and your life.

To Embody

Embodiment is intertwined with *embracing* and *inhabiting*. If you unplug embracing or inhabiting then embodiment, as we will be exploring the subject, disappears and your life becomes disembodied in some shape or form. Embracing means to cast out or reach outwards, thus enabling to you to encompass or envelop something. This movement involves an encircling and including. For example, when your mind considers a novel perspective your mind opens and expands as it reaches out and includes this novelty. This is a movement of embrace just as your arms reach out and extend to embrace a loved one in a hug.

To embody is not simply to embrace though, it is also to *inhabit*. When you inhabit something you are on the inside. When you are standing across the street from your home, looking back at the front door, the windows, and the form of the rooftop, you are not inhabiting your home. You are looking at it. When you cross the street and walk along the path to the front door you are not inhabiting your home until your hand reaches out, opens the front door, and you step inside. Only when you are actually inside your home you can say you are inhabiting your house. Similarly embodiment requires you to inhabit, not merely look at, your body. To embody you must also inhabit—that is, be on the inside of your body.

Looking at your body, witnessing your body, interpreting your physical and emotional sensations through a series of stories, and conceptualizing your experience all largely miss the mark of embodiment. Embodiment requires you to inhabit your embodied experience, meaning you perceive your embodied experience from the inside. The location or origin of your perception is the differentiating criteria. Just as I can ask you if you are perceiving your home from the inside or the outside, a useful inquiry to ask yourself is: Am I perceiving my embodied experience from the inside or the outside? *To inhabit requires than you rest your faculty of perception into an intimacy with the inside of your embodied experience.*

To some degree you are always inhabiting your body, yet take a look and you are likely to see that often you are drawn out of large swaths of your embodied experience; that is, you are no longer on the inside of these dimensions of yourself, but rather you are perceiving them from the outside. This is often the case with the body and the direct immediacy of sensations, emotions, and felt senses that reside therein. Instead of living these dimensions of life from the inside, often habituated defenses eject your faculties of perception out of your immediate aliveness. As such we see our embodied truth from the outside or perhaps we ignore dimensions of our lives altogether. When this happens, we do not embrace nor do we inhabit. Life becomes disembodied.

Your body, the physical form and structure of you, is a basic part of an embracing movement into your life. Your whole body from your toes to the crown of your head is actually a beautiful gesture of embrace. Your body is an expression of you reaching out into the world, literally pressing

Chapter 10 - Embodiment

"you" out into the vast terrain of life. From the physical resonance of your posture, the felt sense of your embodied fluidity as you move about in your life, and the emotional textures flavoring your experience, to the felt sensations of the inside of your thoughts, stories, and beliefs, this embodied reaching out (from toe to crown) enables you to embrace, receive, and envelop every facet and nuance of the intersection of you and the world. When you inhabit your body—that is to say when you flower your capacity for perception from the center of your embodied reaching out—you become the synthesis of embrace and inhabitation. This is what it means to embody.

Why Is Embodiment Important?

Embodiment is not just something to consider when you are working out, having sex, or doing an activity that is overtly physical. Embodiment can reach out and inhabit every facet of your life. To embody your sexual desire is fundamentally not different than how you embody your passion at work, play with your children, aspire in your spiritual practice, or embody the love and tension that arises within intimate relationship. The fashion with which you embrace and inhabit your life is an ever-present invitation, thereby making embodiment an essential fabric of who you are and how you engage your life.

Your embodied truth, in any activity, is your aliveness. Deny embodiment and you deny your aliveness. Push some part of your embodiment away, see "it" from the outside, and your vitality becomes split and divided; you are now identifying with merely a fraction of the aliveness that you are. Aliveness then is not something that is binary, meaning it is not something that is either on or off. You are not either alive or dead. Aliveness is a spectrum, a continuum spanning from low levels of vitality (or none at all in the case of clinical death) to high "wattages" of aliveness. To expand the field of what you embrace is to increase the aliveness in your life. Similarly, to expand and open your inhabitation is to grow your connection with aliveness. As such, embodiment is an essential piece to the aliveness that you are able to conduct into your life.

Unfortunately, it is precisely due to the body's power to dictate and command aliveness that so many of us habitually pull away from our embodiment, situation after situation, day in and day out. Most of the

The Coming Waves

time we prefer to feel as though we are in control. When this happens, you often stop embracing your embodied experience and inhabit distracted and disconnected ways of functioning in life. In some shape or form the direct immediacy of your embodied truth is traded in for some kind of manufactured fantasy.

Perhaps it is floating disembodied through your day focusing upon your agenda and the most pressing "to-do" items. As your faculty of perception is largely consumed by your capacity to predict, your predictions begin to determine your life's flow with greater and greater command. All the while you lose touch with the uncontrollable nature of what is already present right here in your embodied experience. You may be so consumed by your agenda that you do not even feel the interiority of your own agenda; you only look at it and press onward to the next item. The refined attunement with the present moment's aliveness and texture of your life is traded in for a map of what may happen next, where you should be already, and what needs to happen in order for something else to happen. While this map of predictions may vary in accuracy, the fundamental process is often a similar disconnect from embodiment. You draw out of the inside of your embodied experience and trade in this luminous source of intelligence for a guesswork plan that is divorced from a large spectrum of your life that is continually arising.

Let us presume that most of your day has been disembodied as you have surfed from one activity to the next. As such your habituation may lead you into a fascination with entertainment. As much of your life has not been embraced nor inhabited you become fascinated by watching others embrace and inhabit their characters, be it on TV or in movies. Over time these characters become more and more important to you because they offer you a small glimpse into your own embodiment. This may even go so far as to where you might begin to predict someone else's fabricated life on TV as you feel into the possibilities and their implications. All the while you are largely distracted and disjointed from the embodied unfolding of your own life.

Disembodiment yields greater disembodiment. As such, when you become more and more distracted your aliveness becomes more and more disorganized. You embrace less and inhabit less as you embody less. As a result you want more. Maybe it is more clothes, more food, more money, or perhaps more social power. The formula is simple: the greater the poverty of embodiment, the more you desire in order to fill the hole

Chapter 10 - Embodiment

birthed by not inhabiting and embracing the fullness of your life as it is right here and right now within your embodied truth. Maybe it is an enslavement to work, a fascination with entertainment, an compulsive draw for another glass of wine, or an insatiable desire for relationships to fill a void. Regardless what the distraction and disconnect is from your embodiment, its essential function is to avoid the raw aliveness of who you really are. These often unconscious strategies enable you to move around the immense potency of truth, power, and purpose within your embodied life. As such you commonly sever yourself from the source of feeling the full beauty and pain intrinsic to your life's most basic textures.

Embodiment is so important because in so many ways this embrace and inhabitation is your doorway to your unbounded vitality and aliveness. Whether you are aware of it or not, this aliveness has an inherent gravity within your being. While the open aliveness of who you are may often scare you into more habituated ways of living, the unconditioned aliveness at the center of your embodied truth is an essential part of the fullness your heart seeks and yearns for in your life.

Integral Embodiment

So what is integral embodiment and how is it different from embodiment? Integral embodiment expands upon what it means to embody yourself and your life. To embody is to embrace and inhabit both yourself and your life. Integral embodiment moves with this same process, yet you expand the scope of your embodiment in both intention and practice. Let us investigate each component, as there is a significant shift occurring when we move from embodiment to what we are calling integral embodiment.

First, integral embodiment involves an expansion of scope, both in what you embrace and what you inhabit. While the essence of embrace and inhabitation remain the same, the qualitative scope with which they are lived grows, opens, and refines. We will refer to these qualitative changes as integral embrace and integral inhabitation. Together these form two major pieces of the foundation of integral embodiment.

Integral embrace expands the scope of what you are able to include and welcome in your life by enabling you to move beyond your preferences. Embrace is conventionally governed by your preferences. You are able to embody the parts of your life that fit within the sphere of your conditioned preferences. Sadly, this sphere is typically fairly small. It is only these preferred dimensions of yourself and your life that can be embraced with more ease. The parts of yourself and your life that reside outside of this sphere of preference are quickly and often reflexively defended against. Most of the defenses involve some strategy to get out of or distance "you" from the direct embodiment of your full experience. While this was a necessary and healthy developmental step growing up as a baby and child, it is not congruent for healthy ongoing adult development and the general movement to embody greater spheres of intelligence, aliveness, and skillfulness as you grow.

When you step beyond the conventions of your conditioning you are stepping into the territory of what we are calling integral embrace. Integral embrace qualitatively includes more space, *much more space*. It is this spaciousness that now governs your embrace. No longer are your preferences in the "driver's seat." Instead the intrinsic curiosity, acceptance, and attuned spaciousness within you guides your embrace. This spaciousness reduces the necessity for defensiveness toward your experience and it simultaneously allows your habituated defensiveness to arise without being unconsciously consumed by conditioned responses. This space can hold your habituated defensiveness instead of simply being (and thus acting) defensive.

Your journey into integral embrace starts just beyond your conditioned preferences, so as you feel beyond your habitation you are beginning to cultivate your capacity for integral embrace and as such your integral embodiment. Your preferences all stem around pleasure and pain, joy and suffering. Your most basic habituated preference is to move towards that which brings pleasure and away from that which brings you pain. Integral embodiment invites you to go beyond this core conditioning. When you step beyond the basic preference to move away from experience that is painful and to move toward pleasurable experience, your capacity to embrace the full territory of yourself and your life now surfaces.

Your embrace is then dictated by spaciousness. You can only include and accept what you have space for. When you step into the very center of integral embrace you step into a spaciousness that is *unconditioned*. What this means is that the spacious resource you have access to is not conditioned by any experience—this uncollapsible nature of your integral

Chapter 10 - Embodiment

embrace is capable of embracing every facet of you and your life. This enables you to accept, open to, and work with yourself and your life with much more skill than your more fragmented functioning stemming from habituated preferences. This spaciousness is a function that can be felt into precisely when life presses you right into the location where all of your habituated preferences point to you not being able to embrace this facet of your experience. Where closure, denial, and dissociation conventionally have governed you, now you find an unshakable space that finds room for everything. This includes the parts of your experience and life that your preferences have no room for. Whenever this happens your embodiment qualitatively grows, you have become much bigger in your embrace. For the first time there is no corner, no facet, and no dimension of your experience that your embrace leaves out. This is the essence of integral embrace.

The next piece is, of course, the expansion of that which you are able and willing to inhabit. Again, embracing is only a part of embodiment. To embody is to embrace and inhabit. The essential heart or center of integral inhabitation also stems from this same unconditioned spaciousness.

A basic quality that co-arises with this spaciousness is curiosity. In the open field of your embrace, curiosity naturally arises. This curiosity is a vital link to your embodiment. Spaciousness does not get lost in its own open expanse, nor does the nature of this space just witness and look at the form of your life as you and your life arises. Curiosity draws your spacious presence closer and closer to the fullness of life. Ultimately, the only position that satisfies this yearning curiosity is the complete inhabitation of every facet of your life. When your spaciousness follows the completeness of your curiosity integral inhabitation is born. You are on the inside of every facet of your life.

Where conventional inhabitation is governed by your preferences, integral inhabitation shifts into your larger sphere of functioning enabling your unconditioned spaciousness and curiosity to guide your faculty of perception. It is from this greater functioning that you are able to move to the inside of the full territory of your experience. In this way, you go beyond your habituated preferences as to what you are conventionally willing to experience as you grow into the full intimacy of your perception.

To perceive means to receive, to take in or collect and apprehend within your body-mind. Perception is then a gesture of embrace as we have been discussing this term. Every facet of perception is, to some degree, an act of embrace. But to truly take something in, to fully perceive something in your life also requires inhabitation. If you are not on the inside of your perception, you in some way are not receiving in completeness. Thus all perception, in its mature expression, is an act of embodiment. Integral embodiment releases the barriers to perception enabling you to take in and receive whatever arises without habituated distortions and manufactured boundaries.

Thus far we have been talking about your faculty of perception; we have been doing this to simplify our discussion. In actuality you have many faculties of perception, both for the perception of the exterior world, your interior world, as well as the myriad of relationships in your life. With that said there is one faculty of perception that holds a central place within embodiment and inhabitation in particular: feeling. Your feeling-consciousness is the central faculty of perception needed for your embodiment.

Feeling-consciousness is the very faculty that can rest on the inside of all of your faculties of perception. How does a song sound and how does a particular melody feel? How does dinner taste and how does your meal feel? What is your partner doing and how does this relationship feel? What does your idea look like and how does your idea feel as you think about it? Feeling-consciousness is a fundamental fabric of your inhabitation. There is no boundary to that which you are able to feel into. Your sight is limited to vision, your interoception is limited to the inner felt sense of your physical body, taste is limited to your mouth, mindsight is limited to sensing aspects of your mind's activity. Your feeling-consciousness is however a faculty of perception that is unbounded in its nature and thus is capable of resting on the inside of all of the ways you perceive yourself, others, and the world at large.

The third component of integral embodiment is that your sphere of inclusion envelops all of the territory of yourself and your life. Your feeling-consciousness is a powerful vehicle of embodiment, enabling to you feel beyond the duality of self and other. You do not merely embody yourself, you extend your feeling-consciousness out into and through all of your life as well as into all of the dimensions of yourself. Integral embodiment then is a "presencing" into every facet of you and your life. In this way you step beyond your attachment to your habituated

Cultivating Integral Embodiment

preferences and step into the full territory of yourself and the life that you lead.

Cultivating Integral Embodiment

The final component of integral embodiment has to do with your intention and practice. These are your primary vehicles through which you can cultivate your integral embodiment. Intention is your starting point. As you read this chapter, your perspective on embodiment has hopefully grown and expanded. If so, you have likely already begun to feel into, consider, and see some new perspectives on how you can embrace, inhabit, and ultimately embody yourself and your life in novel ways. The intention to *liberate yourself into the fullness of your embodied experience* is a powerful orientation enabling you to transition into a larger sphere of embodiment. When you find yourself caught in some form of disembodied habituation return to this central intention.

Your practice always begins right here and right now in the direct immediacy of the embodied truth of your experience. The following practices outline several keys to help you reach beyond the confines of your habituation. Ultimately the integrative gesture remains the same: embrace and inhabit the full territory of yourself and your life without any conditions, restrictions, or boundary. Embrace and inhabit the completeness of what is already present within your life.

The first practice involves practicing "space and embrace." The simplest and often most effective way to engage this practice is to open up your breathing. When you notice that the vast amount of your functioning is trapped in some expression of disembodied habituation open your breath up, breath more deeply, and feel into your intention to embrace your life. When your breath is habituated the rest of your body-mind tends to be habituated. When you begin to inhabit your breathing while opening and expanding your breath you are likely to find more spaciousness within your experience. This enables you to "breath into the fullness of your experience." The more space you are able to free up through your breath the greater your capacity to embrace and ultimately embody your life.

Another simple way to practice space and embrace is to move your body; that is, change the form, posture, and alignment of your body.

When you get stuck in habituation and are defensively pushing away some dimension of your experience you probably have a strong tendency to organize your body into a habituated posture. Moving your body, finding fluidity within your spine, opening up your hips as you walk, and freeing up your shoulders and arms loosens habituation's grip upon you. If you want greater access to spaciousness move your body through more space. When you do so oftentimes you will find that you have greater access to a spaciousness within, thus opening you up to greater embodiment.

The second practice is called "going in" and is tailored to expanding your capacity for inhabitation. This practice depends upon you noticing when you stop feeling into some aspect of your experience. When your feeling-consciousness recedes from some part of yourself or your life connect with the intention to "go in." Use this cue to extend your feeling-consciousness into yourself and life. This simple instruction to feel into your experience can help you refine your ability to step into the inside of your experience with your feeling-consciousness. This practice can be used in any aspect or dimension of your life. The greater the resistance to inhabiting your direct experience, the greater reward to feeling into these dimensions of your embodied truth.

The third practice is called the practice of "embodied immediacy." This is a direct path to embodiment where you radically dive into the complete truth of your direct experience. Regardless what is arising in your experience you embrace and inhabit what is present without condition. There is no agenda to get somewhere else, to move beyond your habituation, or to gain more spaciousness. This embodied immediacy is a leap into what is without condition. This is the ultimate test to actually find out what your most alive vitality is in this very moment. This is integral embodiment in its pure essence, the complete embrace and inhabitation of your experience without condition.

Reaching beyond your habituated preferences to embody the fullness of who you are is a rich practice with limitless opportunities. The above practices coupled with a strong and clear intention to *liberate yourself into the fullness of your embodied experience* will expand your capacity for integral embodiment. Your life and this moment is ultimately an invitation to do something elegant, most notably to embrace and inhabit every facet of your life with grace. Even more central to this, your life is an invitation into a greater participation with who and what you genuinely are. Your full embodiment is typically the most neglected dimension of this

Chapter 10 - Embodiment

realization of who you are, yet the center of the integral impulse within your heart cannot allow your liberated embodiment to remain unlived.

Chapter 11
Activism

Jana Espiritu Santo and Eliot Bissey

Meta-Perspectival Cognition with Integral Meta-theory

Our goal in this article is to examine how activism looks, both to and from different developmental levels and perspectives. We wish to share a spectrum of mental and experiential worldspaces, which can open the potentials to and offer the possibility of actually inhabiting these diverse perspectives with feeling and compassion, as well as integral cognition. First one feels subjectively, then one learns to think subjectively, and then one may learn to think objectively and mentally conceptualize different perspectives. Then one may learn to "feel into" those new and diverse objective mental perspectives with subjective feeling. The idea of "integral" is integration; in this case the integration of thought and feeling into teamwork as being.

We will use several models to help us describe the content of "activism" within the context of three tiers of consciousness that unfold developmentally. This includes (1) the Integral Meta-theoretical model (Wilber-V iteration);[1] (2A) Gravesian theory (Dr. Clare Graves) and (2B) Spiral Dynamics[2] (SD, Don Beck and Christopher Cowan); (3) Harvard psychologist Robert Kegan's Constructive Developmentalism;[3] and (4) the teachings of nondual sages, such as Jiddu Krishnamurti (J. K.), Lao Tzu, and Ramana Maharshi. This article can be relevant for those with little or no knowledge of these models and teachings as well as advanced students (one may skip the parentheses, and return later to go more deeply).

Spiral Dynamics provides the cross-culturally verified definitions of 1st and 2nd tier developmental structures and their levels (vMemes), based on Gravesian theory. (As a side remark, we consider the SD model of a single *spiral* to be an oversimplified interpretation of the Gravesian *double-helical* model, and this will not affect our analysis.) In Gravesian theory there are six levels per tier, and the levels that have emerged so far are as follows: 1st tier: beige, purple, red, blue, orange, green; 2nd tier: yellow and turquoise. The rest of 2nd tier is currently emerging (coral) or still dormant; we are referring to the emergent levels when we say "2nd tier." Integral Theory is a model of reality (with the main features of quadrants, lines, levels, states, and types) that can be useful for those with an integral consciousness, which we define as "at least" a 2nd tier consciousness.

(Theoretical note: We may refer to an individual as "a level" [or tier] in order to fit more content, yet this is not to be taken literally. Individuals *inhabit* levels [or perspectives, worldspaces, vMemes] in a very fluid and dynamic manner. SD/Gravesian theory states that an individual that "tests out" as centered in one particular vMeme will have approximately 50 percent of their self-system center of gravity at that vMeme, and 25 percent at the vMeme above and 25 percent at the vMeme below, which is a general description of their distribution of energy in consciousness. Also, Integral Theory adds a dimension to development called *lines* [similar to Howard Gardner's multiple intelligences], as an individual can have different stage acquisition in different lines.)

Generally, 1st tier (and the first six levels) describes our primitive and animalistic nature, driven by subsistence needs, and is the foundation for the more cognitive and uniquely human aspects that emerge in 2nd tier. The chasm between the tiers is described by Clare Graves:

> Here we step over the line which separates those needs that man has in common with other animals and those needs which are distinctly human ... we are just approaching this threshold, the line between animalism and humanism.[4]

Our purpose in using a three tier model, rather than a two tier model, is to more fully illustrate another dimensional shift in development between 2nd and 3rd tier. We could call 3rd tier the "total human-being" (J. K.), following Graves's metaphor with animalism (1st tier) and humanism (2nd tier). This distinction should be used loosely, however, as there is some debate on the validity, evidence for, and definition of "3rd tier consciousness." Our meaning is based on individuals we think and feel have stably attained this stage as mentioned earlier. "Nondual perspective" can be used in place of 3rd tier for those concerned with theoretical accuracy. Ultimately, the map/model (with finite detail) is not the territory (with infinite detail).

Activism from a 1st Tier Perspective

First tier activism is based on subsistence (SD) or deficiency (Maslow) needs, ranging from ego needs to the need to belong to a group. For the (1st tier) individualistic levels, one can become a leader of an activist group to make a living (beige), gain ego power (red), or gain profit and status (orange). For the (1st tier) collectivist levels, activism can hold the core values to form a group or tribe. Communion with others offers individuals safety and security (purple), mythic membership (blue), and pluralistic social resonance (green).

Preconventional levels: Instinctive beige activism is driven by survival needs and fear for the environment (i.e., "Save the planet or we might all die!"). For magical purple, activism can help create a tight knit tribe to bond against a common enemy (i.e., bad omens and evil spirits). For power-driven red, activism may trigger the king and warrior archetypes, where the ego can exert power and control over the tribe through an activist cause (i.e., imperial conquest and cult leaders).

Conventional to *Postconventional levels*: For mythic blue, activism can offer eternal salvation and connection to a higher power/God (i.e., the Crusades, spreading the Gospel) and security in an ethnocentric tribe (i.e., patriotism, nationalism). Activism can reflect valuing the individual for rational orange, found in some of its political philosophies concerning rights and freedoms. Orange leaders can consolidate political power and status through activist causes (i.e., wars for democracy, globalization). For pluralistic green, humanitarian activism is a means to serve and help the planet evolve (i.e., civil rights, worldcentric values, environmentalism). Infinite level/line combinations can manifest in an individual psychograph (healthy and otherwise, including level hijacking, transitioning stages, etc.).

For example, "Boomeritis," a pathological combination of red and green, is described by Wilber:

> This strange mixture of very high postconventional memes with preconventional narcissistic memes is Boomeritis. A typical result is that the sensitive self, honestly trying to help, excitedly exaggerates its own significance. It will possess the new paradigm, which heralds the greatest transformation in the history of the world; it will completely revolutionize society as we know it . . . it will save the planet and save Gaia and save the Goddess; it will be the most extraordinary . . .[5]

(Also, as a side note, we very seriously question the acquisition of green consciousness, which requires the transcendence of orange, where the capacity for grounded rationality and multiplistic cognition emerges when actually stably developed. It has been our experience that magical thinking, biases, and cognitive fallacies are rampant in green and so-called integral communities.)

The Content of Activism from 1st to 2nd Tier

According to the Oxford online dictionary, activism is a noun defined as: "The policy or action of using vigorous campaigning to bring about political or social change." First tier "Action-Man" (SD) will join a *social movement* to campaign worldviews and take immediate action, supporting identifications with social payoffs. While some movements have been successful in achieving their goals (e.g., the Civil Rights Act), the actual accomplishments can be nothing more than endless "organized" discussions, parties, and selling of merchandise, or what Malcom Gladwell calls "slactkivism." While 2nd tier has no problem with these types of functions, they are not confused with actually achieving a humanitarian objective, or somehow being "spiritual"; they are seen with clarity and objectivity and enjoyed with subjectivity.

In order to take action, campaign, or attempt to bring social change, one should have ideas to define the meaning of each. These ideas (concepts), the content of activism, are comprised of the goals of activism (i.e., better environment, education, or socio-political systems), and the

Chapter 11 - Activism

method and means to achieving these goals (i.e., type of change and/or system).

For 1st tier these ideas form ideologies (or "isms") due to thought-identification based on animalistic (body-mind) attachment. Specifically, they reflect the values, needs, desires, and agendas of a particular 1st tier worldview (i.e., fundamentalism [blue], capitalism [orange], environmentalism [green], etc.). First tier ideologies create a sense of identity, accessorizing one's self-image.

In development, the subject of one stage becomes the object of the subject of the next stage (Kegan). The move from 1st to 2nd tier can be described as the move from *thought-identification* to *thought-objectification* in terms of content, and as the move from *structural unconsciousness* to *conscious self-deconstruction* in terms of context. Second tier is very aware that activism is based on ideas and that "few ideas are sacred; all are subject to review and upgrades to more functionality" (SD, 276).

Graves called the first level of 2nd tier (yellow), "the cognitive level," while SD calls it the "problem-solver." From this level, the content of activism is composed of theories attempting to describe possible reasons for and solutions to social problems.

The goals of 1st tier activism are usually based on positive ideals. Second tier understands that attachment rarely leads to virtue. Humans are often tempted to rationalize or hide their shadows, and when persona identifies with ideology, shadow dissociation and projection usually result; dogma, hypocrisy, and self-righteousness ensue. Second tier realizes that thoughts about good intentions which result in actions that make one feel good may not have any relationship to actually doing any lasting good in the world (i.e., the local manifestation over time, plus chain reactions, the "butterfly effect," etc.). For 2nd tier, positive ideals are held in the form of universal principles rather than ideologies to impose on others. While these principles give purpose to an activist theory, they are not necessarily part of the theoretical content, just as one's intentions aren't the same as one's actions.

A methodology is merely a means to an end, the goal. First tier often confuses the means with the end and so it may appear that when an individual does not support the local idea (methodology), that individual may be accused of not supporting the global ideal (activist goals). For example, those who disagree with the conclusions drawn from political global warming theory have been accused of being anti-environmental (straw man fallacy), which may or may not be the case.

With a tendency towards dualistic and ideological thinking, 1st tier can only see *support* or *denial of support* for a particular activist cause ("You're either with us or against us!"). Activist agendas often have contracted motives (such as popularity, sex, money, power, etc.) hiding behind a positive, global ideal. First tier seeks to satisfy these desires through manipulation with confirmation, validation, and groupthink biases.

For 2nd tier, a more objective evaluation without the biases of 1st tier is desired. The 1st tier duality of support or no support is replaced with "Integral-aperspectival" (the ability to inhabit all relevant perspectives with attachment to none of them, Wilber) analysis. Consider the various constituents of a social problem (e.g., multiple subjective descriptions, possible reasons, and potential solutions), made up of data sets containing different degrees of epistemology (what can be known), speculation, and accuracy. In a multidimensional context, the question of support or no support is a crude oversimplification; both the Right and the Left have their partial truths, and integral wants them all.

From a 2nd tier perspective, activist theories are evaluated with a scientific method that goes beyond scientific materialism (orange) to include the analysis of subjective perspectives and interior meaning (Wilber's "Kosmic Address"). Theories are not confused with pregiven realities ("the myth of the given," Wilber), they are known to be explanations of interpretations of data and these interpretations are not all equally valid (post-pathological green "flatland," Wilber).

Contrary to the rigidity and certitude of ideologies, theories are based on finite data (data not being synonymous with fact), containing limitations and biases (both technological and mental). Adequate extraction of meaning requires this progression: (1) analysis of data acquisition methodology, (2) data acquisition, (3) data validation, (4) data processing, (5) comparative analysis of data processing output with reality, and (6) repeat. This is a multidimensional process of continually integrating new data and deconstructing one's data acquisition methodology and interpretative framework and comparing the output of this process with reality. Evolving one's interpretation of data and being open to higher orders of pattern recognition, as it may arise, is of great significance to 2nd tier. Application of this theory inserts an action step prior to repeating.

First tier has a tendency to form opinions and jump to conclusions during data acquisition and may be unclear as to the boundaries of data acquisition and data processing. Once a conclusion has been drawn and attached to, the mind has stopped functioning optimally. Conclusions create the illusion of identity and security and can activate shadow charges against those who question (threaten) them, because the cognitive unconscious cannot tell the difference between a physical attack on the body and the perception of an attack on something with which it is identified/attached/stuck to. Unlike 1st tier, 2nd tier completes data acquisition first before consciously beginning data processing. Second tier does not cling too tightly to a perspective as it may be relativized, reframed, and/or proven false with new data (which is always arising). Second tier will perpetually question the adequacy of all theories and methodologies and their manifestation with an agenda for more, higher, wider, and deeper truth; nothing is taboo. Any method that rejects valid truth because it does not support a particular worldview is not up to an integral standard.

First tier can be influenced by media propaganda (and in fact, they are targeted) and social conditioning that supports their worldview. For example, a blue patriot is less likely to question the validity of a war his or her country has entered into than a red anarchist. Even green, the peak of 1st tier, is prone to cognitive fallacies, with a bias towards immanent social resonance, as SD remarks: "Green is susceptible to group think. The pressures to be supportive of collective decisions and actions can be extreme." (266)

For example, Michael Coffman, a scientist in ecosystem research has unexpectedly discovered what he considers to be hidden agendas behind some environmentalist movements (i.e., seizure of property for political power, redistribution of wealth); SD cautions about "orange in green clothing" (263). Whether this has validity or not in this case, the possibility may have difficulty gaining recognition in a green worldspace.

The "autonomous self" (Wilber/Kegan, describing 2nd tier) is capable of radical and independent thought, having outgrown the need for social validation, and is less swayed by peer pressure, propaganda, and socially accepted beliefs. Not only are the activist theories evaluated and analyzed, so too are the agendas and support behind the activist theories, which may reveal different goals and endgames.

Social Change Recontextualized

Breaking down the Oxford definition of activism, we will examine the difference in the meaning of "social change" from 1st and 2nd tier perspectives. First tier vigorously campaigns its particular worldview to be the vehicle for social change. On the other hand, 2nd tier can see the necessity of *each* worldview as they unfold developmentally, and therefore does not campaign for one particular 1st tier worldview. The manifestation of the healthy aspects of each worldview *as appropriate to life conditions* is preferred (taken from SD):

Free of 1st tier compulsions—must haves, need tos, afraid ofs—YELLOW activists are uniquely qualified to remove blockages and smooth out flows between and among vMemes. In short, YELLOW is able to move in and out of various 1st tier systems in order to (1) make them healthy and (2) show their connections with other systems on the Spiral. (283)

A common objective of 1st tier campaigning is to create social consensus. The goal for everyone to inhabit the same perspective is impossible to 2nd tier and is based on an erroneous flatland (relativistic pluralism) perspective, which excludes developmental differences and depth. Even when a group can appear to hold the same values (herd mentality), under inspection each individual's interpretation will be unique according to his or her structure of consciousness ("zone 2," Wilber). And that interpretive structure will change through time, which may or may not involve evolution (i.e., higher stage acquisition), while mutation, regression, and stagnation are also possible. Graves describes the vertical diversity of human values:

The error which most people make when they think about human values is that they assume the nature of man is fixed and there is a single set of human values by which he should live. Such an assumption does not fit with my research. My data indicate that man's nature is an open, constantly evolving system, a system which proceeds by quantum jumps

Chapter 11 - Activism

from one steady state system to the next through a hierarchy of ordered systems.

Consensus is not only futile, but if forced, dangerous to individual freedoms and rights. The desire from our (American) Founders was to protect individual rights and freedoms (a Republic), not the majority rule (a democracy), or minority rule (e.g., wealthy elite, secret societies). Looking at history, social consensus has been proven wrong/untrue in science (i.e., the geocentric model debunked by Copernicus and Galileo) and as immoral in politics (i.e., Nazi Germany). Cutting edge thinkers at the peak of evolution have always been the minority ("greater depth, less span," Wilber).

First tier often projects a positive image and feeling sentiment onto the term "social change," without defining what that means (clarity impedes people's ability to unconsciously project their hopes; precise definitions may create conflicts causing positive feeling to dissipate). Second tier realizes that the definition of social change is relative to the individual using the term. Also, change can be looked at from many perspectival locations (Wilber's "quadrants" and "zones") and seen as many different types: positive and negative, vertical (evolution or regression, ascending/descending) and horizontal (translation, inclusion or exclusion), and multidimensional (expanding/contracting). Without context, the term change is too general and abstract to have grounded meaning (ambiguity can be quite effective in some contexts). Change is the very breath of the universe (life/death, order/chaos cyclic oscillations).

Activism can attract elevated self-assessment. First tier tends to exaggerate individual influence on the collective, sometimes to the point of "heroic self-inflation" (Lentriccha in *Boomeritis*, Wilber). One may believe that s/he can save the world. This is not only unrealistic to 2nd tier, but also relative, as "saving the world" entails a different meaning for each worldview (i.e., for everyone to be Christians or Muslims or integralists [1st tier self-system center-of-gravity with 2nd tier rhetoric]). In some cases a "tipping point" (Malcolm Gladwell) can take on a viral character and exponentially spread like wildfire (e.g., Martin Luther King, Gandhi). Yet these cases are generally the statistical outliers (the 100th monkey theory has been debunked). One may be able to appropriately contextualize his or her individual range of influence without ego inflation.

Those who have a truly global span of influence might comprise a tiny minority (i.e., the 1 percent, global elite, international bankers, etc.). With the monetary ability to affect large populations through technology, media, and socio-politico-financial systems ("Lower Right quadrant" [LR], Wilber), they have the resources to create "humanitarian" activist propaganda to accumulate and centralize their wealth and power (red, orange). Graves' cautions us of a possible future: a "blue-orange-green tyrannical, manipulative government with glossed over communitarian overtones" (SD, 13).

The research of Anthony Sutton and G. Edward Griffin have shown how this may be done by financing both sides of social movements, wars, and political parties. This may be what we call a "rigged game" of higher order (orange) strategies, when the amount of money and effort it takes to spread activism is considered and the line between big corporations and governments blur (corporatocracy). After all, could not capitalism and socialism both be ruled by the wealthy? Michel Chossudovsky, Professor of economics at the University of Ottawa, researched how the Occupy Movement may be a colored revolution or controlled politically correct opposition, actually funded by the wealthy. Whether these statements have validity or not, 2nd tier is more interested in evolving into a more global perspective, rising above the "system" and the duality and opposition it breeds, for more practical reasons, with little time for speculation.

"A plan to save humanity is almost always a false front for the urge to rule."

—H. L. Mencken

There are different spans of the social dimension, starting with individuals and extending outward (i.e., family, community, state, country, continent, planet, etc.). For 1st tier, "global" means the largest span (greatest number of people) in the social dimension, the "global-social." This dimension is frequently associated with human salvation (blue), freedom (orange), and mystical transcendence (green, i.e., singularity and unification [pre-rational/rationalized] theories). The goal of social change is for humanity to become one single unit. Yet Wilber clarifies the distinctions:

Chapter 11 - Activism

... the we is not a super-I. When you and I come together, and we begin talking, resonating, sharing, an understanding each other, a "we" forms-but that is not another I. There is no I that is 100% controlling you and me, so that when it pulls the strings, you and I both do exactly what it says. (*Integral Spirituality,* 153)

While individuals can physically come together in space-time and share interior worldspaces with dialogue, they do not create a single individual; all individuals have different psychographs, different development and experience in the different lines, and occupy different worldspaces. Each individual has a unique context of consciousness. For 2nd tier, 1st tier's desire for global-social unification and "planetary change" can reflect the spiritual desire for oneness, evolution, and universal perspective, yet contains a mental error as these desires can only occur within an individual and be shared be others on that level (similar, not identical). (False) Gurus and political dictators have used the faulty reasoning of collectivism to wield power and control by prioritizing the group over the individual, while (behind the curtain) the leader's individuality (or the leader's inside group) is prioritized over the (larger) group. Second tier, described as the "holistic level" that takes a "global view" (SD), can see a whole new dimension of global: as a level of consciousness in an individual, rather than a collective idea.

Activism for 2nd Tier

Consider the following quote from SD (with our comments in brackets for clarifying examples):

Besides the notable dropping away of fears, other significant differences between 1st and 2nd tier may include a marked increase in conceptual space [zone 2 gets "bigger" and can hold seemingly opposing thoughts and beliefs with ease and comfort, rather than confusion, paradoxical conflict, or cognitive dissonance; from diametrical opposition to complimentary opposites] the dropping away of compulsions ["imperatives" start morphing into "choices," and what were previously thought of as needs become differentiated into real needs and mere preferences], impulses tend to arise as objects of consciousness rather than as the subject ["I feel irritation/hunger/arousal" rather than "I am irritated/hungry/aroused"], and an ability to learn a great deal from many sources [increased curiosity and comfort with uncertainty, ambiguity, and the unquantifiable unknown], and a trend toward getting much more done, with less energy and/or resources [multidimensional efficiency optimization with higher order strategic thinking and action]. (66)

Based on the Oxford definition, "activism" evolves to not really "activism" with the "momentous leap" into 2nd tier (Graves). There is no need to campaign for 1st tier ideologies as these needs, impulses, and worldviews are being and/or have been differentiated/integrated and transcended (which is shorthand for "transcend and include and negate and destroy," Wilber). It is not that these needs disappear at 2nd tier, but that needs (air, water, food) and preferences (clothing styles, entertainment, attention) are differentiated, contextualized, and prioritized rather than rationalized. The metaphysical baggage can be shed for (Wilber's) postmetaphysics, in the way a butterfly sheds its cocoon to open its wings and fly. Activism becomes (1) inner activism and its intersubjective sharing with like-minded others, (2) humanitarian projects, and (3) planning for the future.

And so, you see, once you subscribe to flatland, all you can do is try to fix the exteriors—you try to stop people from polluting, you try to force them to recycle, you try to legislate a moral response to Gaia. And of course it doesn't work very well, because you must resort to force, legal or otherwise. (*Boomeritis*, 295)

Exterior change on the societal level, the *outer activism* of 1st tier, occurs when people's behaviors and actions are directed and controlled by artificial (LR) systems that connect individuals, such as laws, policies, and bureaucracies, as activism often involves politics. If history and its totalitarian cycles have been any lesson to us, we can see that not all laws exist to protect the rights, freedoms, and well being of individuals (the Patriot Act?). "Power corrupts and absolute power corrupts absolutely" and some laws can be passed to exercise political power, control and domination involving the violence of genocide, war, and bloody revolutions. Therefore, 2nd tier focuses on *self-government* to guide our lives as "politics" is replaced by "ethics" and "campaigning" may be replaced by "being good and doing good" from a universalized perspective (e.g., Kant's "categorical imperative").

Inner activism radically turns activism inside out. Rather than trying to change the world "out there" or exert power and control over others, desires shift to becoming a more whole and healthy individual, inhabiting a more global perspective. An integral self-analysis is engaged, including persistent self-questioning, self-deconstruction, and the self-examination of ones' biases, opinions, and perspectives, in a process that attempts to bring the unconscious to the conscious, integrate the persona and shadow and become more free from irrational, mythic, metaphysical and other limiting beliefs (1st tier baggage).

The efficiency-oriented lifestyle of 2nd tier prefers reasonable goals in clearly defined contexts that can actually produce real results. For 2nd tier, social movements are simply membership to an organized group and are not confused with development to a global perspective or actual problem solving (not to say that they cannot manifest positive outcomes). One is aware that changing patterns in society does not change people (e.g., the Civil Rights Act did not end discrimination). Consequently, 2nd tier usually prefers to embark on a humanitarian project after 1st tier needs are met. These projects can be rewarding as acts of real goodness, when desired results are yielded (which is not always the case as multiple levels of risk, uncertainty and the unknown exist).

Requiring hard work and determination, with little or no ego pleasure (the cost/payoff "re-equilibration," Kegan), humanitarian projects can resemble the operation of a business, beyond the capitalistic self-interest of orange (meritocracy), and are less likely to be distracted by the potential problems that may arise in group dynamics of individual belonging and ego needs (i.e., over-identification/attachment, narcissism, the consensus problem, leadership power struggles, etc.). Second tier (turquoise) is not too eager to take action (sensitivity to exterior contexts determines appropriate interior urgency), does not act from impulse, fear and insecurity, "seeing-everything-at-once before doing anything specific" (SD, 289), and carefully examines the multidimensional contexts of self, collective, analysis, methods, contingency scenarios, multiple time frames, and probability and risk/reward ratios (probabilities tend to be inversely correlated with risk/reward) in his or her project assessment.

While the green system is often full of idealism and human-centered concerns, yellow may be abrupt in wanting to get on with it . . . yellow does penetrate to the core of an issue. (SD, 280)

Einstein once said: "The difference between genius and stupidity is that genius has its limits." At 2nd tier one does not waste time and energy on problems one cannot solve due to lack of expertise, clean and clear channels of information, resources, power, authority to execute, etc. Donations to well-researched organizations and charities may be alternatively chosen. The immature hero will challenge the unbeatable foe, while the seasoned warrior chooses his battles carefully.

Second tier has the cognitive capacity to understand the complex relationships involved in an ecosystem (feedback loops, trade-offs, chaos theory, objective/exterior errors and tolerances [technological; applied theory, measurement, etc.] and interior interpretive biases [zone 1 and zone 2 relationships, potentials, and blind spots; the advantages and disadvantages of any one particular interpretive context]). Simple answers fall prey to reductionism. According to Wilber's Integral Semiotics, it is not until turquoise (2nd tier) that the term "ecosystems" (signifier, sign) has actual grounded meaning (referent). SD warns, "Be wary of green speaking turquoise . . ." (276). On that account, green environmentalists may do more harm than good, due to their cognitive biases and overly simplistic models that represent reality more inaccurately and inadequately than higher levels of consciousness. This can lead to the wrong actions, or actions that don't achieve the intended goals. For example, well-meaning 1st tier environmentalists banned DDT (a pollutant) in Africa, causing the crops to die and millions of people to starve to death.

> "Half of the harm that is done in the world is due to people who want to feel important. They don't mean to do harm but the harm does not interest them."
> —T. S. Eliot

Chapter 11 - Activism

It is generally difficult for 1st tier to change course with activism for the reasons of ego identification and attachment. Contributing to their developmental stuckness is their general inability to recognize higher-level logic (exclusivist tendencies, SD). Being over-committed is somehow equated with strength, and time investment is a reason to remain static/stay the course (the "sunk-cost fallacy"). First tier tends to fulfill security needs and assuage fears through mental inflexibility, by wanting to appear right, whether one happens to be right or not, subjectively oriented to assertions rather than outcomes, until the pain becomes great enough and the cost/payoff equilibration is too disadvantageous. On the other hand, 2nd tier can completely revise a theory and its application ("flexflow," SD), and in fact Wilber is in his fifth iteration of Integral Meta-theory. Giving up an erroneous thought, useless belief, or wrong assertion immediately is the most efficient path to being and becoming more correct and adequate (dynamic, process view, objective, results oriented). This is much easier for an individual to do in a humanitarian project than for a collective to do in a social movement (e.g., Malcolm X).

A great disparity exists between the average-mode level of consciousness and our technological level of advancement, as well as a financial disparity between the wealthy elite and poorer global populations. As a result, the potentials for chaos and destruction increase (i.e., the purple terrorist with orange nuclear technology, Wilber). Sustainability movements seek to prepare for the future and these movements contain the issues we have addressed, such as the errors of collectivist thought, the "consensus" impossibility (flatland), and political corruption for an occulted agenda.

For 2nd tier, sustainability is a realistic endeavor that an individual may plan to do for him or herself and those close to him or her as the means for continued survival during times of crisis (i.e., economic, natural, geo-political). This could mean the creation of wealth, forming a survival group, learning self-defense, relocating, the gathering of resources both internal and external, and preparing for emergencies. It could also mean the practices of evolutionary exercises such as UZAZU, ILP, and meditation as the saying "evolve or die" can be prophetic. Planning for the future is not entangled with pre-integral ideas of metaphysics or spirituality; it is authentic, raw, and in the name of the first level (beige), the least significant/meaningful and most basic/fundamental, upon which the entire Spiral is built (early Wilber, SD).

Third Tier Activism and Putting the Pieces Together

Ultimately, in the relative universe, there will *always* be problems to solve (both socially and individually) that demand ever-increasing intelligence, sensitivity, and technical ability, as life conditions become ever-increasingly more complex. The solution to one problem creates the next problem, ad infinitum (Graves, SD). All social movements have a life cycle and eventually dissolve. Even though 2nd tier has the ability to solve problems with greater cognitive ability, 2nd tier is not an omega point. Evolution of consciousness is an open-ended system (Graves and Maslow, just prior to the latter's passing). Thus, becoming an activist for 2nd tier (or ANY particular type of) consciousness is a performative contradiction, and 1st tier in nature.

Higher developmental levels have different values in a different order than their juniors; one must first see, and then care, and then stably manifest that care through consciousness and action. Each tier defines social change differently. While 1st tier focuses on social change through activist movements, 2nd tier focuses on inner activism to grow and evolve in all aspects of life, as the individual is the backbone of society. The next quantum leap into 3rd tier reframes change to include a type of change that does not require time at all and is a complete revolution in the dimensionality of the context of consciousness (structure-stage acquisition), rather than merely changing the content (moving to a bigger house, rather than just buying new furniture).

Interestingly, pathological green and the higher tiers use similar language to describe this type of change with very different interior realities. While pathological green asserts immanence and "living in the moment" with its persona and shoves the truths of genealogical development into its shadow (e.g., the dysfunctional guru or psychotic mystic), the higher tiers actually integrate these truths, and embraces both the process of becoming/evolving through time-bound development AND radical instantaneous transcendence and transformation (J. K.; vertical and horizontal enlightenment, Wilber).

The purpose of 1st tier activism is to end social conflict and suffering with the hope that activist ideas somehow convey spirituality. Since activism is based on ideas, a 2nd tier postmetaphysical perspective

Chapter 11 - Activism

may consider this a form of "spiritual materialism" (Chogyam Trungpa); thought (content) comes from perspective (context), which can be located and relativized (is not the "be all, end all"). For 3rd tier, thought cannot grasp that which is immeasurable, whole, and timeless, and thought will always be fragmentary, so must know its limits and boundaries (J. K.).

From 1st to 2nd tier, ideologies evolve into theories, which are differentiated from 1st tier needs and agendas by the adequate functionality of actual problem solving from an integral-aperspectival view. For 3rd tier, enlightenment cannot be found in thought at all, which is a dead thing, the residue of psychological time and limited experience, however beautiful and subtle. This is not to say that high quality thought is not needed, it is just a warning not to allow it to become a "gilded cage." Even the thought to transcend thought is not real transcendence; in fact, the desire to transcend time keeps one rooted in time (J. K.).

First tier activism has a subtextual agenda to strengthen the self-sense as important and the so-called "spiritual ego" (an oxymoron) as "sustainable." Second tier activism deconstructs the self, getting the "me" out of the way, to more objectively assess specific conflicts in order to provide solutions. Third tier sees the entire self-concept as a product of the mind and the root of all conflict. It is the primal dualism that separates one from his environment. (Even the concept of Self [or higher self] falls into this dualistic trap [self vs. Self]).

At 1st tier, one is trapped in duality (e.g., me versus the environment, persona versus shadow and us versus them). After all, the very term "activism" is dualistic (i.e., active against who? and active versus passive). The conflict between the real and the ideal exists in the quest for utopia, as ultimately all social revolutions have failed to change human nature at its core. Conflict will be generated by activism, as the purpose of one's life is based on being in opposition to an enemy (or one's own projected shadow). Conforming to the establishment or rebelling against it (conforming to the anti-establishment) does not lead to freedom but to its opposite, slavery and co-dependency; it is a reaction to a stimulus and therefore is determined by that stimulus, it is not independently created in freedom by intelligence (J. K.). Also, a dualistic context of consciousness holding a concept of "nonduality" as content really has nothing to do with nondual consciousness.

Second tier consciousness can resolve 1st tier conflicts with an integrative perspective, bypassing the indulgence of ideologies. For 3rd tier, solving conflict becomes freedom from conflict entirely. This is based on the nondual realization that the "observer is the observed" (we begin all subject: baby/pre-rational, no distinctions, and evolve to all object: unattached with clear distinctions, enlightenment, sage/trans-rational, Wilber/Kegan).

In summary, 1st tier activism is a dynamically stable imbalance (Kegan's Dynamic Equilibration), where one seeks to remain safe and static regardless of life conditions, staying comfortably embedded at one's location on the spiral of development. Second tier activism is a dynamically unstable, continual re-balancing and self-deconstruction, where one seeks to evolve, embracing uncertainty, and adapting to life conditions. Third tier replaces both animalistic and humanistic needs with pure transformative awareness and is dynamic—integrating stability and instability, balance and imbalance, sensitively flowing with life conditions, in the context of a "silence that is not stagnant" (J. K.). At this stage, one is the "total human-being," who sees and acts in totality, transcending and including the division between the individual and collective, the interior and exterior. "I am the world and the world is me" (J. K.) becomes a reality, not a metaphor. In such a worldview, real love and bliss become manifest, and nothing is excluded.

> I feel that revolution is necessary at the most profound level, not fragmentary revolution, but integrated revolution, a total revolution starting not from the outside but from within.[6]

In an integral embrace (the capacity for movement in all three tiers to counter-balance life conditions), one takes care of his or her survival needs first (1st tier) so that one can continue to evolve and be present, and solve problems for self and other (2nd tier being needs) and live in love and harmony, free from conflict, with teamwork between thought, feeling, and being/ontology (3rd tier).

Notes

1. Ken Wilber, *Integral Spirituality* (Boston, MA: Integral Books, 2006).

2. Don Beck and Christopher Cowan, *Spiral Dynamics.* (Oxford, UK: Blackwell Publishing, 1996).

3. Robert Kegan, *The Evolving Self* (Massachusetts: Harvard College, 1982).

4. C. Graves, "Human Nature Prepares for a Momentous Leap," *The Futurist* (April 1974): p. 72–87, www.clarewgraves.com/articles_content/1974_Futurist/1974_Futurist.html.

5. Ken Wilber, *Boomeritis* (Boston: Shambhala Publications, 2002), p. 37.

6. Jiddu Krishnamurti, *Total Freedom* (Krishnamurti Foundation of America, 1996), p. 178.

Chapter 12
International Development

Gail Hochachka

In this chapter, I describe how an integral approach is being applied to alleviate poverty and enhance human well-being in remote corners of the planet. In the following pages, I explore the question, what is integral? in the context of current global statistics that report 1.75 billion people living in multidimensional poverty, with indicators reflecting acute deprivation in health, education, and standards of living (Human Development Report, 2010), and another 1.24 billion living on less than $1.25/day. Here, I share some of the principles for integral action and give examples from development projects in Peru, El Salvador, and Nigeria. I hope at the close of this chapter, you'll leave somewhat inspired as to how Integral Theory in action brings greater comprehensiveness and deeper compassion, worldwide.

Interior Sources of Change

"So, *how* did you get through in the refugee camp? What did you draw on to gain strength?" asked my colleague to a local man who'd survived the twelve-year civil war in the 1980s in El Salvador. It had been a time of massacres, injustice, and bloodshed. Not one that is easy to talk about. "What did you rely on to move through it?" my colleague asked again, and I felt my chest tighten, fearing that he was pushing too hard on a topic that is clearly traumatic and sensitive.

Sitting back into his seat, with a firm yet spacious resolve, the man said, "Fe." *Faith.* A woman chimed in saying, "Hope." And another said, "Positive thinking."

All of these answers point to the strength and resilience that people draw on from inside in times of turbulent change. And these answers point to some of the very questions we are exploring in international development; namely, how do we integrate the human dimensions of consciousness and culture with the other more common economic and systemic interventions for development? And how does our engagement with development become more nuanced when we include an understanding of human psychology?

In many of the approaches used in international development, these questions are answered with empirical, factual, and exterior solutions. Or, they aren't even asked in the first place. Instead, human experience is reduced to dollars and cents; human development is measured by changes in markets; multidimensional needs are met through building things. Human interiors, such as dignity, empowerment, and meaning-making, are less welcomed and in some cases actively ignored.

Global issues keep shifting the ground beneath our feet. Deaths from HIV/AIDS shift entire demographics of nations. Emerging democracies teeter in their enactment of good governance, as age-old dictatorships sway and fall. Unpredictable weather events disturb the very patterns on which global food systems depend, such that new climate scenarios will literally shift entire development strategies for nations. In other words, while, on the whole, development indicators are looking better for greater swaths of the global population, there are certain wild cards in the game that give rise to unpredictability and turbulence, and require us to plan for development for *contexts that we cannot yet see.* How does human resilience arise in the face of this turbulent, uncertain change? How does development actually occur in consciousness, cultures, and systems? And, what approach is dynamic and inclusive enough to best support development in all these dimensions?

These are the questions we are exploring with an integral approach to development. As we do so, we recognize that it is often the interior domains of human experience that people draw on to source strength, resilience, and evolution in the face of hardship. We take seriously the core assumption in international development, which is that *we are developing.* Using innovative methodologies, we seek to integrate interior (consciousness and culture) and exterior (behaviors and systems) dimensions of development.

What We Disagree On Is How

"Every age has its massive moral blind spots. We might not see them, but our children will."

—Bono

The world has really changed. Unlike in any prior moment in history, today, on the whole, most nations of the world *agree on the value of supporting the well-being of nations.* International development reflects that shared sentiment. It is one of the first disciplines on the planet to situate from this worldcentric care. That is, the goal is not the well-being of *one* nation, as per most national endeavors and disciplines; it is not the bottom line of a corporate entity, as per most companies and transnational companies; nor is it the prosperity of one geographic community or tribal group, as a more parochial view from village or community would hold. The final analysis of the effectiveness of international development is nothing less than improved social, economic, political, environmental, and human development indicators of all countries on the planet! For the first time in history, humanity possesses the knowledge and skill to relieve suffering of vast numbers of people across the world, and for the first time in history, *humanity has the moral inclination to want to.*

As this worldcentric morality arises and sets the global discourse, it is increasingly less and less tolerable for there to be a billion people living in abject poverty and many more suffering from malnutrition and illness. Although often the message in the news is one of clashes between perspectives, the countries of the world actually *agree* on the Millennium Development Goals and in their own ways are struggling to enact them.[1]

What we *don't* agree on is how to go about it.

In this section, I go into why this is the case. Beginning with an evolutionary view of development itself helps us to see more fully how much we know as well as to explore our blind spots. And, through discovering and owning those blind spots the field can continue to evolve.

International development grew out of a post–World War II era, when the objective was to get economies and democracies going and not fall back into conflict and war. "To increase the productivity of the poor" was a phrase used at the time, and it set the predominant view of seeing the word "development" to be synonymous for "economic development." That was, and remains, the *modern, conventional approach*—that is, to find economic and technocratic solutions to underdevelopment. This relies on a linear conception of development, much like a competition or race in which countries are evaluated based on the economic indicators alone and are then categorized as first world, second world, and third world.

Later, a pluralistic worldview deconstructed the former conventional view, and brought a more nuanced understanding to the field. First of all, the pluralistic view recognized that the linear competition model wasn't fair, since not all countries started from the same place and some benefited at the expense of others. So, it's objective was to level the playing field sufficiently for the countries at the bottom to recover from poverty and get ahead. In fact, some modern theorists, inspired by the analyses of the Dependency School and the Latin American Structuralists, came up with policies to advocate nonmarket preferential treatment for LDC's (Least Developed Country), a kind of affirmative action which was, in effect, an economic way to "level the playing field" for a country. Yet, many extreme relativist postmoderns, it seems, simply refused the game; they refused to acknowledge that there was such a thing as economic underdevelopment along a linear scale. They celebrated cultural diversity and concentrated on values, particularly for the oppressed, and worked at a unit of analysis that was not of countries but communities or disenfranchised groups within those countries. Many astute technologies and methodologies were used to doing this, such as methods of accompaniment, participatory approaches, and recipient-led programming, for example. It is really this worldview and approach that fleshed out in greater detail the needs for gender equality, human rights, workers rights, community organizing, empowerment, and social justice. The pluralistic view deconstructed the linearity, suggested that going forward would actually involve a "going back" to more romantic traditional times, and questioned the terms "first world" and "third world." The critical inquiry of pluralism was a gift, and

Chapter 12 - International Development

many of these methods inform the field in a normative way. If the conventional approach could be depicted as a line, then the pluralist approach would best be represented as a circle: a circle of inclusivity and sensitivity to the inequities and injustices of history, as well as a "going back" to the romantic precolonial era.

The integral approach to development sees that all approaches are partially true and partially needed at certain moments in going about addressing complex issues today. We don't ask which one is true, but rather which integration of approaches is needed for a certain moment in time, in a certain location on the planet. If the conventional approach could be depicted as a line, and the pluralistic approach as a circle, then an integral approach would be depicted as a spiral. It takes as its beginning point the core assumption of international development: *that the world is developing, evolving, and changing, and that we can participate in that development.* We take that seriously and have included the evolutionary theories for how systems change, the social psychology theories for how social discourse changes, as well as the developmental psychological theories for how individual consciousness changes. And, we've included ourselves in the development process, through a focus on the self-growth and evolution of the practitioner, similar to the *inner activism* described earlier in this book:

> Rather than [only] trying to "change the world out there," one attempts to change oneself with Integral consciousness: the continual process of analysis (both theory and practice). This includes self-questioning, self-deconstruction, and self-examination of one's biases, opinions, and perspectives, in attempt to bring the unconscious to the conscious, integrate the persona and shadow and become more, free from irrational, mythic, magical, metaphysical and limiting beliefs.

In other words, it's not just that the world out there can and is developing, but we have to admit that we are too, and both are engaged in our integral practice of international development. This is held in a moral balance with the world, as Quinn and Prieto explain in chapter 14 of this book, warning us to be careful to keep this balance or, we may find we "have gone deeply within only to realize [it] is of little use to the 80 percent of humanity that is living on less than ten dollars a day." This dynamism of deep personal work and engaging the world is central to an integral approach.

What Makes the Integral Approach Unique?

> Everyone has in him something divine, something his own, a chance of perfection and strength in however small a sphere which God offers him to take or refuse. The task is to find it, develop it and use it. The chief aim of education should be to help the growing soul to draw out that in itself which is best and make it perfect for a noble use.
> —Sri Aurobindo

There are a handful of key distinctions that make an integral approach unique. First, probably one of the defining features of this approach to development is the recognition of an inherent pulse of evolution throughout manifestation. Called *eros* in philosophical texts, this is the very impulse that moves natural, social, and psychological systems towards greater complexity. Like an oak seed matures into the greater complexity of a fully developed tree, a small zygote matures into an incredibly complex human. The natural tendency for any situation is to develop and to evolve, and this development tilts towards greater complexity, wider circles of care, and expanded capacity to include more perspectives.

Integral Theory describes this developmental unfolding as a "holarchy"—a spiraling unfolding of nested *wholes* that themselves become *parts* of the next order of complexity. Every entity is first whole in and of itself, and also part of a greater whole. Each stage births a new perspective and fills out that perspective with ways of knowing, being, and doing—eventually coming to its own limits and then transforming to a new stage.

When, however, there is an obstruction or imbalance, then stasis or regression from that natural unfolding occurs. When the flow of development gets stuck, our work is to inquire into where it's stuck and why, and to work towards how it can be released for the inherent development to reengage.

This is important because it helps us see our future more clearly. It doesn't fall into the retro-romantic view of development being a return to

Chapter 12 - International Development

a golden era of indigenous perfection. Nor does it fall into the industrial, neocolonial view of "third world" and "first world" countries participating in a linear race to a Western and economically defined endpoint. Instead, it sees that healthy development arises as a series of "nested wholes" *where overall well-being results from each stage of society being healthy and well-integrated.*

Second, working with an integral approach we don't assume that every context is the same and will respond well to the same intervention. That statement might seem really obvious to you reading this, and yet again and again that assumption is made. An economist, for example, will see every problem in an economic light and will propose and instill an economic solution. An engineer sees primarily the context in engineering terms and puts forth an engineering solution. A civil society organization with pluralist values may see that greater equality is needed and will layer on a rights-based solution. Do people *really* surrender their pet theories and preferred perspectives to clearly perceive what the situation actually needs? Infrequently. What if we could truly surrender our own disciplines, skill sets, and self-identities to act more responsively, instead of prescriptively? How can we listen and become sensitive to a situation first, to inform us what methods and modalities are needed?

That is where we begin with an integral approach, assessing the quadrant-dimensions and *levels of development* of a particular situation (what we call the AQAL context, for short). This includes the interior and exterior of the individual and the collective, described as quadrants by Wilber. The Upper Left (interior of the individual) includes experience, values, and consciousness of people in the society. The Upper Right (exterior of the individual) includes such aspects as physical health, biological indicators of development like infant mortality rates, and behavioral practices like hygiene as well as land use practices. The Lower Left (interior of the collective) includes shared worldviews, social discourse, and culture. And the Lower Right (exterior of the collective) includes economic, political, legislative, judicial, and ecological systems. We first assess this AQAL context, not just as a categorizing of all that is going on in the Four Quadrants, but a more nuanced assessment of *where there is flow and where there is stasis*, and then looking carefully at *why*. For this reason, *what* is done using an integral approach only arises in coherence with the context, culture, and consciousness of that situation; sometimes an integral approach will intervene to support economic growth, in other situations to restrain growth for greater sustainability, in other situations to support personal empowerment and community resilience.

All the ways we currently engage in development are important perspectives that we'll invariably need, at one point or another. Debating which is better than another is not the point. Rather, our task at hand is to identify what is needed where and when. This involves being willing to use perspectives that are not necessarily our favorites, surrendering our preferences enough to really meet the situation on its own terms, and not forcing it to comply with our own. With an integral approach, we are not "delivering" development to anyone or any country, but rather honoring what is the inherent, natural unfolding that is *already occurring* and that can be fostered and enabled more fully, supporting ways that a situation can release itself back into its own unfolding eros.

On the whole, this is a radically appreciative stance to development: appreciating how naturally development occurs when blocks and sticking points are alleviated; appreciating the vast array of human perspectives that exist and can be brought to bear on a problem; appreciating the inherent wisdom and trajectory that is a birthright of being manifest.

In the following sections, I'll go further into how we use quadrants and levels in international development, sharing some examples from work in Latin America and Africa.

Integral: A Wider, Deeper Development

Change arises both internally and externally, both in individuals and the collective. So, if we want to change an economic system, or a cultural habit, or a social institution, that will include working with the interiors and exteriors of individuals and groups that make up that system, culture, or institution. The quadrants of the integral approach serve to integrate perspectives and paradigms of development (see figure 1, below).

Chapter 12 - International Development

Upper Left: Subjective, Qualitative (consciousness)	**Upper Right: Objective, Quantitative (behavior)**
How do people make meaning? What do they care about, what motivates them, what inspires them? **Involves:** the psychological and cognitive processes involved in making meaning, constructing identity, structuring reasoning, and forming worldviews; perspectives of roles within the community, society, environment and world; attitudes, feelings, self-concept, and value systems. **Methodologies include:** self-reflection, introspection, contemplation, emotional capacity building, self-inquiry, counseling, body scanning, journaling, goal-setting, meditation, prayer, rituals, vision quests, wild nature experiences.	*What do people do?* **Involves:** the quantifiable, measurable, exterior individual components of development, land use practices, resource management practices, economic activities undertaken, income generated, roles and behaviors of both sexes, behaviors that demonstrate (or not) gender equality, actions undertaken for religious or traditional rituals, and so on. **Methodologies include:** diagnostic tools and other quantitative data collection to gather statistics on individuals of a society (e.g., health and education indicators, fertility rates, data on resource and land use practices, indicators of gender equality, empirical data for physiological health); also includes methodologies that attempt to change behaviors such as skill building workshops, technical capacity building, and educational programs.
Why do people make meaning as they do; what is the subtle shared context; how does the culture hang together? **Involves:** worldviews, social norms, customs and values that (subtly or explicitly) inform relationships, community processes, mutual understanding, social discourse, social appropriateness, and processes of communication. **Methodologies include:** dialogue, participatory methodologies, focus groups, collective visioning, trust-building exercises, group facilitation, participant-observer techniques, storytelling, appreciative inquiry, collective introspection, and other cooperative approaches of reaching a common vision and shared goals.	*What do the interlocking systems look like; how do they operate; how do they press upon and influence development?* **Involves:** the quantifiable, measurable, exterior, and collective components of development, such as economic growth (i.e., economic feasibility studies, marketing and/or fundraising, management and administration, etc.), ecological conservation (i.e., resource management, sustainable land use practices, and pollution control), social institutions and political arrangements (i.e., the councils, associations, cooperatives, etc.), and the modes and means of communication (i.e., formats of information transfer and communication technology). **Methodologies include:** quantitative research, scientific studies, gap analyses, diagnostic testing, assessments, rapid rural appraisals, policy making, technical capacity development, and systems theory.
Lower Left: Inter-subjective, Qualitative (culture)	**Lower Right: Inter-Objective, Quantitative (systems)**

Figure 1 (previous page): Integrating Ways of Being, Knowing, and Doing in Development Practice. The Four Quadrants as described by Wilber (2000, 1999, 1996, 1995) applied to how an integral approach integrates ways of being, knowing, and doing in development issues.

Each quadrant brings an important dimension of reality. Since these quadrants describe consciousness inherent to every human, practitioners in the field often intuit their importance. Says the Human Development Report (HDR) 2010:

> Human development is not only about health, education and income—it is also about people's active engagement in shaping development, equity and sustainability, *intrinsic aspects of the freedom people have to lead lives they have reason to value.* (Human Development Report, 2010, p. 8)

Often, however, practitioners are trained to work in one discipline only, and though they might be aware of the subjective, intrinsic aspects of development, they are not trained in, or don't feel comfortable engaging, these subjective change processes. With a particular emphasis on quantification in the field of development, most practitioners have not been trained on how to engage these intrinsic aspects in quantifiable ways. However, "lack of quantification is no reason to neglect or ignore them." (HDR, 2010, p. 8) In fact, we neglect or ignore interiority to our own peril. Endless "white elephant" projects exist in development in which resources and funding were thrown at "things" like infrastructure or equipment without a complementary investment in the interior aspects of understanding, capacity, and cultural norms. As a result we see new buildings that stand empty and gradually erode into the soil, expensive technologies that never get used for lack of capacity on how to run or fix them, fancy equipment that ends up covered in moss at the edges of the village—precisely because interiors and exteriors were not integrated.

Integral Theory helps us to understand the change dynamics of all four quadrants and encourages us to find tools to work with them. The principle at play here is that sustainable development arises quite spontaneously and naturally as the quadrants become integrated in healthy ways. To overemphasize any one quadrant, to the exclusion of others, can cause problems and an unbalanced development. Interlinking any one intervention or activity with the other quadrants—or, tetrameshing—can help to ensure a coherence to the overall development vision.

The example below explains the integration of quadrants at the scale of organizational development for enhanced effectiveness in Amazon rain forest conservation in Peru.

All-quadrant Amazon Rain Forest Conservation

> "At first I thought I was fighting for the rubber trees, then I thought I was fighting for the Amazon rain forest. Now I realize I am fighting for humanity."
> —Chico Mendez

As we move into an example of quadrants in international development, recall the "acupuncture" style attitude that an integral approach takes. This attitude sees that development is a natural, healthy unfolding that can get stuck or blocked in certain particular ways. This can occur at the scale of an organization, community, nation, region, bio-region, or at a global scale. Development work, seen in this light, involves discerning those blocks and assisting in releasing them. The approach trusts the natural intelligence of a system, and may only intervene in pointed and specific ways—like an acupuncture needle—to liberate the natural flow and well-being of eros. For this reason, a wise assessment of the situation is important, and that's where quadrants come in.

Using Quadrants in Enhancing Organizational Capacity

At an organizational scale, the Canadian nonprofit organization I work with uses the quadrants in an integral assessment process to discern where our capacities are stuck and where they might need more attention. In a recent project with a Southern partner organization, we shared this self-assessment methodology as part of an organizational capacity-building project. The main goal of the project was to contribute to developing the capacity of the Peruvian NGO for enhanced effectiveness in Amazon rain forest conservation. We began by looking at the quadrant-dimensions of the organization's current capacity with our Peruvian colleagues, noting where there was flow and stasis, to discern where best capacity development was needed. Explaining the quadrants during our first meeting was met with an enthusiastic resonance. The executive director at the time immediately recognized there was some stasis in using social methodologies and with the community engagement of the Lower Left quadrant.

This NGO works to promote conservation of the cloud forest of the high Andes through to the lowland Amazon rain forests of Peru and Bolivia. The region has incredibly high biodiversity, is the source of countless foods, fibers, and medicines, and significantly shapes the world's weather and climate patterns—all of which is threatened by human interventions, such as road development, logging, industrial agriculture, and mining.

In this context, we quickly found that the organization's scientific, research, technological, and financial capacity was notably strong—that wasn't a gap that needed any further capacity development. But, was there a gap or an aspect of the organization's approach that was stuck? And if so, where? Using the integral assessment tool, we began to explore these questions.

At that time, the Peruvian NGO was beginning conservation efforts in a watershed about ten hours from Cusco, but was having some trouble with community engagement. In a previous project in a more remote region, the organization's "land-purchase approach" to forest preservation had worked. But in a more populous region with better organized communities, such a land-purchase approach was hotly contested. This approach essentially puts forested lands into private ownership and thus out of the threats of deforestation from community overuse. It essentially avoids the "tragedy of the commons" by making forested lands private. Communities tend to critique this approach since it also means that they increasingly get pushed out of the landscape—a landscape that supports their livelihoods and connects with their culture. And so in 2007 the communities in this region near Cusco pushed back, demanding that the NGO get out of the region entirely. The NGO was a bit baffled and unsure how to proceed.

Using this integral assessment, we found that the primary challenge the Peruvian NGO faced was ineffective community engagement and insufficient knowledge on the "human dimensions" of working with communities. In terms of the quadrants, these were the LL and the UL aspects of rain forest conservation. In other words, conservation of an ecosystem (LR) and the introduction of new land use practices (UR) are not enough to conserve rain forests, particularly if the local people value the landscape differently (for sustainable livelihoods rather than preservation, UL) and have different cultural ways to relate and interact with the forest (LL).

With an understanding of quadrants as irreducible dimensions of reality, one can see the need to include all quadrants at least to some extent for the conservation efforts to be successful. With an intervention including only one or two of the quadrants, conservation efforts were almost shut down entirely. Our subsequent three years of the project sought to develop capacity in these particular quadrants. Our interventions were specifically oriented to the precise places where there was stasis or blockage, and included workshops on social and interpersonal methodologies, processes for self-reflection to foster awareness of human interiority, strategic planning to take a big-picture view of conservation efforts, and an integral curriculum for community engagement.

Ripples of Change, Inside and Out

Over the next three years, the organization shifted its approach in the Cusco region. Said former Executive Director, Cesar Moran-Cahusac, "We're shifting you see, looking more to the social, integral approach in the region." (Personal communication, January 2009) The organization developed social diagnostic tools to use with communities, to have a more comprehensive sense of community needs and to define appropriate intervention strategies. This included being more attentive to local worldviews by using new social methodologies and approaches to complement their existing ecological methodologies, and carrying out a participatory approach with communities to co-create the conservation concession. Speaking about the need for self-identity (UL) and interpersonal alignment (LL) in this participatory work, one of the NGO's community development practitioners explains:

I believe that with the participatory work, the primary thing we have to do is talk authentically with the community about various alternatives of the project, so that they can self-identify with it, and identify what they want to create, and then based on that write the project proposal. . . . Because if we go to communities with the project already elaborated, with funding, etc., . . . we are going to have the same problem: the people won't feel committed [and the project will stall], as what happens with many other NGOs.

Combined with several other important influences, the results of the integral capacity development work could be seen in a marked improvement in community engagement. The organization went from being practically kicked out of the region in 2007 to signing a seven thousand hectare conservation concession in the name of the indigenous community a year and a half later. The Reserva Ecológica Huachipaire Haramba Queros is held in the name of the Queros Native Community, which is significant not only because it is a first for Peru if not the world, but it also demonstrates how the conservation NGO shifted to include both its own conservation objectives as well as the community livelihood objectives in its focus.

This example demonstrates how using the quadrants can be woven into existing programming both implicitly and explicitly. Implicitly with the Canadian NGO, we used a light-touch, acupuncture-style of attuning to the points of flow and stasis in the organization and in the context, with an appreciation and trust that the sustainability would arise naturally and spontaneously as the blockage points were released. Then, together we explicitly used the quadrants in an integral assessment so that the Peruvian NGO could self-reflect on their own approach, and discuss and examine where the flow and stasis was at the organizational scale. This helped to then orient subsequent activities and interventions to the precise quadrant-dimensions that were stuck, releasing the whole back into flow.

What arose was not only a balancing of the quadrants and the successful result of a rain forest conservation concession, but also the transformative shift in the Peruvian NGO. It went from a more conventional land-purchase approach to rain forest preservation (orange altitude), to a more alternative, postmodern, and participatory approach to conservation (green altitude). The integral approach describes how "balancing quadrants" helps to translate the existing worldview of an individual or group, so that quite seamlessly a transformation can arise. This is what we witnessed in Peru.

In the next section, I look at this dynamism of development arising in self, culture, behaviors, and systems.

Unfolding Worldviews in Development: A Case Study from West Africa

"Mankind," said Plotinus, "is poised midway between the gods and the beasts." . . . For if men and women have come up from the beasts, then they will likely end up with the gods. The distance between man and the gods is not all that much greater than the distance between beasts and man. We have already closed the latter gap, and there is no reason to suppose that we shall not eventually close the former. As Aurobindo and Teilhard de Chardin knew, the future of humankind is God-consciousness. . . . But if men and women are up from the beasts and on their way to the gods, they are in the meantime rather tragic figures. Poised between the two extremes, they are subjected to the most violent of conflicts. No longer beast, not yet god—or worse, half beast, half god: there is the soul of mankind. Put it another way, humankind is an essentially tragic figure with a beautifully optimistic future—if they can survive the transition. (Wilber, p. viiii, *Up From Eden*)

Looking at humanity's cultural development, we find throughout the ages an increase in consideration and compassionate care for others, both for other humans and other species. These cultural waves of development follow the trends seen in the psychological development of individuals. In this section, I explore some of the key points to consider regarding stages of consciousness in international development with examples from our work in Nigeria, West Africa in leadership development for sustainability. I begin with an introduction to the Nigerian leadership project.

Leading from Within, Nigeria

One Sky's project, Leading from Within: Integral Applications for Sustainable Development, engages thirty leaders from civil society organizations in Nigeria over three years. The main purpose is to support people who have awoken to their own human potential and to greater depths of care for greater well-being and sustainable development in Nigeria. The thirty participants in the project have this quality of openness of heart and mind, and in a certain way, find themselves at the emerging edge of consciousness in the population. They include a female lawyer and gender equality activist who successfully advocated for women's legal rights to own property in Cross River State in Nigeria, a village chief who started a community forestry initiative that has won UN awards focentric, ethnocentric, sociocentric, worldcentric, and kosmoscentric (see the appendix at the end of this chapter).

There are four things to keep in mind regarding these stages:

1. These are deep structures, not surface structures.
2. There are healthy and unhealthy versions of each stage, and in the context of international development, we need healthy expressions of all stages (not for the society to get to one particular level, such as worldcentric).
3. Translation at one stage assists seamlessly in transformation to the next stage, such that translation and transformation are in fact two facets of the same developmental process.
4. Individuals and groups go through different developmental dynamics: that is, while an individual can't skip stages in their psychological development, a society can change dramatically as the social discourse shifts.

Here, I take up these key points about stages that we consider in our practice of international development, giving examples from our Leading from Within project in Nigeria. The leadership curriculum was designed with an integral approach, and has particularly engaged an understanding of levels in the four ways listed above, which I'll describe in the following section.

Chapter 12 - International Development

Discerning Surface and Deep Structures

Just as the skeleton of an adult human is comprised of 208 bones, human consciousness develops through some distinguishable "deep structures" that are common to all. It doesn't really matter how you divide up these stages—as it doesn't matter if you describe length with centimeters, meters, inches, or feet—what does matter is that there are some features to how we *make meaning* that are recognizable across time, geography, and culture. In other words, nowhere on the planet are babies born with the cognitive capacity to talk at birth, or to take the perspective of another, let alone know that he or she is even an individual self! These are all capacities of human consciousness that appear later in the developmental process. However, *what language that child will eventually speak* is not common across time, space, and culture: such things as language, culture, and personality are surface structures. Superficial features and characteristics are diverse among humans; even though we share the same number of bones in our skeleton, these surface structures invariably differ and are diverse, even though the deep structures are common.

When we talk about stages in an integral approach to international development, we want to be sure we are talking about deep structures. Discerning surface structures from deep structures lets us retain the vast diversity present on the planet, honoring the cultural expressions worldwide (i.e., the unique), while also recognizing that there is a commonality of deep structures that we work with (i.e., the universal). (Kiray, 2009, personal communication)

Attending to both *the unique and the universal* in the Nigeria leadership project has encouraged us to lay emergent conditions for transformative learning in the ways that are unique and particular to Nigeria. Understanding that the action-logic of this group of leaders is approximately the same as a similar group in the United States for example, helps us to select exercises and activities that are sufficiently challenging. Yet, the ways this is done, the actual features of these leadership workshops, have a characteristically Nigerian expression. In other words, when we facilitate workshops, we create a challenging learning environment that is aligned with the general stage of action-logics of the leaders, and yet ensure that the curriculum is "empty" enough for the Nigerian participants to fill it with their own cultural content. So, for example, in teaching early worldcentric material (achiever action-logic

[Cook-Greuter], rational cultural worldview [Gebser]), we use as many local examples as possible from the participants' work in Nigerian villages on microfinance, sanitation and hygiene, and environmental activism, often bringing in local guest speakers to highlight certain aspects of this. The balance of the surface structures and deep structures, or the unique and universal, is a central principle in how we apply levels in this work.

Humanity Needs Pathways To and Through Each Developmental Stage

Since we cannot skip these stages or altitudes, it does not help to ignore or repress any of these stages. Nor does it help to simply layer a new ideology or system (from a higher altitude) on top of a lower altitude. Rather, an integral approach to development recognizes that healthy expressions of every stage are needed. Pathways to healthy expression of each stage and pathways onward to the next stage are necessary to identify and foster. While stages cannot be skipped, they can be expressed, manifested, or translated differently with greater or less health. Knowing humanity moves into and through these life stages, as integral development practitioners, our task at hand is to foster *healthy* expressions, manifestations, or translations of these particular stages. Health arises with an *overall integrity of the stage*, where there are fewer disowned aspects and shadow elements at play. So, for example, given there are 208 bones in the body, we need to make sure all those bones are present, healthy, strong, whole, and demonstrating overall integrity. Similarly, if we have a gaping hole in our interior development—an entire stage largely repressed, or more often, a stage not completely integrated—then our overall psychology is somewhat skewed and incomplete, not fully whole, without integrity.

The integral leadership project in Nigeria is actually not about getting individuals to an integral worldview or an integral stage of development. Rather, it is about providing a leadership curriculum that helps individuals become as healthy as possible at the current stages they are at. This honors each person, as well as recognizes that for a global sustainable development we'll need healthy leadership at every level of development. In developmental psychology, this is referred to as *translation*, whereas *transformation* refers to shifts to the next higher order stage in an unfurling spiral of growth and evolution. While transformation can be more alluring and exciting, in fact, the vast majority of the time we are translating an existing stage, with transformation occurring much more rarely.

In the leadership curriculum, we've included activities from all quadrants of the integral approach, as a balancing of the quadrants has been found to support translation. These quadrants point to the four native perspectives that is part of being human, namely, "I," "we," "it," and "its." The curriculum was designed using the quadrants to orient these four central themes into four modules, depicted in the following table.

Developing Self Leadership Vision and Personal Capacity: - ILP and personal ecology practice - Mind (perspective taking, learning elements of Integral Theory) - Shadow work - Moral span	**Building Skills** Workplace performance: - Writing skills (email, reports, blogging, Internet) - Visioning - Strategic planning - Fundraising - Media - Monitoring and evaluation
Engaging Culture Organizational Culture and Learning - Interpersonal skills (communication, group dynamics, facilitation) - Conflict resolution - Team building - Diversity and gender	**Influencing Systems** Organizational and Societal Systems - Policy analysis and dialogue - Multistakeholder engagement - Networking - Applied learning of systems theory

Figure 2: Applying quadrants in leadership curriculum for sustainable development.

Translation and Transformation Are Different but Related

Of course, there is a relationship between translation and transformation. In fact, translation and transformation are two facets of the same developmental process. As we saw in the example from Peru, as healthy expressions of an existing stage are stabilized, transformation can arise. When we began in Peru, our partner organization demonstrated a

Chapter 12 - International Development

predominately rational, modern approach to rain forest conservation. Through the work to balance quadrants, quite naturally a new way of engaging with communities arose, at a new stage. This more collaborative, participatory way of working is distinctive of worldcentric pluralism. This example illustrates how *translation* (or, living into and filling out an existing stage) is seamlessly connected to *transformation* (to the next stage). So, practically speaking, it is worthwhile to focus on translation, knowing that a) it assists with fostering health at that stage, and b) it lays the emergent ground for transformative change.

In Nigeria, through laying emergent ground and balancing support with challenge, we expect to see some of the participants transforming to the next stage of leadership expression. For example, some participants have demonstrated this transformative shift through a keen interest in the perspective-taking exercises in the curriculum on interpersonal dynamics. As Quinn and Prieto describe in chapter 14 of this book, "That [one is] truly capable of taking someone else's perspective, not just as a concept, is evidenced by overwhelming action on the ground where it is most needed." This perspective-taking capacity and ensuing action will expand out, to include and enact wider and wider circles of care. Certain participants began the program identifying primarily with their own organizational group and with their own particular agenda (sociocentric). Through the program, their worldview has expanded to listen to others, to be open to radically shift their own agendas with other neighboring communities and with other organizations in the larger network, and they have begun to assist other Africans to play a greater leadership role in global development through creating the African Integral Development Network (worldcentric).

Over 80 percent of participants said they'd received positive feedback on changes in their leadership, particularly on perspective-taking during group meetings and during conflicts, in public speaking, and presentation skills, suggesting a transformative shift in how they are leading. One of the participants, Nneoyi Ofem, used to be involved in political violence, but now works devotedly for a true democracy in his country. He says now, "Development work has changed me, my family, and gradually changing my community. One day I will change my nation and the world." This leadership project is helping him to hone these changes into stabilized ways of knowing, doing, and being.

These individuals are supported within the leadership cohort of thirty others, but what about when they go home to their organizations, families, or villages? These tastes of transformation can become supported or thwarted by the social holons in which individuals participate.

Working with Stages in Social Groups

While individuals' own consciousness has to grow and develop through these stages at their own pace, as the average mode of consciousness shifts in a group, the entire group can skip a stage. For example, imagine a company that orients from a traditional worldview (fosters a protestant work ethic, has religious underpinning such as a sense of charity and helping, and is well-ordered with a strict sense of place and role), and suddenly a new CEO is hired from a higher altitude. Quite suddenly, the leadership team may decide that the organization is going to adhere to sustainability more explicitly, creating codes of conduct and purchasing policies with green values. They may begin to hold this social discourse, and perhaps put in place a certain code of conduct, with which all employees, regardless whether they agree or disagree with his or her vision, have to comply. Suddenly, a company that may have been centered at traditional (amber) suddenly skips the stage of rational (orange) and stabilizes at green. (Individuals who remain at an amber altitude then compose their own interpretations of these changes—as stewards of God's Earth perhaps—and adjust to the new higher predominant level of social discourse and policy.) It is possible for groups to "skip stages," though it is not for individuals. International development is essentially about global social change, and so knowing the limits and the possibility for growth through developmental stages in individuals and in groups is important.

Attending to these nested social holons is the central axis of the work we are doing in Nigeria, in three different ways. Firstly, anywhere in the world, one can notice how frequently individuals are inspired while on retreat but then slide back into old ways of being when they get home. Our social groups become really crucial in moments of transformation. "You will always become the company you keep. Keep great company." (Dr. Gopala Aiyer Sundaramoorthy, quoted by scholar Douglas Brooks, 2011, personal communication.)

Chapter 12 - International Development

With this in mind, we designed nested learning communities to support each individual in stabilizing any transformative changes they experienced in Leading from Within. First, we set up learning communities of about three to five individuals in which participants would relate and converse during the months between the four retreats each year. Second, we combined individuals into small groups to carry out *breakthrough initiatives*. By working together, they could hold each other to new ways of engaging and new ways of thinking that goes beyond "business as usual." Finally, the cohort of thirty individuals gather at least six times per year (four formal retreats, at least two interim group meetings), to assist them in providing a larger community in which new ideas could take root in their lives. A testament to how well this approach to nested social holons worked was the group's spontaneous initiative to found the African Integral Development Network. This was something we had hoped for, but were surprised to see emerge far earlier in the project.

The second way we have included an understanding of levels in social groups is in our assessment of the larger economic challenges that Nigeria faces. This country is ranked number 124 on the Economists Democracy Index out of 167 countries. On the one hand, it supposedly functions as a democracy, yet when assessed on the specific criteria for a democratic system, it is actually categorized as an "authoritarian state" (Economist Democracy Index, 2008). Extremely excessive corruption continues to constitute a major challenge to Nigeria, and vote rigging and other means of coercion are practiced by all major parties in order to remain competitive. The country's lucrative oil wealth has not supported the country's development, and in fact may be a cause of its underdevelopment. The oil dollars bring in foreign currency and thus devalue the local currency, eroding the national economy from thriving.[2] Also, elected officials and government workers feel they have a right to a share of government revenues, such that the political elite continues to drain a low leak from the state coffers, leaving less for everyone else. In other words, the "social center of gravity" of the electorate is ethnocentric rather than sociocentric (that is, care extends to a certain social group, but not sufficiently to the national social holon). And, millions of Nigerians are suffering because of that. Oxford's Paul Collier (*The Bottom Billion*, 2007, p. 101) explains how the country has made approximately 280 billion dollars in oil revenue over the past thirty years, and yet on the Human Development Index the country remains 158 out of 182, with over half of the population living on less than $2 per day. He explains, "This is far larger than any realistic scale of aid to a bottom billion country. Yet Nigeria has depressingly little to show for it."

For the country to develop sustainably, this ethnocentric worldview and social discourse of the electorate that allows the system to run on corruption has to be reckoned with. But, how does one do that? How does one get at that political elite? One way is through the people.

Almond and Verba (1989) identified the role of political culture in a democracy as vital. They suggest that the political element of many voluntary organizations facilitates better awareness and a more informed citizenry, who make better voting choices, participate in politics, and hold government more accountable as a result.

That has become a design principle of this project which seeks to support a group of leaders in civil society organizations that are developing from a healthy ethnocentric to an emerging worldcentric level of consciousness. We believe the number of individuals holding a higher worldview need not be that many for new ideas to take root. It is possible that this corruption is perpetuated by under ten individuals—perhaps even less than five!—at the top of the power hierarchy, and that the majority at the grassroots hold a different intention and participate in a different social discourse. Many Nigerians have tremendous intention for positive change and, given the enabling conditions, have the human potential to realize it. So, the project is designed for this group of thirty individuals to become "strange attractors" for the social center of gravity toward worldcentrism, and more effectively press upon their electorate to show up more ethically. The goal, ultimately, is to promote sustainable development in the country and region.

To reach that goal, we created a *holarchical scaffolding* for individuals to be enmeshed in increasingly larger social groups—from pairs, to learning communities, to small group breakthrough initiatives, to a larger network. We did this knowing the national social holon will exert a downward pull on this smaller cohort of thirty participants in our program, and would also pull upon the developmental achievements of individuals. By ensuring that the participants can collaborate in smaller groups between retreats and as they apply their leadership skills in action, hopefully they can retain their learning and transformation beyond the bounds of the One Sky project itself. And even begin to become strange attractors for the society as a whole.

Chapter 12 - International Development

With this in mind, I was truly heartened to hear at the end of the year Obio Owai Obio, a participant from the small rain forest village of Ekoasi, explain:

> I am grateful [for Leading from Within]. I am really grateful because through this program, I know how to move forward in my work. My vision is to liaise with other communities that use the forest near my community—which is one of the largest areas of rain forest remaining. If I only work with Ekoasi, we will not be able to stop deforestation, but if we can liaise with other communities as well, we have a chance.

Conclusion

"You cannot separate the epistemology of a knowing human from the ontology of what is revealed."
—Ken Wilber, 2006

At its essence, as integral practitioners in international development, we are looking to the context, culture, and consciousness that gives rise to situations of "underdevelopment." We then recognize the evolutionary unfolding and note where it is stuck and where it is flowing, so the situation might liberate itself back into its natural evolutionary flow to greater depth and complexity.

As a result, we are less looking to lay upon a situation what we think is important for development (such as greater gender equality, human rights, food security, etc.); rather, we are looking to the context, culture, and consciousness to find where it is stuck, how it's stuck, and to what extent. It *may be* that gender equality, human rights, and food security are what are needed, but we don't go into a situation with that as our assumption. Laying down our preferred "building blocks" of development on a situation and a people falls into the same error as the modern and postmodern approaches: that is, whether I am coming into communities instituting an economic agenda for growth or whether I am coming into communities instituting a set of green values, I am still not listening to the situation, being sensitive to what is present, and responding to what the context, culture, and consciousness most need for their spontaneous, natural evolution. The radical shift in this approach is not what is done, but how we do it: through listening, being sensitive to what is arising, being responsive to how to proceed, and staying deeply aware of the enactive nature of the universe.

Our work as integral practitioners in international development, then, is to assess where those obstructions and imbalances are, and work to release them, at which point *development* can continue spontaneously. We don't deliver development, we don't do development, we don't work in thematic areas that we feel are needed for development, and we don't institute our pet theory of how a developed society should look. Rather, we recognize development to be natural, spontaneous, and inherent to every situation, and work to reveal the places where development is snagged, and assist in releasing blocks for greater flow. So, *what* we do using an integral approach may end up looking very similar to other development approaches. However, *why* we are doing what we are doing is usually informed by different assessments and orientations compared to other approaches—with notably different results. This orientation is the most unique aspect of how we do what we do.

In this chapter, I have explained quadrants and levels in greater detail in the context of international development, giving some applied examples of engaging in development challenges in Peru and Nigeria.

Chapter 12 - International Development

Appendix

These are the stages of development used in international development (based on Wilber, 1985, 2006, Gebser, 1985, and my own experience working with these stages in international development).

Egocentric: Includes archaic and magic worldviews (both pretraditional), make meaning based on a paleo-logic unlike the reason that most adults rely on today. Here, power is held in blood and semen, and so familial lines are important and power displays often include violence. A healthy expression of this stage may be seen with the animistic cultures and shamanism in some indigenous cultures that have remained largely separated from the modern world, such as in the voluntary noncontact peoples in the Amazon rain forest. Healthy versions may also be seen in the tribal chief structure of local villages as well as tribal customs and practices that connect people to place. Unhealthy expressions, however, are seen in the despot rulers whose moral span supposedly should include the nation and yet only extends to one's tribal group. In international development, when a politician has a magic worldview, he or she construes governance to be using one's power for one's own family or group benefit. The sense of doing right for the nation is not present, even though they are making decisions that affect the entire nation.

Ethnocentric: Includes a mythic worldview is prevalent across the world in many traditional societies and groups. This traditional worldview begins to order reality in specific forms, where each thing has its right place. The healthy expressions of this stage are the rules, roles, and policies that become incredibly important in fiscal accountability and financial management in international development. Other healthy expressions are the sort of ordered thinking that guides bureaucracies and public services. In fact, the concept of "public service" arises for the first time at this stage. Power shifts from the self and its tribal group, to a great Other, be it God, Allah, or Jehovah, and individuals are encouraged to conform socially. While an important and healthy degree of self-surrender occurs at this stage, unhealthy expressions at this stage arise if there is such conformity that individual expression and innovation are stifled, or if people align with the power of their chosen great Other (Allah, God, etc.) and enact violence, injustice, and inequity in their name.

Sociocentric: Includes a rational worldview (modern), characterizes much of the global economic discourse, and relies on science, reason, and facts. This worldview is one of the first to expound a universalistic sense of care for all individuals, and so many of the secular expressions of modern society that demand universal rights for all (including all women, children, minorities) is a healthy expression of a rational worldview. Power is held in facts and empirical evidence, as well as held by those who have control over the facts and evidence, and is also held in the universal injunctions for moral care. In international development, some healthy examples of the rational worldview include the engineering efforts to build infrastructure, transportation, and communication systems, to increase a country's access to the global market, and to advocate for universal human rights. Whereas unhealthy examples of a rational worldview are a disenchantment of the world, with an over-reliance on technology and scientism, as well as unexamined assumptions of privilege and power.

Worldcentric: Includes a pluralistic worldview (postmodern), is seen more and more in the international development discourse where diversity and cultural sensitivity are held up as central to human wellbeing. Many of the "isms" arose with this worldview, such as multiculturalism, environmentalism, sexism, feminism, etc. and the idea of "context" became incredibly important. Pluralistic approaches in development work for community-based, rights-based, recipient-led, and people-centered approaches. Power here is held in "political correctness" and the deconstruction of traditional and modern truths. Healthy expressions include its ability to be self-reflective, to critically question assumptions and power dynamics, and to prioritize individual self-expression. Unhealthy forms include the tendency to view green values as better than all others, and yet to simultaneously deconstruct the idea of ranking. This is not only contradictory but also takes away the very pathway of human development, which arises through a hierarchy of whole-parts (or, holarchy).

Kosmoscentric: Includes an integral worldview, is newer to our human community, though had forerunners as early as the turn of the century with philosophers like Aurobindo. It enables, for the first time in human evolution, a way to value all the previous stages and worldviews that came before it, as each arose in a particular time for a particular reason, and gives important insights for this moment. Early expressions can see and sort contexts (strategist action-logic), and later expressions become aware of constructs (construct-aware action-logic). integral practitioners in development tend to resonate with whatever is most appropriate in each moment. As such, they will notably embrace a pretraditional, traditional, modern, or postmodern form of engagement where appropriate, which is a healthy expression of this stage, namely, that previous stages are integrated and thus able to be drawn upon when necessary. Unhealthy expressions fall into hyper-masculinity, hyperbole, hubris, and over-categorizing reality.

NOTES

1. And when a nation doesn't, they are seen to be out of step with the global whole.

2. To explain this in more detail: The country earns so much foreign currency from exporting oil that it is much cheaper and more rational to import anything they need with that foreign money, rather than produce it locally. Local industries, enterprises, other export sectors languish under competition from cheap imports. This is referred to as "Dutch disease" in economic theory. A kind of de-industrialization occurs or, more to the point for Nigeria, commercialization and market formation cannot take place in a widespread way, which is key for higher economic complexity and transformation into amber and orange altitudes of social organization.

References

Economist Intelligence Unit's Democracy Index: 2008, retrieved on April 8, 2011 at en.wikipedia.org/wiki/Democracy_Index.
The UN's Human Development Report: 2010, *The Real Wealth of Nations: Pathways to Human Development*, accessible at hdr.undp.org/en/reports/global/hdr2010.
Gebser, J. *The Ever-present Origin*. Athens: Ohio University Press, 1985.
Collier, Paul. *The Bottom Billion: Why the Poorest Countries Are Failing and What Can Be Done about It*. Oxford: Oxford University Press, 2007.
Almond, G. and S. Verba, editors. *The Civic Culture Revisited*. Newbury Park, CA: Sage Publications, 1989.
Wilber, K. *Integral Spirituality: A Startling New Role for Religion in the Modern and Postmodern World*. Boston: Shambhala Publications, 2006.
———."Excerpt D: The Look of a Feeling: The Importance of Post/Structuralism," 2002, retrieved July 31, 2008, from www.kenwilber.com/writings.
———. *A Brief History of Everything*. Boston: Shambhala Publications, 1996.
———. *Sex, Ecology, Spirituality: The Spirit of Evolution*. Boston and London: Shambhala Publications, 1995.
———. *Up from Eden*. Boston: Shambhala Publications, 1985.

Chapter 13
Leadership

Mikyö Clark

What are the essential qualities of tomorrow's emerging leadership? Our's is a time on planet Earth in which the many systems that humankind has built over the course of its history are being rendered obsolete by the sheer size and complexity of the problems that we face. In both our public and private institutions, the growth of a globalized informational marketplace has rendered the rules of traditional economics and twentieth century business practices extinct. We have seen countless firms closing their doors, and even more new ones springing up in their wake. When I first began researching this article, protestors from around the world had been occupying public spaces from Wall Street to Bangladesh continuously for more than six months in opposition to the injustices being incurred through a massive and ongoing financial crisis. The multifaceted and interwoven human systems that have carried us into the new millennium are today collapsing under a tremendous weight.

The roots of these dysfunctional systems live within the hearts and minds of societies both past and present—we have inherited them from the elders who came before us. It is the role and purpose of today's leadership to transform these structures into newer, more complex, and more adequate forms which are suited for the world that we are leaving to the generations of the future. Successful leadership today requires more than rote learning of new technologies and the incorporation of an expanded framework for action. We are going to need more than a few skills and some knowledge of integral or other meta-theories in order to effect real change. To affect this transformation, to be resilient and regenerative in our leadership today, requires modes of continual epistemological overhaul in the face of ever-changing circumstantial and environmental factors.[1] Building such capacities is perhaps the single greatest challenge that we millennials must face as a generation, not only professionally but personally as well, in our roles as children and parents, husbands and wives, friends and mentors. Such growth requires entire networks of deep support and challenge, which can help to incubate and structure our experiences of the higher capacities we are being called to explore, and eventually master.

My proposal, then, is that it is the role of today's leadership to design these types of leadership networks, and to weave relationships between the disparate parts of the many systems that we live in and through. As leaders we must tend not only to the outsides of these systems, to their aesthetic, form, structure, and scaffolding, in order to insure that they will provide beauty, integrity, stability, and support. Simultaneously we must tend to the insides of these complex systems, to their cultures and subcultures, families and tribes, in order to insure their sense of safety, mutual reinforcement, healthy competition, well-defined boundaries, and commitment to specific values or value systems. We must begin to architect not only the size and shape of our teams and committees, but the interior cultures and interpersonal dynamics in which they function. The micro-communities in which we live must reflect our own complexity and internal capacity for change. This shifting of our interpersonal engagement reforms the riverbanks of our social world by changing the exterior structures[2] of our relationships and the way that values and other interior phenomena[3] can move through our organizations and communities.

Integral, Action-Inquiry, Tribal, and Developmental

There are a number of leading-edge leadership paradigms which address both the interiors and exteriors of culture within a larger meta-systemic framework, namely integral leadership (Wilber, Esbjörn-Hargens), tribal leadership (Dave Logan), and developmental action-inquiry (Torbert et al.). Each is based in an ontogenetic understanding of the individual human life cycle, which points to different potential stages of cognitive (oneself-world), interpersonal (oneself-other), and intrapersonal (oneself-oneself) modes of identification and maturation. In each of the models, alongside individual growth, two differing modes of collective development are also acknowledged. The first is as a "deep time"[4] evolutionary processes—the (phylogenetic) unfolding of human potentials throughout the course of our history into more and more complex civilizations and forms of social interaction. This same arc of cultural evolution can be seen in smaller (ontogenetic) micro-movements, which happen throughout the course of a single human lifetime, as an individual transitions between a previously held set of values and an emergent set of values tied to new sets of communities with different social practices.

The developmental component of these models serves as their ontological and epistemological backbone by emphasizing the increasing complexity of structures of human consciousness as they connect with the world to make meaning. This developmental lens is an indispensable cornerstone of emerging forms of leadership for two reasons. Firstly, within leadership communities which are immeasurably diverse, it allows us to map and place individuals along a recognizable spectrum and thus better support them in taking their next steps into the elaborate terrains of human life and work. Secondly we realize that, as Einstein mused more than fifty years ago: "No problem can be solved from the same level of consciousness that created it." Then the moral imperative for us as leaders becomes the continuing evolution of our own consciousness to match and overcome the many complex problems that we face.

But, as we know, the process of maturation and healing never happens in isolation; it is only with the support of a strong community that we can step more fully into our own deeper capacities for love, vision, and action. Weaving these communities, committed both to undying support and fierce challenge, has become the focus of my work, and has led to the development of a social technology called Cultural Evolutionary Ecosystem's Design, or CEED for short.

I feel that CEED's potential as a transformative tool for the development of tomorrow's leaders is unrivaled for a number of reasons: 1) it runs on IOS, Wilber's (2003) postmetaphysical framework, which allows for a) the coordinates of its ontological and epistemological zones of enactment to be specified,[5] and b) its methodological injunctions to be determined in relationship to the realities they are designed to reveal,[6] all of which helps to frame the enactive nature of the technology's various functions; 2) it employs Torbert's (2000, 2004) triple-loop feedback system for highlighting the relationship between our actions, strategies, and awareness or attention itself, allowing us to incorporate more moment-to-moment feedback and perspectives on the current decisions we face and identities we hold; and 3) it draws on Dave Logan's (2009) concept of tribal leadership, first and foremost operationalizing the triadic structure that he presents as the basic unit or "building block" of CEED communities. The integration of insight and praxis from these rich emergent leadership paradigms is the basis for CEED's developmental approach to ecosystem creation and cultural design. It is with these tools in hand that I offer the beta version of this leadership technology in hopes that it can be revised and incubated in its own network of theoretical and practical application and critique.

Pilot Research on CEED's Applications

Given the need for robust developmental ecosystems in leadership training and capacity building, it is clear that CEED technology's time has come. Yet it remains unclear to what extent the more theoretical aspects of this praxis can start coming online in real-world situations as embodied functional capacities of a diverse group of leaders. In attempting to drill down into the source code of CEED's platform, I have begun to conduct formal research and beta-testing on this technology over the past three months, in the context of a course on integral research held at John F. Kennedy University. In the following pages I will outline a pilot research project that utilizes the platform of integral research (Esbjörn-Hargens, 2008) to explore a number of the core components of CEED applications through a mixed-methods research design. For the purposes of brevity within this version of my exposition, I have cherry-picked the most relevant insights and consolidated them here—a fuller version of this article with detailed research notes can be found online.[7] My current inquiry into the application of CEED is meant as a generative preview of an ongoing revision and restructuring processes, which will give way to newer versions of this technology as it is birthed from a theoretically aligned set of practices into a fully operationalized living system for leadership support.

Before proceeding I would like to describe a few of the assumptions I hold about this topic, and about the art of leadership as a whole. First, the limitations of my own awareness and development (my Kosmic Address)[8] will dictate my direct experience of the terrains that I enact (i.e., my data sets). This includes the first-person research that I have conducted on myself, which constitutes a picture of myself that only I could have taken. Second, my own interest in, and involvement with, my research topic (i.e., CEEDbeta as a whole) is based on unseen and unnamable forms of identification, desire, and repulsion (karmas)[9] which play into my every interaction with my topic and the world. Third, the support and challenge that I have received from my own leadership ecosystem which I have been engaged with throughout my research process prevents me from wholly objectifying CEED, as its core components are constitutive of my present sense of self as a researcher. These are important for me to name upfront in the knowledge-building process, as they have formed the bedrock of my entire inquiry process.

The potentialities of CEED technology must be viewed as enacted through the developmental capacities of the leaders operationalizing it, and so, in an attempt to shed light on my own hidden and unhidden structures of consciousness, I will be presenting original, first-person research in two different horizons of inquiry according to Wilber's (2003, 2006) division of eight methodological zones. This movement will serve as a part of the "drilling down" process described above, by which the roots of CEED's source code in my own body and mind can be explored and examined at length.

First-Person Research Methods

The research conducted in phase one of this project is designed to explore my own subjectivity as CEED's designer, including my own thoughts, sensations, perceptions, emotions, and state experiences. Here we will be exploring these experiences qualitatively as they connect to the practice of leadership design. These direct experiences will be inquired into from two different perspectives or horizons of inquiry. The first horizon, oftentimes referred to in Integral Theory as phenomenology, examines the insides of my own subjectivity—in this case my own direct experience of myself and of leadership and leadership design. In researching my own interiors, I chose to utilize a form of autobiographical archaeology, in effect asking "Who am I?" and "What is (and has been) my experience of leadership and leadership design?"

The second horizon of inquiry, oftentimes referred to as structuralism, approaches my subjectivity from the outside, revealing the structural (i.e., developmental and typological) components of my own perspective which pattern my internal experience but are invisible to me. In examining the structures of my own conscious awareness, I utilized both a developmental metric and a typological test, coupled with my own processes of research and resonance with the literature surrounding both, in addition to a coaching session with my SCTi rater (who is also an integral psychologist), Elliot Ingersoll. I asked the questions, "How is my identity constructed?" and "How is my personality structured?" These structural inquiries and their relationship to my phenomenological research will be examined in the discussion section.

It is through these two horizons of inquiry that we will attempt to explore my own subjectivity and its relationship to CEED technology as a platform for leadership design. Through this process the strengths and limitations of my own perspective in relationship to the topic will hopefully become clear through the revelation of my own personal experience and the deeper structures which set the limits on that experience. Now that we have set some context for the first phase of this research endeavor, let's turn to the first-person methods themselves.

PHENOMENOLOGICAL METHODS
Research Design

The subjective component of this research is an important gateway into myself as a tool in the research and understanding of leadership design. Such an inquiry stems from the postmodern recognition that any form of research is mediated by the structures of the knowing subject, in which the developmental capacities of an individual (in this case, me) are employed in the examination of a particular topic (in this case leadership design and CEEDbeta technology). My own subjective experience of leadership design, how I experience it, is an important data set for the full elucidation of what leadership design is. My choice of methods for this exploration have been grouped under the title "Autobiographical Archaeology."

Chapter 13 - Leadership

Autobiographical Archaeology Data

The data offered here should be contextualized by offering a brief but poignant look into the cultural ecosystem which gave rise to this research process, as this article is an artifact of that ecosystem and my place within it. I am presently situated in the context of many triads which I have cultivated as an act of implementing CEED technology in my own life. The triads that I have running as of today are: 1) a horizontal triad of fraternal peers who are well versed in AQAL and aspects of the wisdom traditions, who's developmental scope ranges between Cook-Greuter's individualist stage at the lower end, and autonomous to construct-aware stages at the higher end (more on these developmental levels can be found in the section below titled "Structural Assessment Methods"); 2) a vertical triad of Dzogchen-practitioner-integral-scholars spanning three generations, who are aligned in a common mission, of which I am the youngest; 3) a pyramidal triad of two third-wave integral leaders (myself included), led by a second-wave practitioner, who's primary focus is waking up to deeper and deeper vantage points[10] in the moment; 4) a second pyramidal triad of conscious creatives with varying levels of familiarity with AQAL, who together are building a guild structure for cultural stewardship; 5) a vertical shadow triad, who's other two members are my mentees, coming together in a context focused on the healing of "dark" and "bright" disowned aspects of self; and 6) an emerging pyramidal triad, led by a significant second-wave researcher, which will be focused on the writing and publication of integral texts.

These six triads constitute my personal deployment of CEEDbeta technology, with the specific recommended number (six) being sourced in Dave Logan's work on tribal leadership, and much of the developmental and state-based metrics and language used being sourced in AQAL and the larger integral tradition. The live feedback practices occurring in each of these triads can be seen as expressions of developmental-action-inquiry, as the organic capacities being lit up in each feed into their own evolution, and the evolution of the larger interwoven system of micro-communities. This platform has not yet fully launched, but is expected to do so soon with the completion of this research process and the integration of its findings. Now, let's move on into those findings.

In my synthesis of the data sets that emerged from my different modes of inquiry, I distilled a set of four themes in relationship to my own experience of leadership and leadership design. These are: 1) leaders produce artifacts which are meaningful to their leadership ecosystems; 2) artifacts represent (i.e., are symbols of) the developmental complexity of the systems that generate them; 3) certain artifacts may be used as leverage points for a system to transition into a higher-order of complexity; 4) each developmental level represents an artifact itself. I will now present an abbreviated description of these themes in order, drawing direct examples from my research on myself to illustrate these higher-order principles. A certain familiarity with the AQAL language is assumed in relationship to different elements of my meta-analysis of these themes, as has been true for the entirety of this article.

Data: Theme 1: Leaders Produce Artifacts Which Are Meaningful to Their Leadership Ecosystems

The first theme that emerged had to do with the relationship between individual leaders and the leadership ecosystems which house them in spheres of concomitant meaning-making and value creation. The intersubjective realm of a leader's life will have a great deal of influence on his or her worldview, this much is clear. But what I explored in this theme had more to do with what leader's produced, the actual artifacts of consciousness, whether songs, soups, or subpersonalities, which were tended to during their creation processes. These artifacts will always exist (i.e., be interpreted) differently for different developmental levels of consciousness, as explained by Esbjörn-Hargens's (2010) notion of integral ontological pluralism. They will always "show up" differently, and be related to differently, by people at different levels of consciousness. What is interesting to explore, then, is what leaders do produce—and what I found in my own case was that I always produced artifacts that were meaningful to those in my larger ecosystem at the time of their creation. I found that I exemplified developmentally different performances of higher levels of complexity when I was in communication with a higher-order "audience," or group of leaders.

This theme exposes the relationship between artifacts and the leadership ecosystems which produce them, with the process of meaning-making being highlighted as the thread connecting the two. If we utilize this insight as a lens for the examination of current leadership systems and the artifacts they produce, we can more readily create relationships between the complexity and meaningfulness of an artifact with the many systems which gave rise to its form. In the context of CEED's implementation as a technology for leadership design, we can operationalize this insight by first assessing the current ecosystems which form the back-end support system of any leader's life. We can asses such a system through any number of lenses, looking into deep structural (i.e., developmental) components, as well as surface structural (i.e., cultural, temporal, geographic, and other such contextual circumstances), chronological (i.e., how long have the various components of a system been online), linguistic[11] (i.e., how leaders speak about themselves, others, and their work), narrative (i.e., how such a support system came into being from the leader's perspective), and others. This sort of investigation can offer a variety of inside-out perspectives on the back-end leadership ecosystem, which gives rise to front-end artifact creation processes in gross, subtle, and/or causal spheres.

An inverse approach would start with the artifacts themselves, and attempt to discern (using a variety of the lenses mentioned above) information about the back-end systems which gave rise to them. This is a sort of outside-in approach, which is similar in some ways to psychotherapy and traditional medical sciences,[12] wherein one starts with a symptom (which itself can be seen as an artifact) and then works backwards to discover the root cause (or set of causes) which gave rise to it. When CEED is operationalized in such a way, it can explore the genealogies not only of problems and less-than-desirable outcomes, it can also trace successful and brilliant forms of emergence "upstream" to their own root systems in order to reveal some of the causes of both healthy and diseased forms of leadership. This article is an example of this mode of outside-in investigation into an artifact (namely CEED technology), by which research is conducted into the context in which the artifact came into existence.

The capacity to relate the back-end systems with their front-end production capacity is an extraordinarily valuable asset within the context of leadership design, and one which is not yet being taken advantage of by many of today's top leadership professionals. CEED's capacity to meaningfully integrate these dimensions within the personal and professional lives of its users exemplifies its breadth and depth of potential application.

Data: Theme 2: Artifacts Represent (i.e., Are Symbols of) the Developmental Complexity of the Systems that Generate Them

In each of the previous examples I have noted the generation of particular artifacts. It should be clear by this point that my use of the word artifact is in no way limited to concrete objects or material things. I am using the term to point to objects in the most general sense as expressions of a particular consciousness. The second theme has to do with how these "things" are related to the various systems (both intra-, inter-, and extrapersonal)[13] that give rise to their existence. The shape and texture, size and weight of a thing, in fact all of its gross, subtle, and causal attributes, are symbols of the many systems which gave birth to it—they are indicators of the ecosystem in which it participates and thus has meaning.

This theme keys into an artifact's meaning, and the process by which objects interact as symbols within the networks in which they participate. These front-end artifacts have their life cycle as the carriers of those back-end systems which gave rise to them, as we learned through our examination of theme one. But once birthed into the world, these artifacts (again, gross, subtle, and/or causal) become the symbolic carriers of their mother system's generational DNA (or AQAL blueprint). Throughout this process, the artifact's DNA interacts autopoetically with the surrounding system, forming newer and exceedingly more complex forms of communication and interaction within the expanding world. These interactions in turn serve to amplify meaning and help to shape future systems which give rise to more complex artifacts.

As a leadership design platform, CEED's primary function is the continuation of meaning as the blueprint of the Kosmos. It's capacity for understanding the living nature of the participatory systems in which humans and other life forms generate their realities allows for its functional participation in the lives of it's users as a dynamic platform for the regeneration and reconstitution of their own meaning-making. Such regeneration allows for more dynamic and healthy front-end expressions

Chapter 13 - Leadership

within user's own professional environments, in addition to back-end stabilization and integration within user's personal and familial environments.

Data: Theme 3: Artifacts May Be Used as Leverage Points for a System to Transition into a Higher Order of Complexity

In outlining the symbolic relationship between artifacts and the ecosystems which give rise to them, I hope it has become clear that artifacts themselves have multiple meanings. These differing meanings are based upon the levels of development of the subject in the various lines through which the artifact is apprehended and interfaced with.

This theme examines the transactive nature of artifacts as levers for whole systems to undergo transformation. This relates to the concept of artifacts as keepers of a genetic code, which interact dynamically within the systems which consider them meaningful. When an artifact is transacted between two systems, the DNA of that artifact couples with the DNA of the receiving system, and something entirely new is born. When the releasing system opens itself to release or birth the meaningful artifact, its structure inevitably changes, as does the structure of the receiving system, but what is interesting to note is that the artifact itself changes as well, as its meaning shifts simultaneously to stabilize within its new context. The entire interaction is almost sexual in nature, and it is through such intimacy that both systems have the potential for constitutional transition.

CEED exists as a platform for such transactions to take place between systems which couldn't have otherwise found commonality. It's users will find through its platform the triangulated spaces in which their own personal and professional growth can take place through a demand for increasing quality of deliverables (i.e., more complex front-end artifacts being produced; more challenge), as well as a deep network of professionals who can assist them in legitimating their own failures and regressions (large or small). This can open the gateways for the growth of richer support systems both on- and offline (i.e., more complex back-end ecosystems; more support). In this way CEED itself can act as a lever within its user's lives to help them transition their personal and professional life systems into more satisfying, genuine, and successful forms.

Data: Theme 4: Each Developmental Level Represents an Artifact Itself

As evidenced in the discussion of the three themes above, it is clear that artifacts are generated at each level of consciousness in both the gross, subtle, and causal realms[14] of existence. In such a way, each of the levels of consciousness can be seen as an artifact of the ecosystem that produced it—each can be conceptualized as the emergent technology necessary for the leveraging of a system into a higher order of complexity. These artifacts are then transacted with the full AQAL matrix that they inhabit, as the self continues its process of meaning-making from that level of development. When that meaning-making system breaks down, due to newer and more complex challenges, life circumstances, or any other number of unforeseeable causes, then the mode of self-identification, the form of the ego, becomes an artifact to be metabolized by another emergent form of self-identification.

In such a way, the human body-mind itself can be seen as an artifact of the evolution of consciousness through forms or bodies which can house it with increasing sensitivity to the more subtle realms of perception and awareness. And, as with many of the other artifacts discussed in this section, the human body-mind most definitely exists at multiple levels. It can be seen as the lever for consciousness on this planet to make a sort of macro-transition into the higher-mental (and perhaps transmental) plane(s) of existence. This transition into a more complex form of being, namely the increasing awareness and field density of another few billion people living on the planet, may be the springboard for new forms of social and ecological interfacing in the coming generations.

This theme deals with situating each level of human existence, or each chapter of a user's life, as an artifact of its own. This frame allows us to look at the entirety of our front- and back-end systems, at the entirety of our ecosystem (at the entirety of our self) as a living process with its own DNA which will inevitably act as a lever for our own continued evolution deeper into the depths our own potential and manifestation. We can view this transaction as taking place between the entirety of our self-system and the Kosmic or total AQAL system itself, part of which is unmanifest or latent at the point of such an interaction. This sexual act in which the DNA of our present self is released allows for the influx of a structurally novel set of potential horizons for both our front- and back-end systems. We can also conceptualize such a transaction as the overflowing of awareness beyond the boundary of the current system, which results (with the satisfactory environmental conditions; i.e., support and challenge) in a metabolizing process (the aforementioned sexual transaction) through which the boundaries of the self are redrawn to include larger spheres of being. This is epistemological overhaul in action.

The role of CEED technology in such profound growth rests in its own living, open-source nature. Its users upgrading their own interface will result in CEED's DNA changing along with their own, as the quality and quantity of support and challenge requested from this platform deepen as more and more users begin to engage it.

Discussion

The themes outlined above point to the continued process of the evolution of form, and draw from my own experience of evolution and simultaneous production of gross, subtle, and causal artifacts along the way. I have attempted to outline some of the processes by which leadership (or the "leading edge" of either individual or collective evolution) creates the necessary technologies for the purposes of the continuity of the system of which it is a part. Through this process, it seems that the systems themselves have the opportunity to become increasingly self-conscious in their utilization of emergent artifacts as gateways into newer and more complex forms of self-organization. It is my hope that CEEDbeta can be such an artifact for its front-end users, albeit scaled accordingly to their own current level of development.

We are seeing, in the examination of these themes, a story emerging which surrounds both the growth of leaders and the growth of CEED technology as an artifact produced by a group of leaders. This story is one of the dynamic potential exemplified by human beings which has been translated into an active platform for the development of future generations of leaders who, because of the enormity of the challenges they face, will undoubtedly require the developmental edge that they can gain through its use. CEEDbeta, having emerged through my own back-end support structures, can today begin to be operationalized as a front-end user interface for those desiring to pioneer the future of leadership.

STRUCTURAL ASSESSMENT METHODS
Research Design

The structural perspective is an important one for the revelation of the hidden ontological and epistemological structures of my own consciousness which bring into being my phenomenal world, my leadership, and thus this version of CEED technology. It is through the examination of these exterior structures that we can assess more readily where CEED is being sourced from, both vertically (in terms of structure-stage origination),[15] horizontally (state-stage, or vantage point origination)[16], and typologically (personality structure orientation).[17] It is through locating my own Kosmic Address as the originator of CEEDbeta that we can more readily begin to situate this technology within the ecosystems in which it can be of the most benefit. My structural assessment also took place via first-person, second-person, and third-person methods, which I will now detail.

The first-person component of my vertical structural self-analysis consisted of a thorough process of review of the current developmental literature, especially the Harvard-based lineage[18] of scholars in which Integral Theory is most deeply rooted. I examined aspects of the different stages as they corresponded to my own inner experience of the different stages of my own life.

The second-person component of my vertical structural self-analysis took two forms: a) weekly feedback and biweekly class meetings with a professor, Mark Forman, himself an integral psychologist, who's up-front dialogue with me about my own constructions of reality was deeply informative as well as grounding; and b) an hour-long coaching call with Elliot Ingersoll, also an integral psychologist, who scored my SCTi and reviewed the results with me in the context of my own life and growth. These two more formal modes of engagement with elder scholars were complemented with feedback that I received continually from peers versed in development, in the context of the many triads that I am engaged with

Chapter 13 - Leadership

surrounding my own centers of gravity in differing lines of development, as well as in my overall level of ego-identity.

The third-person component of my vertical structural self-analysis consisted of my engaging a developmental metric designed by Cook-Greuter and Associates, the SCTi, which is designed to measure ego-identity.

The data and metrics for the third-person measurement of horizontal state-stage and vantage point being quite limited, I will refer only briefly to my own first- and second-person inquiries into this dimension of my Kosmic Address. It seems to me that various theoreticians hold differing viewpoints on the nature of development with regard to state stabilization, with some emphasizing more heavily than others the subtle dimensions of being. That being said, my own interest in, and practice of awakening has had little to do with some of the more eclectic aspects of subtle growth, and has focused more on the depth of my nondual presence as awareness itself. Having been born into the Tibetan Dzogchen[19] tradition of which my father was a lineage holder, I have been steeped in a transmission-based nongradual path of awakening for my whole life. With the help of mentors from various[20] Dzogchen streams, as well as students of its "sister," the Mahamudra tradition, I have come to know what awakening is. I have begun to conceptualize this process primarily through DiPerna's (forthcoming) notion of vantage points, which is based on the work of Daniel P. Brown. From this standpoint, through a) first-person investigation both through daily sitting practice and the practice of moment-to-moment recognition of awareness; and b) second-person peer feedback from various friends and mentors who have stabilized deeper vantage points than I have; I've come to a better understanding of my own wakefulness.

With regard to the typological elements of my own perspective, I investigated thoroughly (in the context of John F. Kennedy's quarter-long course on the Enneagram taught by Jordan Luftig) my own typological orientation also via first-person, second-person, and third-person methods. The first-person methods consisted of personal reflections upon the literature of the different Enneagramatic traditions, and my felt resonance with the characteristics and behaviors of the different types presented therein. This was coupled with second-person feedback that I received from classmates regarding my posts and insights about my own typology, in addition to ongoing feedback that I was receiving from the triads I was engaged with at that time. The third-person method that I engaged was the RHETI 2.5 metric, which I took online on May 30, 2011.

Data: Vertical Structures

Scoring at 5+ on the SCTi indicates that my self-identity is most often associated with Cook-Greuter's autonomous stage,[21] though I may be in the process of entering the early construct-aware stage (indicated by the +). There are a number of different elements of this stage which both resonate strongly with my own sense of myself, and are relevant for our discussion of leadership design. These are as follows: 1) meta- and systems-thinking as modes of cognitive perspective taking; 2) a preoccupation with personal development; 3) an intergenerational temporal horizon; and 4) a sense of responsibility for one's own meaning-making. Each of these themes contributes to my own sense of myself, and has shaped CEEDbeta throughout its gestation process.

Data: Theme 1: Meta- and Systems-Thinking as Modes of Cognitive Perspective Taking

The cognitive dimensions of Cook-Greuter's autonomous and construct-aware levels of ego-complexity are considered to be systemic and cross-paradigmatic, respectively. These modes of cognition are capable of the integration of the multiple, complex, and ever-changing variables which are constitutive of a leadership ecosystem, the awareness of which must be present throughout its design and implementation. As discussed by numerous scholars[22] in the field of leadership, the capacity to cognize complex systems with multiple interdependent variables is one of the cornerstones of tomorrow's management capability. The coordination of complex variables couples with an ability to see and distinguish multiple worldviews and differing mental frameworks and strategies which come into play within the field of an organization or team. The meaningful synthesis, dialogue, and coordination of such perspectives, however, can only begin when this mode of cognition is housed in a self-system which exemplifies an equal level of complexity (i.e., autonomous or higher in the self-identity line). My own embodiment of such complexity allows for the requisite nuance and integrative capacity of these modes of cognition to be expressed healthily through the creation of artifacts such as CEED technology.

Data: Theme 2: A Preoccupation with Personal Development

At the center of the autonomous self lies a cognitive understanding of the developmental processes which gave rise to its own being—the occupational focus of which is a life of practice strategically geared towards self-actualization. Having come from a background which implicitly recognizes adult development, namely the guru-centric Buddhist tradition, my own intense desire for personal growth has spanned territories both personal and professional, exoteric and esoteric. This deepest drive has at times created obstacles for me in my own natural movement towards wholeness, causing perfectionism[23] and a fierce willfulness towards growth. My own focus on development is what has led me to develop technologies which aim to accelerate and harmonize this process, creating the living laboratories for actualization which are both safe and malleable.

Data: Theme 3: An Intergenerational Temporal Horizon

Another feature of the autonomous level which resonated strongly with my own process of personal investigation and peer and mentor feedback, was the mode and range of temporal engagement. This "intergenerational" mode is considered to span the entirety of one's lifetime, and extend into an accounting for both grandparent's contributions to one's own sense of self and psychoemotional patterning, as well as the potential effects of one's actions and attitudes on one's grandchildren. This widened horizon couples with a deep sense of personal responsibility and self-authorship to create the basis for truly sustainable action in the world. Such a widened temporal perspective is necessary for the design of systems which are adequate to meet the needs of human beings for the entirety of their own life cycle. It seems that the temporal mode identified with the next (construct-aware) stage is most suited to the design of multi-life-cycle, self-regenerating system meshworks, of which later versions of CEED will hopefully become a living example. These capacities for understanding the long-term global and historical effects of systems design are the baseline for tomorrow's higher-end leaders who are attempting intricate, regenerative, psychological, and outcome-driven work with groups who hold different worldviews, values sets, interests, and desired futures.

Data: Theme 4: A Sense of Responsibility for One's Own Meaning-Making

In my own life there is a very direct sense of personal accountability for the creation of meaning and fullness, which is both tremendously empowering, and can at times appear effortful and arrogant to others. This sense of being the author of one's own life story allows for the concentrated efforts of personal and professional growth, healing, and integration to coagulate as the core principles by which one lives. In my own case, I have found that the creation of a meaningful life, and the wish for the revelation of other's own authenticity led me to create a platform for the further growth of such capacities. Although CEED users will vary in their level of identification with the responsibility of creating their own stories and meanings about their lives, the platform's origination within my own self-system lends it to the increased generation of meaning and value at multiple levels of development, including those beyond my own.

Data: Horizontal Structures

I now recognize that I am "into"[24] awareness more than 50 percent of my waking life. My vantage point cycles between rigpa,[25] emptiness/causal recognition, and subtle witnessing/personality involvement during sitting practice, while throughout the day I can range on the shallow end into submersion in personality structures of varying density. The number of hours per day that I find myself in the recognition of awareness is increasing rapidly, however, through personal practice coupled with the completion and integration of cycles of deep trauma which have tied up my energy in innumerable ways. This healing and integration process yokes with a moment-to-moment inquiry practice into the source of my awareness, which is leading to an overall growth in my identification as pure presence. In fact, through the course of the writing of this article (perhaps because of the single-pointed nature of my daily engagement) I have found myself "into" awareness for upwards of 75 percent of each day.

The capacity to identify oneself with the field of awareness, rather than with one's own emotional "storyline" or sense of self, is foundational for tomorrow's leaders.[26] To offer a framework for this discussion in brief: there are different vantage points which can become embodied and stabilized over the course of state training, each of which offers deeper levels of inner sanctuary from the unpredictability of phenomena and their relationship to mind (i.e., the appearance of duality) which can manifest as obstacles in the domain of a practitioner's leadership. Each vantage point allows for a deeper intimacy between oneself and the objects or obstacles that are presently arising, as one begins to realize in a nonconceptual manner that they are not, in fact, things separate from the practitioner herself, but are deeply interwoven with her being by the fabric of the Kosmos. This perceptual interrelationship opens up a space for action that is uniquely appropriate to the circumstance that one finds oneself in—wherein whether the said action entails a great deal of effort or not is of little concern. The residing in this recognition of the nature of mind[27] is an important element of CEED technology; it serves as the space in which its complex ecosystems take form.

Data: Typological Structures

The conclusions of the various typographical metrics that I have taken over the past year have been in agreement that my personality is structured most prominently by components of the Enneatype One, called the Reformer. This type is known for being highly critical, both towards his or herself and others, often in the name of a deeply held set of moral values. The corresponding passion[28] is Ego-Resentment, which points to the reactivity and frustration experienced by this (my) type in relationship to life in general. The visionary capacities of the One often lead to an experience of how things should be, and when they do not turn out that way Ones experience anger which they often direct towards themselves or others. On the brighter side of this type, One's are often deeply principled, purposeful, and perfectionistic—they hold their values deeply within their minds, and want to act from those values, rather than just speaking about them. This can lead to a flavor of activism in their work in the world, wherein their judgments can be transmuted into discerning and decisive action.

This typological preference evidenced in my personality forms the backdrop for my desire to create the CEED platform as an emancipatory tool for the future of leadership. My desire for perfection and resentment towards the messiness of the world could lead to a limiting of CEED's user-interface to those whom I may unconsciously deem as developmentally capable of operationalizing it "properly." It has been my intention, however, throughout the process of its design, to offer a wide bandwidth of users the capacity to skillfully implement it for the design of their own ecosystems. The aspects of perfectionism and attention to detail, coupled with my own deeply held convictions surrounding the future's possibilities, will serve this technology in its continued evolution into more and more complex iterations.

Discussion

This latest look into the structural components of my own awareness as CEED's designer has offered a window into the inner ecosystem of self which gave rise to this technology. The vertical structural components of my own ego-identity have shaped the horizons of CEED's capacity for temporal management, while the cognitive styles of the two levels that I appear to range between shed light on the levels of systemic complexity which CEED is prepared to coordinate and synthesize. The horizontal state-based components of my identity point to the depth of presence and wakefulness which CEED is equipped to transmit to and recognize in its front-end users. Lastly, the typological components of my personality structure point to the overall orientation from which CEED has been birthed, as well as the potential limitations of its interface as indicated by my own identification patterns.

It is clear from our discussion above that such a technology is well suited to serve future leaders in the building of their back-end support systems, as well as their front-end production capacities. CEED's complexity is clearly sufficient for the nurturing of leaders whose mental models and communication styles are geared towards sustainable development in the spheres of self, culture, and nature (or more popularly: people, planet, and profit), which constitute the potential basis of future forms of accounting for value[29] within a business, organization, or team.

I would argue, based on the current assessment of my own development and the likelihood of the continuation of that development (and CEED technology along with it), that elements of future versions of CEED could become useful for individuals and organizations at vastly divergent levels of complexity, though its resources will likely find their best fit in circumstances and groups that are evidencing formal-operational or higher modes of cognitive expression. This investigation of my own structural capacities and limitations has served to situate CEEDbeta in relationship to its origins within my own consciousness, in addition to providing a backdrop for its prolonged evolution in and through my own process of post-formal development.

By examining CEED's origins within my own developmental constellation from both a phenomenological and structural perspective, we have been able to more clearly situate its applicability as a social technology for leadership development and design. Our inquiry has provided us with a rich set of perspectives for understanding the mandala-like nature of this platform and its potential for scalability across contexts and worldviews. As we take the next steps to rollout CEEDbeta across a range of projects and initiatives, we would love your feedback. If you are interested in beta testing this technology, please contact me using the information below. With your input we can continue to innovate and build a better world.

Acknowledgements

I would like to thank my two second-wave integral mentors, Dustin DiPerna and Edward West, for showing me what it means to walk this path with ferocity, heart, and genuine deep purpose. You have guided my words, my actions, and my being. I would like to honor my lineage, specifically my Dzogchen teachers, Khyentse Yeshe, Chögyal Namkhai Norbu, and my father, Jey Clark. Without your blessings and infinite compassion I would be lost in the ocean of samsara. Finally, I would like to express my deep gratitude for my loving partner, Day, for her support, innocence, levity, and sense of humor. Without your laughter in my life I would be taking all of this much too seriously.

Chapter 13 - Leadership

NOTES

1. See Kegan (1994). This means that our ideas of who we are must be updated and reiterated, tested and redeployed as quickly as our ideas about what the world surface. We must engage in deep inquiry and feedback such that we can come face to face with our assumptions and test them against reality in the most sober of ways.

2. See Wilber (2003c). Social systems and the techno-economic paradigms through which they operate are perhaps the singular most important driving force in the average level of consciousness cultivated within a particular group. iPhones and social media being current examples of my generation's immersion into a participatory postmodern world, which attempts to deliver (at the culmination of the standard formal educational process, usually around the age of 25) largely worldcentric values.

3. See Wilber (2003c). These are the values themselves that flow within the riverbanks. The worldcentric feelings of mutuality that drive us to illegalize racial prejudice and legalize gay marriage. These feelings are mediated through our interface with the riverbanks, which, increasingly, are technological and web-based.

4. Wilber sometimes uses this language to describe a view of the evolution of consciousness over vast stretches of kosmic time. For our purposes, we can think of deep time as the 14 billion-year evolutionary history of what we call "universe." The patterns that have caused matter to evolve into life and into mind are the same patterns that can carry our leadership from its current expression into a wider field of impact, resonance, and emancipatory legacy.

5. See Wilber (2003a, 2003b, and 2006). This means that we can locate this research in a larger context, and position it according to the deeper patterns of human development in order to synchronize it's meaning.

6. See Wilber (2003a, 2003b, and 2006). This means that we can put limits on what this research can and should tell us about reality, and about our topic of investigation. We do this by locating the methodologies selected within a larger field of meta-inquiry, namely the framework of IMP and Integral Research.

7. The full version can be found at: www.mikyo.me/wp-content/uploads/2012/07/CEEDbeta-v.2-Mikyö.pdf.

8. See Wilber (2006). This means where I see the world from, including the structures of my own awareness explored in the section titled Structural Assessment Methods. It can also include the specifics of my own life, including cultural and geographical as well as economic, racial, gender, and other such variables that inevitably dictate my own experience—though many of these contexts are largely unconscious to most of us for much of our lives.

9. See Trungpa (1976 and 1987), and also Wilber (2003a, 2003b, and 2006). I won't try to explain karma here.

10. See DiPerna (forthcoming). "Vantage point" has been a key concept in my understanding of what spiritual development is, and I would highly recommend this text as a reference to anyone serious about their own meditative practice.

11. See (Logan, King, and Fischer-Wright, 2009), appendix 1. Logan et. al found that the ways in which leaders speak about themselves and reality is a key predictor of how they are structuring their relationship with that reality.

12. See Pichford (2002). TCP and Ayurveda have been instrumental in my understanding of the nature of the Kosmos, and continue to deeply inform my daily life. I will note here that much of Wilber's evolutionary narrative at times can marginalize the dignity of these astonishingly precise and profound methods for healing and transformation. Far from medieval, these methods represent an unparalleled renaissance in the understanding of the human body-mind and energy system, and its relationship with the larger universe. What is needed for a modern-day synthesis, as Wilber so eloquently recommends, is a jettisoning of some of the metaphysics involved with these systems.

13. By extrapersonal I am referring more to the larger social, cultural, economic, and technological forces which inevitably shape artifacts and consciousness of any kind.

14. See DiPerna (forthcoming). Here I am differentiating between realms of existence and states of consciousness. This distinction is fleshed out in DiPerna's work on the topic, and isn't worth detailing here for the purposes of our discussion.

15. See Wilber (2006) and O'Fallon (2010b). This means what level of consciousness produced this artifact.

16. See Wilber (2006) and O'Fallon (2010b). This means what state or state-stage of consciousness produced this artifact.

Chapter 13 - Leadership

17. See Wilber (2000). This means what typological orientation produced this artifact.

18. Namely the work of Loevinger, Cook-Greuter, Kegan, and contemporaries, which has been cross-culturally validated and successfully applied across sectors in the fields of leader development.

19. See Norbu (1999) for a beautiful exploration of the differences in view and practice of Sutra, Tantra, and Dzogchen.

20. I have two main streams running through my bloodline. My mother's root teacher, Tulku Sang Ngag, is a Nyingmapa lama of the younger generation who is the heart-son of the famous master Dilgo Khyentse Rinpoche, whom I met when I was just two years old. Visit www.ewam.org to learn more about his work. My father's root teacher, and my own, Chögyal Namkhai Norbu, is a great master trained in all four of the Tibetan Buddhist schools, as well as his having receiving instruction from many Bön teachers before his leaving Tibet. His son, Khyentse Yeshe, whom I consider my teacher, has received very little formal training and yet exemplifies an incredible level of wakefully and transmission capacity. Visit www.tsegyalgar.org. Both of these streams have influenced my perception, perspective, and direct experience of awakened awareness, and I pay homage to them here.

21. See Cook-Greuter (2005) for more on this stage. Also Torbert (2004) and Kegan (2009) have written extensively on this topic, from slightly different perspectives and using slightly different language.

22. See Senge (2007) and Scharmer (2009) among many others.

23. This aspect also relates to my Enneatype, which is mentioned in the section on Typological orientation.

24. This language derived from conversations with DiPerna with regards to his lineage through Daniel P. Brown, as well as my own inquiry with my mother, fellow sangha members, and other practitioners who have recognized the nature of mind.

25. See Norbu (1999), but go see him in person if you want to experience this state directly. For his teaching schedule see the website listed in note 20.

26. Sadly, it is not a capacity which is taught, or even recognized as real by the majority of leadership paradigms available today. State-development itself has been largely forgotten by modernity as a whole, and as a result, leaders lack even the most basic understanding of states and the potential energetic, mental, and other (i.e., lucidity, clarity, focus, intentional) benefits which they offer.

27. The phrase "nature of mind" is sometimes considered synonymous with rigpa, mentioned above, but this is incorrect. Nature of mind is used as a conceptual distinction by Tibetan teachers, who are instructing their students in the early stages of Dzogchen practice. The first cycle of teachings, called Semde in Tibetan, is designed to differentiate mind from nature of mind. But the direct experience of the student who succeeds in this differentiation, and is able to rest into his or her real nature, is called rigpa, which Chögyal Namkhai Norbu translates as "instant presence." This instant presence is the goal or fruit of the practice (and also the starting point within the Dzogchen path), while nature of mind is the conceptual referent of this experience or state.

28. See Maitri (2000). This means the poison or characteristic dark side of this type.

28. See Arnsperger (2012) for an integral exploration of value exchange.

References

Arnsperger, C. *Full-Spectrum Economics: Towards an Inclusive and Emancipatory Social Science*, 1 ed. London: Routledge, 2012.

Cook-Greuter, S. R. *Ego Development: Nine Levels of Increasing Embrace*. Unpublished manuscript, 2005.

Cook-Greuter, S. R. *Postautonomous Ego Development: A Study of Its Nature and Measurement*. Dissertation Abstracts International, 60 06B (UMI No. 993312), 1999.

Creswell, J. W. and V. L. Plano Clark. *Designing and Conducting Mixed Methods Research*. Thousand Oaks, CA: Sage, 2007.

DiPerna, D. *The Infinite Ladder: An Introduction to Integral Religious Studies*. Retrieved on January 13, 2012 from www.integralworld.net/diperna04.html.

Esbjörn-Hargens, S. "Integral Research: A Multi-Method Approach to Investigating Phenomena," *Constructivism in the Human Sciences* 11 (1) (2006): pp. 79–107.

Esbjörn-Hargens, S. and M. Zimmerman. *Integral Ecology: Uniting Multiple Perspectives on the Natural World*. Boston: Integral Books, 2009.

Esbjörn-Hargens, S. "An Ontology of Climate Change: Integral Pluralism and the Enactment of Environmental Phenomena," *Journal of Integral Theory and Practice* 5, no. 1 (2010): pp. 183–201.

Gafni, M. "The Evolutionary Emergent of a Unique Self: A New Chapter in Integral Theory." *Journal of Integral Theory and Practice* 6(1) (2011): pp. 1–36.

Kegan, R. *In Over Our Heads: The Mental Demands of Modern Life*. Cambridge, MA: Harvard University Press, 1994.

Kegan, R. and L. L. Lahey. *Immunity to Change: How to Overcome It and Unlock Potential in Yourself and Your Organization*. Boston, MA: Harvard Business School Press, 2009.

Logan, D., J. P. King, and H. Fischer-Wright. *Tribal Leadership: Leveraging Natural Groups to Build a Thriving Organization*. New York: Harper Business, 2009.

Maitri, S. *The Spiritual Dimension of the Enneagram: Nine Faces of the Soul*. New York: Penguin Putnam, 2000.

Meadows, D. H. *Thinking in Systems: A Primer*. White River Junction: Chelsea Green Publishing, 2008.

Norbu, C. N. *The Crystal and the Way of Light: Sutra, Tantra, and Dzogchen*. Ithaca, NY: Snow Lion Publications, 1999.

O'Fallon, T. "The Evolution of the Human Soul: Developmental Practices in Spiritual Guidance." Thesis written 2010, retrieved on January 13, 2012 from www.pacific Integral.com/docs/evolutionofthehumansoul.pdf.

O'Fallon, T. "The Collapse of the Wilber Combs Matrix: The Interpenetration of the Structure and State Stages." Proceedings of the Integral Theory Conference 2010, July 29—Aug 1. John F. Kennedy U: in press, 2010.

Pitchford, P. *Healing with Whole Foods: Asian Traditions and Modern Nutrition*. Berkeley, CA: North Atlantic Books, 2002.

Riso, R. and R Hudson. *The Wisdom of the Enneagram: The Complete Guide to Psychological and Spiritual Growth for the Nine Personality Types*. New York: Bantam, 1999.

Senge, P. M. *The Fifth Discipline: The Art and Practice of the Learning Organization.* London: Doubleday, 2007.
Torbert, W. *Action Inquiry: The Secret of Timely and Transforming Leadership.* San Francisco: Berrett-Koehler, 2004.
Trungpa, C. *The Myth of Freedom and the Way of Meditation.* Berkeley: Shambhala Publications, 1976.
Trungpa, C. *Cutting Through Spiritual Materialism.* Berkeley: Shambhala Publications, 1987.
Wilber, Ken. *Sex, Ecology, Spirituality: The Spirit of Evolution.* Boston: Shambhala Publications, 1995.
———. *Integral Psychology: Consciousness, Spirit, Psychology, Therapy.* Boston: Shambhala Publications, 2000.
———. *Integral Spirituality: A Startling New Role for Religion in the Modern and Postmodern World.* Boston: Shambhala Publications, 2006.
———. "Excerpt A: An Integral Age at the Leading Edge," 2006, retrieved March 10, 2011 from www.kenwilber.com/Writings/PDF/ExcerptA_KOSMOS_2003.pdf.
———. "Excerpt B: The Many Ways We Touch," 2006, retrieved March 10, 2011 from www.kenwilber.com/Writings/PDF/ExcerptB_KOSMOS_2003.pdf.
———. "Excerpt C: The Ways We Are in This Together," 2006, retrieved March 10, 2011 from www.kenwilber.com/Writings/PDF/ExcerptC_KOSMOS_2003.pdf.
———. "Excerpt D: The Look of a Feeling," 2006, retrieved March 10, 2011 from www.kenwilber.com/Writings/PDF/excerptD_KOSMOS_2004.pdf.
———. Excerpt G: Towards a Comprehensive Theory of Subtle Energies," retrieved March 2011 from www.kenwilber.com/Writings/PDF/ExcerptG_KOSMOS_2004.pdf.

Chapter 14
Service

Mick Quinn and Debora Prieto

A man tries hard to help you find your lost camels. He works more tirelessly than even you, But in truth he does not want you to find them, ever.
—Somali poet Ali Dhux

Selfless Action

The discovery of "emptiness" awakens us to our interconnectedness and gives birth to selfless action. Selfless action is a choiceless contribution to the greater whole—*all of us*. Evidence of this way of being is seen in our daily actions and leaves this world a better place. Selfless action is beyond personal desire and is proof of our motive to improve the universe, which is empowering the urge to discover itself.

But the discovery of emptiness and finding your *true self* is often like looking for your lost camels. It can be a seemingly endless search. And, beyond that, in exploring *your world*, you will eventually uncover perspectives that are grander than ever imagined. Frequently these new perspectives reveal that the man who did not want you to find your camels was not acting maliciously, but without experience or knowledge of the existence of higher levels of development that extended far beyond his own comfort zones.

And then, just when you think you are done, and frequently as a consequence of realizing that the camels you seek may actually be ever-evolving and ultimately undiscoverable, even bigger questions arise, such as—how can we live together in harmony, and what might our specific role be in a better future for *all of us?*

At the outset of such a quest, those who can teach and guide us in discovering our Original Face are most necessary. But, to what end do we continue to engage in development and transformation beyond teachers and lineages? So that we can sound spiritual to ourselves and to other people? To feel good about what we have experienced and how much we have come to understand? To feel as if we are contributing with our opinions from the comfort of our couches? Or, to endlessly be getting ready to be ready?

Maps of Human Potential

In our search for answers, the study of traditional practices and beliefs can lead us to grapple with more advanced or evolutionary worldviews. These newer theories and philosophies can sometimes be difficult to grasp and even more challenging to embrace and embody. Yet, should we persist, we will find that they are nothing less than a comprehensive, all inclusive map of our lives; a guide for us to use on an enterprise that not one of us can escape from—*this very life*.

These maps, which have only recently entered our collective awareness, show us how to invest more wisely in the time we have, not only for the sake of ourselves and our family, but for the sake of *all mankind*. But, often we will disregard these radically insightful theories as being too cerebral, too logical, too inclusive or exclusive, or simply *too new*. We can also mistake the maps for the territory and so flounder on the rocks of intellectual debate and superiority. Who amongst us has studied images of a tropical cay, but never wrinkled its sands between our toes? We also run the risk of becoming eternal students, which prevents us from taking personal responsibility, not only for our own lives, but for the co-creation of a better future for *all of us*. Being a scholar in the laboratory of human potential can bog us down in endless seeking.

Yet, after all of the lectures given and received, the peer dialogues and think tanks, if we are bold enough to depart the controlled environments in which we've crafted our knowledge and capacities, we will realize that we have few ideas about how to apply our wisdom in the harsh reality of how most of the world is living. After all our training in the laboratory, life certainly seemed to get a lot simpler. But, now we realize that it's just gotten a whole lot more complicated.

Chapter 14 - Service

And there are other concerns that contemporary thinkers and philosophers are facing: not only how to apply their theories on the ground, but how to get their students, the vehicles of their wisdom, onto that same ground, where they are most needed. A teacher with a view large enough to embrace *all of us* does not want to be saddled with the eternal student.

We may have gone deeply within only to realize that finding our camels is of little use to the 80 percent of humanity that is living on less than ten dollars a day. And, to make matters worse, it's not the dollar amount that's the real issue.

Sense of Urgency

Our greatest leaders primarily value action. This is because they understand the urgency of the task at hand. This urgency is simply: that we, as a human species, as a planet, are running out of time. *All of us* cannot afford to lose this race. These wise teachers realize that if a perspective broad enough to include *all humanity* is going to stabilize, the predominant view that is concerned only with *me* and *us* must not only be surmounted but also absorbed as part of our new, larger perspective.

Moving from the comfort zone of a scope that is limited to *me*, to the bigger view as *us*, into true intimacy with *all of us* is now a necessary step in our future evolution. It is only by detaching from what I need as an *individual* or as a *culture*, that what *I* need as *humanity* can be clearly seen.

To do this, we learn to take someone else's perspective, to see life through someone else's eyes. Only then can we be truly intimate, boldly courageous, and wildly compassionate.

But, we have to be careful not to underestimate the challenges in accessing this level of development. This is because we are conditioned *not* to see the vast majority of our brothers and sisters as fellow human beings. We have been taught, by many generations past, to associate the possession of property and goods as an indicator of depth and self-awareness.

So before we can support change, in a way that is going to make a real difference for all of us, we have to embrace and dissolve this first layer of hidden conditioning.

The Coming Waves

Many of us are privileged to live in developed countries and in nice neighborhoods where the moral standards of the average individual are well worn and rule of law is admired. If we surround ourselves by such safe and sometimes limiting environments, we might see somebody begging once in a while, or even witness a stray dog. We may hear of the abuse of human rights on the news or in the papers.

Blessed with our lovely surroundings, though we can often feel the pain of other human beings, we are essentially safe from deep suffering. Our hearts are guarded with no fear of being truly breached. Even the Buddha himself lived that way for many years. Before leaving the palace he did not truly know what was going on on the other side of the walls; he did not see "them" as human beings.

So, once we have embraced and dissolved this first layer of our hidden habituation that unknowingly prevents us from truly seeing many of our brothers and sisters as humans, we will then enter the second stage: harnessing the power of denial to help us look away.

Look away from what? That the three richest people in the world control more wealth than all 600 million people living in the world's poorest countries. The truth that more than 850 million people suffer from chronic hunger or malnutrition. That twenty-two thousand children die each day due to poverty. And they "die quietly in some of the poorest villages on Earth, far removed from the scrutiny and the conscience of the world. Being meek and weak in life makes these dying multitudes even more invisible in death." And, if the age was say six or seven, the numbers would be even higher.[1]

If such statistics have yet to empower a profoundly evident response, it is reasonable to suspect that our center of gravity still rests with the conditioned view that does not allow us to see all of the inhabitants of the world as human beings, or at stage two, the denial of the responsibility that emerges when stage one is embraced. This is nothing to be ashamed of, nor should we try to cast out blame and responsibility. At least knowing where we are is the first step in getting to our destination.

Another issue to contend with, besides the ten dollars a day that 80 percent of the world is surviving on, is that the reality of day-to-day life for most of the world's population is quite different than what we imagine it to be or what we may have tasted on our last trip to a developing country. And, it doesn't really matter how many National Geographic

Chapter 14 - Service

documentaries we watch, for they simply do not relay how deeply tragic the situation is.

And, while it is true that repeating mantras and doing meditations can raise the vibration of the planet, we now need to go beyond that level of response. If your two-, three-, and four-year-olds, whose cheeks are infected from soiled sleeping conditions, are being looked after by your seven-year-old all day, every day, while you work to provide a simple nightly meal, most of which will be eaten by your abusive alcoholic husband, will prayer and sitting alone be your only solution?

That you are truly capable of taking someone else's perspective, not just as a concept, is evidenced by overwhelming action on the ground where it is most needed. When we make this leap we see how the individuals who are sitting in front of us are not other than ourselves. We have a Buddha sitting in front of another Buddha. It is only then that we can begin taking care of the issues of the world, the issue that *all of us* are facing. The request is to take the vow of the bodhisattvas to save all sentient beings. A small commitment . . .

Stepping into true intimacy with others, by applying our years of spiritual training, is the next stage of moving our center from *me*, to *us*, and to *all of us*. The depth to which we merge with emptiness within is revealed in our ability to merge with fullness without. Being one with fullness without for the sake of *all of us* in practice and action is called *Conscious Service*.

And the reason we can be one with fullness without for the sake of *all of us*, in practice and action, is that we no longer see the suffering of the world as a concept but as who we are. From that arises a natural responsibility for all sentient beings. A hierarchy of our priorities also arises, allowing wise judgments on what must be done. There may, of course, be doubts about the best way of getting things done, but not of the *need or willingness* for massive action.

Conscious Service

Conscious Service is the unfolding of higher levels of awareness in a humanitarian way. The skillful means to implement this work is empowered by an overall sense of well-being, which is mastered in the earliest stages of our development. Traditional enlightenment is only the beginning.

Conscious Service is acting together, now, because the idea of reaching an idyllic "state" and holding that state does not work anymore. Once we've moved beyond that attachment, we naturally become vehicles for awareness to evolve and we no longer get hung up in some mythic *bardo*. From that point forward we are co-creating a better world for *all of us*.

Conscious Service arises directly from the ashes of personal evolution. From our willingness to go beyond the stickiness of unexamined legends and anything else we may have been given and accepted. It arises from an inexplicable inner root that drives us mad at times and eventually allows us to discover, explore, and express our full potential for the sake of all Beings.

Conscious Service is karma yoga on steroids. Conscious Service takes us far beyond karma yoga, because we have already realized that the attainment of any particular state of mind is not necessary in order to fully participate in this next evolutionary progression of humanity. So getting somewhere, reaching deeper states, for the sake of the self is no longer the primary goal and we are fully available for Conscious Service. This means that we *can* act *now*, in Conscious Service for the sake of humanity, without having to wait to be enlightened—whatever that may be!

Conscious Service also means that sometimes we must get our hands dirty. In service of others we truly learn to receive. In service of our fellow humans we discover authentic pride. And surprisingly, it is no longer about us. It is about our family, the world, and the success and achievements that we all co-create.

Conscious Service implants us into the lives of individuals, families, communities, and cultures we didn't know before and could never have imagined we would. A new quality of transformation occurs and suddenly, we are welcomed and appreciated by the others, ourselves, the world. In service of others we are in fact revealing that we love. And this Love is the point of no return in which we have no choice but to serve, selflessly, with open hands in the marketplace.

Chapter 14 - Service

Deepening Perspectives

What we are describing here is a sense of responsibility that arises from our marrow. A sense of responsibility in which there is no separation between us and the starving dog, the helpless man who cannot feed his children, the kid in ragged filthy clothes, the mother who cannot bring her kids to a doctor, the family that is being abused by a husband, a father, a relative, a landlord, a church, a nonprofit, or the local bureaucracy.

What we are describing here is an awakening in which we become the subject of the suffering, until we can be the suffering itself. Only then is there no one to suffer. This presence is perceived, felt, by other people compelling immediate trust. When we are truly capable of taking someone else's perspective, there is nothing false about our motives and intentions. It is not *me, you, us,* and *them,* but a space in which there is only an exchange of intimacy for the human condition. True intimacy arises in these shared moments.

Awakening our relationships to the call of Conscious Service serves as proof of our flight from our comfort zones. And this applies not only to those relationships we have long been comfortable with, but also to new ones that arise as we move to serve. This requires that we embrace a worldview that is large enough to include not only all humanity today, but *all of us* in fifty, one hundred, or five thousand years from now.

The Slums of Guatemala

Both of us work in the slums of Guatemala. We live less than three miles from those integral parts of *all of us.* Curiously, in 2009, Guatemala was ranked as the fourth happiest country in the world by the *Happy Planet Index.*[2]

You can't miss that happiness here. Smiles and laughter abound and you are greeted with a warm glance and greeting, according to the time of the day, by almost every person you pass in the street. There's an unmistakable lightness in the air in this land of the eternal spring. And still, there's a catch.

Many of our fellow brother and sisters here live with a view that only stretches out thirty-six hours. For them, having dinner tonight and getting up the next morning is all the success they can wish for. Beyond that, there is nothing. And this is not the "emptiness" that empowers selfless actions. It is just nothing. And as you may know, to the limited self in its earliest stages of development, a full belly is happily mistaken for immortality.

The vast majority of our global population lives in the unconscious now, so intimately close to nature that they still have dirt floors, torrents of rainwater washing through their homes, a simple diet of tortillas and beans, and when they go to the bathroom, porcelain is a rarely seen.

What then is a slum? An invisible yet convenient container for our collective shadow of hopelessness. A slum is the place that allows us to unconsciously set aside the Buddhist teaching that calls for a "joyful participation in the sorrows of the world."

And, we have also discovered that of those who are blessed to live with affluence here in Guatemala, few have ever been to a slum. The obvious consensus amongst the vast majority of this privileged class is that poverty is not a problem.

Yet, as we will see, a slum can be much more than just a place to hide our shadow of hopelessness.

On Returning to the Marketplace

Before we explore our work in the developing world, we will share a little about the practices and disciplines that have helped us tremendously in our transition.

We have engaged for several years in both spiritual and psychological development. These are practices that empower the overall health of the vehicle, the mind, body, spirit, and emotions, the medium by which consciousness evolves.

Meditation has always been and will remain central to our ability to evolve and prosper. Shadow work, in which we acknowledge, own, and reintegrate those aspects of ourselves that have been repressed or denied, is also critically important. We realized that if we didn't take care of this most subjective aspect of ourselves—the shadow—it would eventually hit us like a freight train at full speed.

Chapter 14 - Service

Therefore, having a healthy sense of self is essential in this journey. To be boldly self-confident, vibrant and effective, to effortlessly recognize and own inauthentic emotions as they arise, requires discipline. To remain centered in the Source, and to also effectively manage diet, energy, and finances, requires dedication. Dedication to what? Dedication to the future of the self as the future of *all of us*.

We even notice that a couple of extra pounds has its affect when we need to do a home visit. The homes we mostly work with here are located where access is quite difficult. Sometimes we'll walk forty-five minutes up a mountain just to visit one home. This territory is land that the mayors of the small towns and local landowners don't want to deal with because it is useless and dangerous. And so it is donated to the poorest families who cannot afford even the smallest plot of land. In the rainy season they become torrents of mud and rocks.

Other practices and disciplines that have had a profound effect on our motives to connect the most evolved minds in the world with those who are not so fortunate include advanced and evolutionary maps of human potential (see "The Kids" section below for more details). These maps point us to the fact that consciousness is emerging in waves or stages, one higher than another. They point to the fact that the farthest reaches of human awareness is always evolving and we believe that by connecting the right people we can change the future of humanity.

We recently published a book called *The Uncommon Path*, which summarizes much of our explorations from the comfort zone of the laboratory. After this project was completed, we were wondering how best to apply this tome on the future of human potential in the reality of how most of the world was living. What better place to start than in Guatemala?

On Work in the Ground

One of the first things we notice when we slip outside the glitz of the tourist districts, is the striking difference between all previous impressions and what the developing world feels like to the body, mind, spirit, and shadow.

The next thing that becomes obvious is that education is not highly valued. Sometimes it does not even cross the minds of the parents. To have a ten-year-old working in a store for twelve hours per day is normal. To see five- or six-year-olds spending their time collecting firewood or picking coffee beans for ten hours a day is perfectly acceptable.

And, as you get to know people better, you will notice, in both adults and teens, that they are often unable to put their thoughts in order. They struggle to organize clear sequential thinking. When important decisions need to be made they seem trapped by a plethora of thoughts arising simultaneously. Since our arrival, we have been working to help them build their own maps and develop a degree of objectivity that is often taken for granted in the developed world.

In response to our experience thus far, we have launched four different programs that comprise the work of the Integral Heart Foundation. They are: Sponsorship, Education, Leadership Development, and Portable Solar Lighting programs. In short, the funds from the sponsorships pay for food, clothes, basic medicines, and ensures that the kids go to school.

Our education program exposes the children to philosophy, meditation, and other advanced tools and maps such as Big Mind, Spiral Dynamics, Integral Theory, and Evolutionary Enlightenment. Our curriculum also includes modules on culture, relationships, diet, energy, exercise, travel, and finances.

Sponsorship

As we mentioned earlier, the challenge here in Guatemala is not only the education of the youngest children, it is also to show the parents that education has *some* value.

Connecting sponsors from within Guatemala and all over the world with the kids here allows us, our staff, and volunteers to look after their basic needs and those of their families. By our regular presence here we ensure that the children receive the opportunity of education. Sometimes, this is just a matter of enticing the parent(s) with the possibility of regular food and clothing visits. Our sponsorship programs also provide an opportunity for teens who can prove their motivation to continue studying beyond the high school level.

Chapter 14 - Service

The Kids

There are over forty modules in our education program. These eight below are currently being taught to both sponsored kids and those yet to be sponsored in the schools of collaborating nonprofit organizations here in Guatemala.

1. Meditation: The kids sit and simply be. And, they love it. Their responses to this practice have been very positive, like "how peaceful this is" and "I never noticed before how busy my mind was." The children are leaning to connect with the Source and eventually to develop objectivity on arising thoughts. This will help them with decision making.

2. Shadow Work: During meditation some of the kids have had deep experiences. Though empowering, these experiences can also be dangerous and can lead to arrogance and abuse. Shadow work teaches them to take responsibility for the good, the bad, and the ugly of themselves and also to make sure that they understand that yes, *I am God*, and so are *all of us*. We use a process called Big Mind, created by Dennis Genpo Merzel, in the shadow work. The Big Mind process shows the kids how to take different perspectives, and eventually to reown those aspects of themselves that have been repressed or denied.

They love to see the self from a distance and to be able to take the perspective of the person they are talking to. For instance, to speak *as* the teacher who wants order in the class and not *about* the teacher who wants order in the class has proven to be quite effective in restoring a productive teaching environment.

3. English Language: We place a big emphasis on learning English. We know that the kids are going to need it in the future if they are going to co-create a wider community and to engage with the rest of the world. We are not talking only from a business perspective but from a way to intimately relate with *all of us*. Teaching English can be quite problematic because we are realizing that the quality of their Spanish, and in many cases, that of their Spanish teachers, leaves a lot to be desired.

4. Sex Education: This program is about raising awareness on the impersonal nature of the sexual impulse. A common belief in countries such as Guatemala is that God sends children. The implication is that there is no way to choose if one has children or not. We reframe this by teaching the children that God also gives them free will. Also, one of the tenets of the sponsorship program contract requires that there are no pregnancies during the term of the support. We also reveal the cost of raising a child per year. This raises many eyebrows. We also suggest that homosexuality is as legitimate as heterosexuality and impress the importance of safe sex regardless of personal preferences.

5. Philosophy Classes: In this class we do not tell the kids *what* to think, but we show them that they *can* think. We teach them not to take anything for granted and that questioning is a great practice. The focus here is not on finding answers, but on the fact that they can begin to question everything. The philosophy class allows the kids to investigate and be curious and therefore nurture the seed of eagerness that can shake the future not only for themselves, but their country, and maybe even the *all of us.*
We also bring in experts, via Skype or in person, who offer the wisdom of their particular lines of development across all aspects of the human experience.

6. Integral Perspectives: We teach the kids that there are basically four ways of seeing reality that are occurring simultaneously. Accounting for only one or two of these four perspectives implies that they will be leaving out important aspects of the events that they are witnessing or being part of. This theory is based on common sense simplicity and reveals that most languages in the world share the pronouns "I," "we," "it," and "its." So, there are at least four essential ways in which we can look at any challenge or opportunity.

7. Evolutionary Enlightenment: This class allows us to plant the seed of understanding that consciousness is emerging in waves or stages, one higher than another and that the farthest reaches of human awareness are continually evolving. In this work, we count on the tremendous help of Jeff Carreira, Director of Education of EnlighenNext. Often the children do not realize what they are learning, they simply know that their minds are stretching and their perspectives are getting wider and wider. They are also learning how to articulate their experiences and to give feedback from these wider viewpoints.

8. Humanitarian Hierarchies: The teens whose participation in our sponsorship program is allowing them to study beyond the high school level are also being taught how to be responsible for the younger children who are being sponsored.

We are teaching the developing world about humanitarian work, which helps them widen their perspectives and develop self-esteem. The older kids are responsible for visiting the homes of two or three of the younger ones each month, and to report back on the situation they are finding so that we may respond accordingly.

We believe that change has to be made at all levels of the society. We recognize, every time we see them, that these children have before them the potential to be tomorrow's entrepreneurs, attorneys, politicians, diplomats, and perhaps even the future president of their country.

The Mothers

We also work toward helping raise the self-esteem and self-confidence of the village mothers. Violent domestic abuse is rife here. One step in healing the traumas directly linked to this abuse is by helping them restore the sense of self-worth, to show them that they are human beings.

In this religious country (60 percent Catholic, 40 percent Protestant), churches are the pillars where the masses rest assured. Unfortunately, their preachers, priests, and leaders frequently declare that current events, life's many struggles, are only God's will. In addition, it is advocated that women must to prove their faith through their willingness to accept whatever God sends them. When a tropical storm, for instance, washes away a son, or when a husband beats and rapes both wife and daughter, that is also God's will. Her perseverance and submission to these situations reflects her God-fearing servitude. Men, on the other hand, are revered as being superior, in Gods image, and can therefore make their own choices, as well as decide for the fate of the women. This, according to their clergy teachings, is honoring God's will.

In another instance of the level of development we are encountering here, we read an article in a national newspaper, which stated that earning income in the home must *now* also involve women. The reporter had no problem in pointing out that this task has been traditionally and exclusively given to the "boss of the home."

And in this struggle, curiously it is the mothers with low self-esteem who are primarily responsible for the education of the new generations, the children. Elevating these women's self-worth and empowering them will help break this chain. Being referred to as ugly, pathetic, and useless is not unusual and contributes grossly to their current sense of self-worth. They firmly believe that they are ugly, pathetic, and useless.

During an interview in a classroom setting, one particular mother revealed that she would love to be an "elegant lady." Using the Big Mind process, we called upon her voice of "the elegant lady," and there she was. As such, she spoke, moved, and walked with a new level of appreciation for herself, as this "elegant lady" she was and she is. From that moment forward, this mother has continually increased her participation in meetings and is helping other women who suffer from similar afflictions. She has also participated in a radio program where we discussed the topic of domestic violence. In short, the increased sense of self-worth perpetuates still deeper levels of healing and empowerment. These have become self-evident by her level of participation in our programs, as well as the ways in which she conducts her everyday life.

In working with these mothers, we find it extremely valuable to speak in terms they can access and reference. For example, when a mother tells us that she is waiting for a sign from the Lord for validation as to whether or not to continue with a particular situation, we remind her that the "Lord" already sent her the capacity to "choose" and that it is now up to her to use it as a gift. We also invite her to see herself as the Lord's temple. We help them to see and appreciate themselves, and their children, as temples of God, and as these temples of God, they need not accept abusive situations to continue. We explain that, in allowing others to abuse God's temple, they allow damage to come to the beauty that God created for veneration. Allowing their husbands to abuse them or their children is akin to allowing vandals to destroy hallowed ground.

For our work to be effective, we need to translate our message into the levels of understanding within these communities. Knowing the cultural background and customs of the individuals before us is a requirement for such intimate communication.

Chapter 14 - Service

For instance, we went to visit a home and the mother had to give medicine to one of her daughters three times a day. Our first thought was, give her the medicine after each meal of the day: one after breakfast, one after lunch, and one after dinner. We took for granted that everybody has three meals a day. But when we looked around the tiny tin shack we realized that there was no food whatsoever. Besides taking the mom and the kids to the local store to buy food, we told her to give the girl one pill after waking up in the morning, another one in the middle of the day, and the last one before going to bed.

To be able to see life through their eyes allows us to take their perspective and to translate whatever it is that it needs to be communicated into their view of the world. Therefore communication arises and we all can understand each other. And in this mutuality, self-esteem is empowered. It is important that we, as teachers, understand their perspective and what they can or cannot do. Telling them how years of study can benefit their children doesn't make much sense as they don't understand the concept of years to begin with. They understand eating tonight and sleeping in the most decent place they can. That is why our work must begin by the basics. If we want the kids to have an education and to change this endless cycle of misery for the new generation, we should provide a meal and bed for the families so the kids can attend school.

Leadership Development

Besides the programs for the kids and the moms, we work alongside local Guatemalan school directors. Through this leadership coaching program we help teachers and school directors run more efficient, effective, and sustainable schools. This program also helps them to maintain their own sanity under the pressure of running a school of ninety kids with only two or three teachers, one administration staff member, and a food program run by local volunteers, which not only feeds the kids and the staff but the local homeless as well.

In these sessions we use a combination of shadow work, structure-building tools, spreadsheets, marketing and presentation tips, and also aspects from the advanced maps of human consciousness that are outlined in our book, *The Uncommon Path*.

The motive to engage as we do emerges effortlessly from having a view that goes beyond ourselves. That is the key that allows us to really engage with the community. Being the community itself, thinking as the community, breathing as the community, and experiencing life as the community is what makes the difference in these times of service.

And, just so you know, not all our work is as "clean" as it seems. Sometimes, we will help out by painting a school or a house, carrying food up a mountain, digging holes, building walls, cutting trees, training with weapons and other self-defense devices . . .

The Reward of a Slum

At the end of the day, a smile, a gesture, one word, or simply a touch are invaluable rewards. Big huge hugs are also the best. True appreciation, genuine caring, authentic compassion, and the palpable mutuality that empowers self-esteem all arise from Conscious Service. Isn't it funny that we have the idea that serving is something that maids should do and somehow we already have transcended that point in our evolution. We studied and became wise, we know better, we make a full investment in our education, we have money, so we believe we are smart enough and accomplished enough to have someone else serve us. We are so wrong . . .

And remember, you are one of a really lucky percentage of the human race that is being exposed to the wisdom of each chapter of this book. Please never forget that. And never doubt that *they want what we have.* With the doubling of some basic commodity prices recently, we now know that without a radical shift in collective consciousness that desire is going to be impossible to satisfy. So, what is the solution?

The developing world must grow through the same levels of development as we did to also realize this quandary. But they must do so with great haste. We have to help them move through those levels. Otherwise, in whose hands are we leaving the fate for *all of us?*

And I, as the planet Earth, am running out of time. I need you and your Conscious Service because there is a part of *all of us* that is beyond both perfection and imperfection. Now your job is to co-create that apex in *all of us.*

Plato told us that in the same way that the head leads the body, there must be philosophers who lead society. But now that we have thought more than sufficiently, we must act.

The Next Step

And in all this work, we also realize that humanity has come a long way in the four thousand years that have elapsed since we first became aware of our individuality, of our distinct sense of self, of our separate sense of self at the level of thought. In language, this evolution is referred to as "I," "me," and "mine." The emergence of individuality also brought with it the amazing ability of "personal choice."

However, a new wave of consciousness is now beginning to wash over our planet. This book is evidence of that. And this cause for Conscious Service is comprised of millions of concerned individuals, whose center of attention has begun to evolve from an exclusive focus on "I" and "we" to include a focus as "all of us."*All of us* is humanity—*no child left out.*

How then can more of us move our center of attention from this naturally conditioned and essential focus on "I," to include and share a focus as *all of us* and so embrace and propel the evolutionary cause of Conscious Service? How can we sustain great choices on a consistent path of growth and development, and so allow more of us to move from a focus on "I," to serve from a focus as *all of us?*

Here is one solution: because of our conditioning, it is considered normal to have separate groups or spheres of values representing the various components of our lives. For example, values related to our career may not be the same as those used in major decisions about our hobbies or our relationships. For four thousand years we have been creating multiple groups of values, one to suit each of our life domains. These value spheres guide our decisions within each role and across our lives in general.

However, this arrangement of what we consider to be important to us, our values, ensures that concealed conditioning remains in firm control of our lives. Because most of us are not aware of the existence of these multiple groups of values, we experience great anguish and confusion in times of making important choices. This drains our attention and leaves us feeling unprepared, unable, and unwilling to engage in Conscious Service.

[3]By making all major life decisions, regardless of the circumstances surrounding that choice, by consciously embracing *a single hierarchy of values*, we will discover that awakening to a perspective that includes *all of us* is not dependent on options or outcomes, but on how consistently our intentions are to live a life directed by a conscious primary value.

Eventually, it becomes clear that we are "choiceless," and we will approach change, transformation, and the evolution of consciousness and culture with unbending confidence, because we now know that our intention to awaken *all of us* is *always* going to be our outcome.

Are you ready to be choiceless?

Practical Tips

1. Make a list of your most important (five or six) life domains or life spheres.
2. Look at how you spend your time across each of the areas of your life.
3. List as many values from within each of those life domains as possible.
4. Arrange your values within each group according to the time you spend expressing each one.
5. Arrange your values into a single list according to the time you spend expressing each one.
6. Is the value at the top of this list consistent with your intention to embrace and sustain the cause for Conscious Service.

Chapter 14 - Service

NOTES

1. Poverty statistics from World Bank, UNICEF, and Global Issues Foundation.

2. Happy Planet Index was introduced by the New Economics Foundation in 2006.

Concluding Remarks

It is with deep joy that I offer a few words of conclusion. To begin, I'd like to thank all of the authors for their contributions. Clearly, this book would not have been possible without all of the brilliance each author shined forth. I'd also like to express my gratitude to H.B. Augustine for his work and diligence to help make this project a reality.

With this publication, the seed impulse to bring together a collection of cutting edge integral thinkers across several generations comes to fruition. My hope then, and my hope now, is that this book helps to introduce the direct experiential recognition of integral consciousness to an even wider audience.

As these ideas enter the currents of transformation presently unfolding on Earth, may it do so in a way that truly serves our next steps together as a human family.

Dustin DiPerna
Sebastopol, California
2013

CPSIA information can be obtained at www.ICGtesting.com
Printed in the USA
BVOW01*1055200114
342188BV00001B/1/P